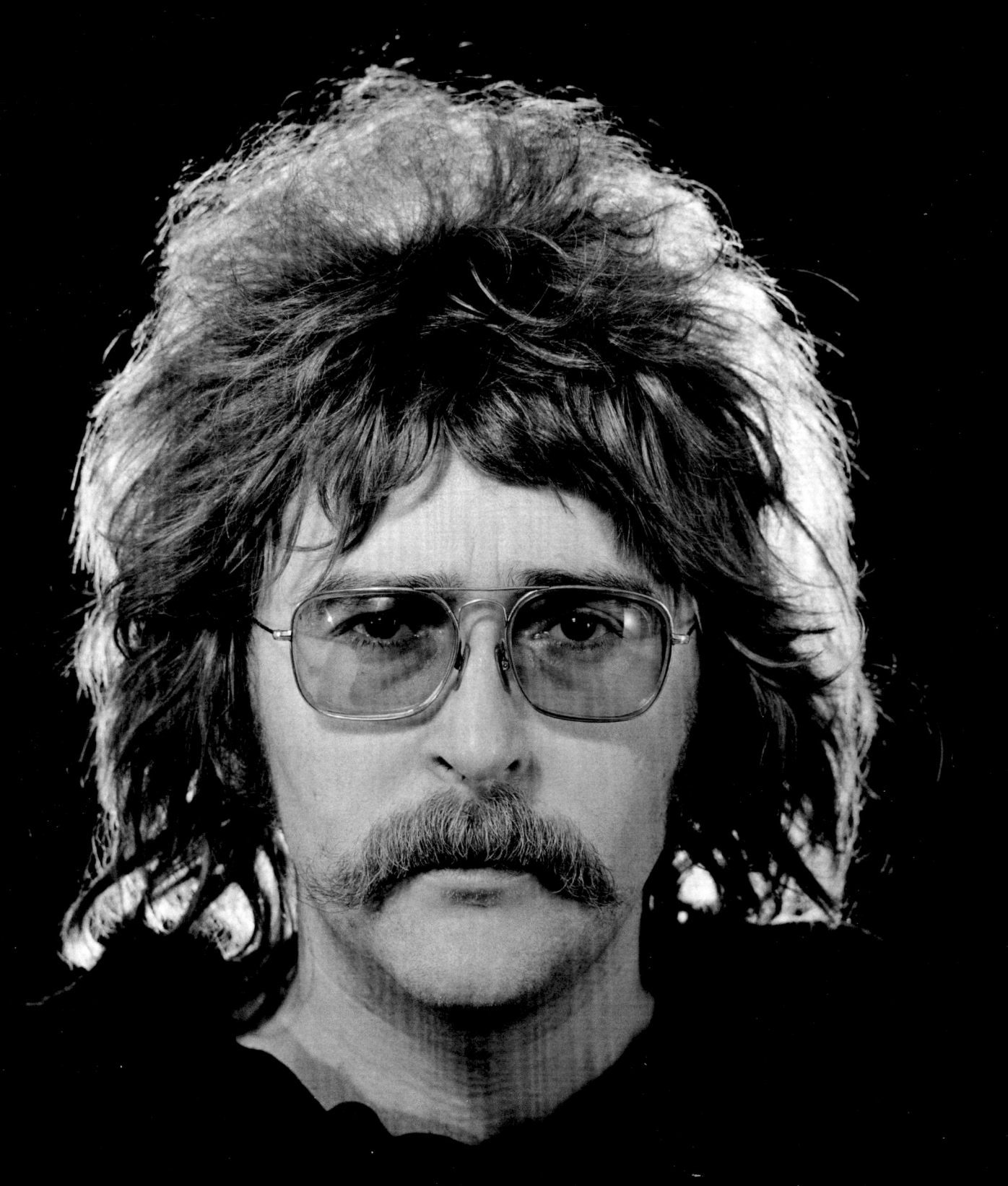

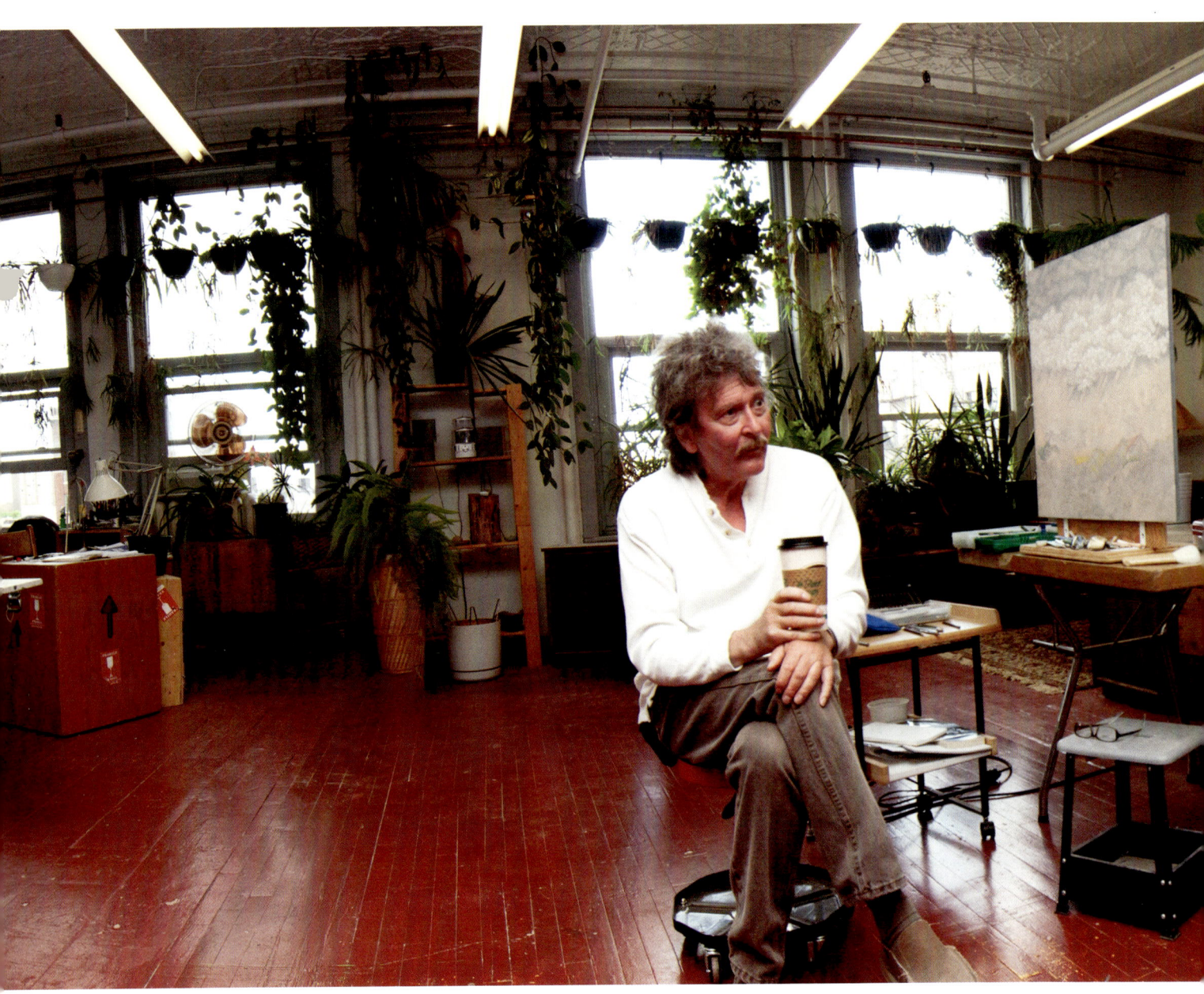

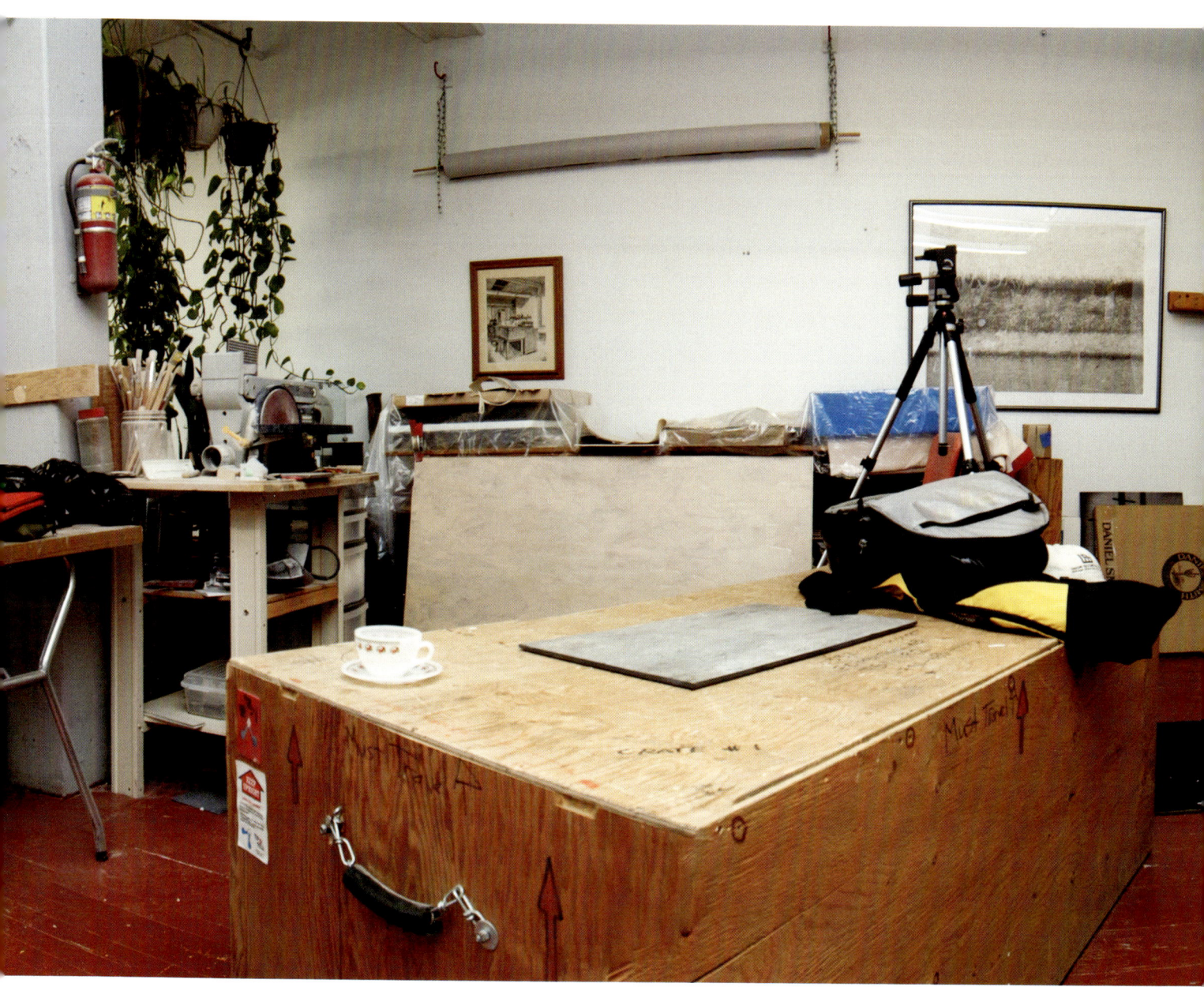

DON

PATRICIA BOVEY

PROCH

MASKING AND MAPPING

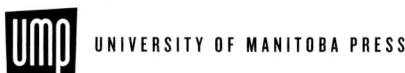

UNIVERSITY OF MANITOBA PRESS

Published in collaboration with St. John's College Press

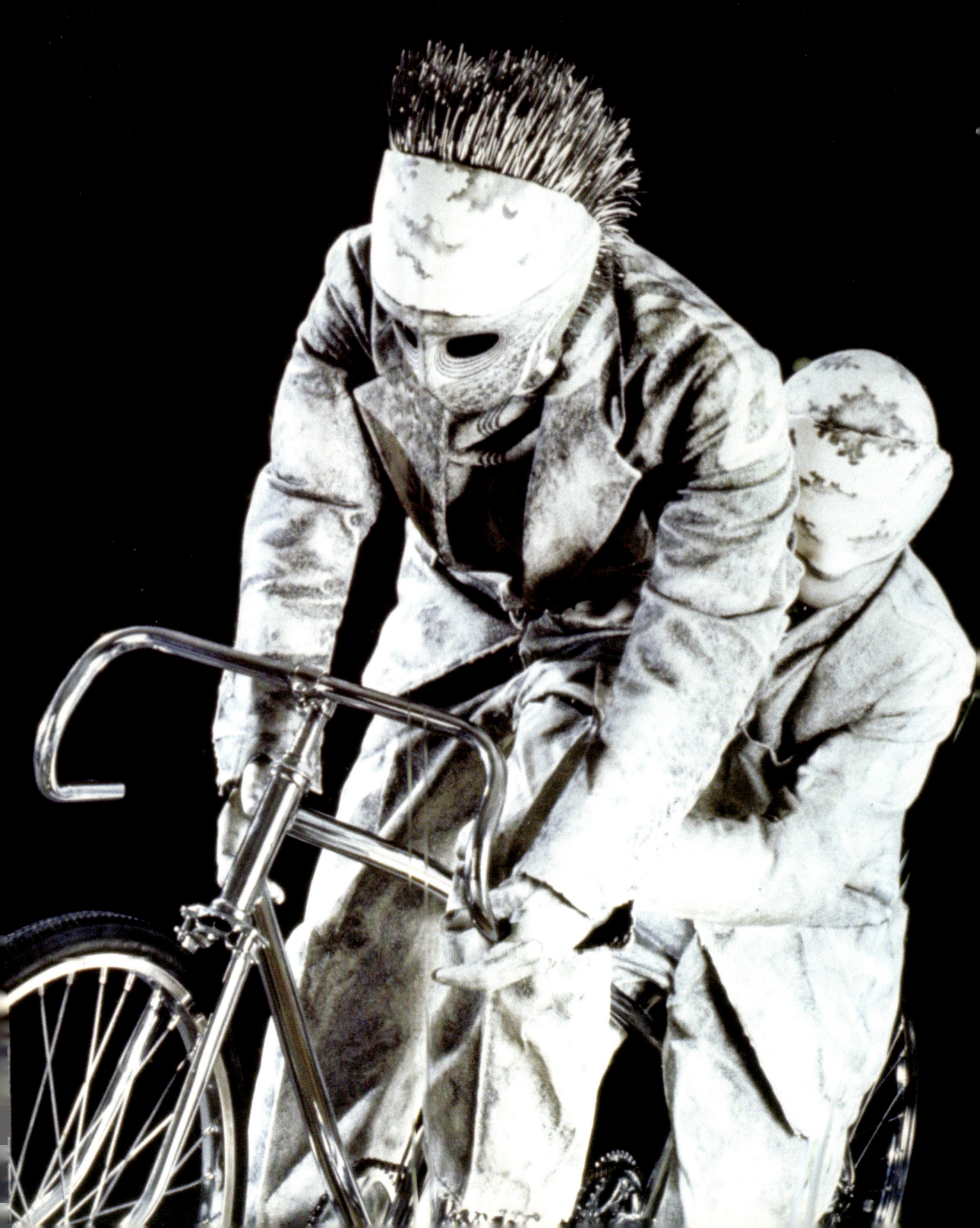

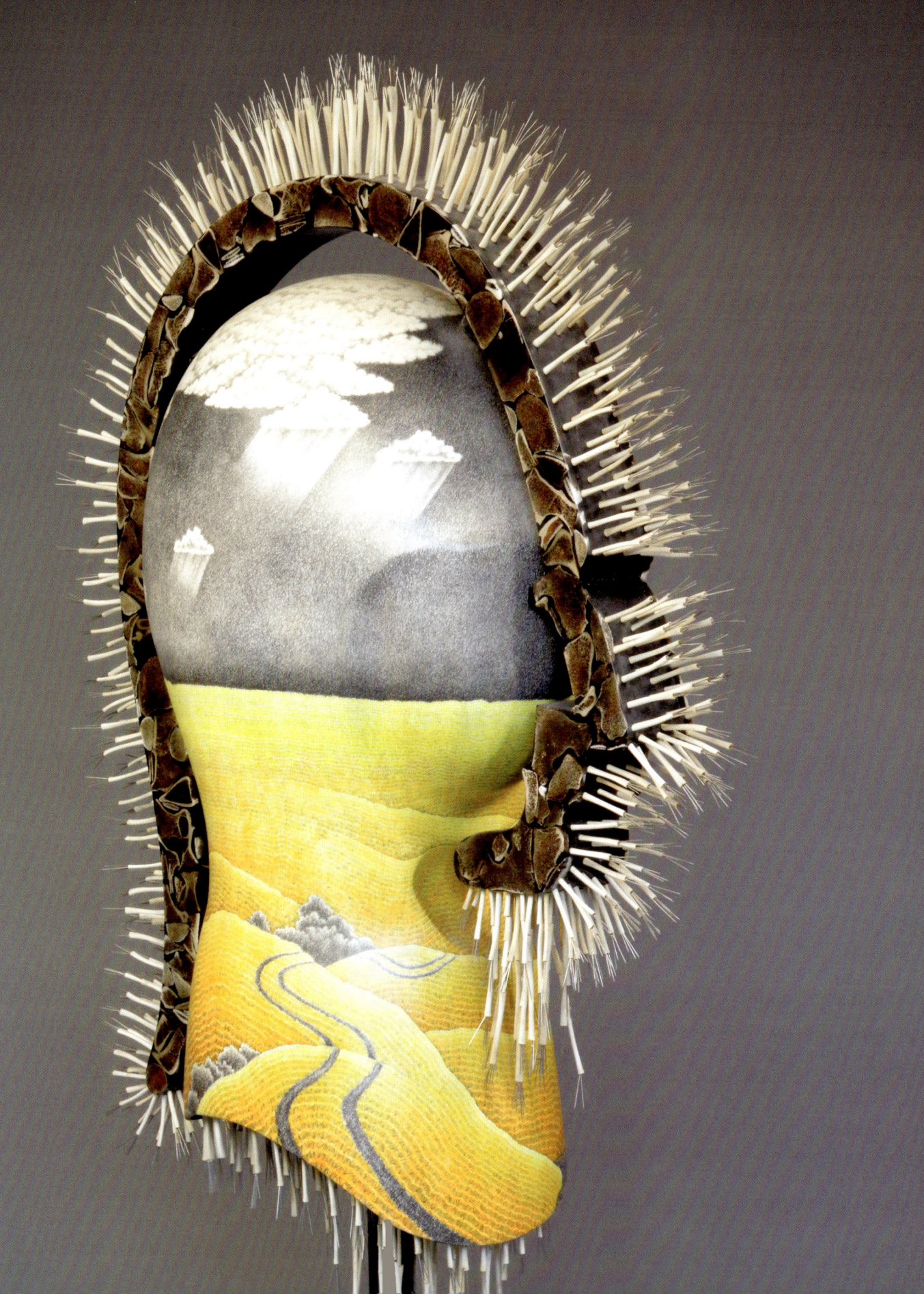

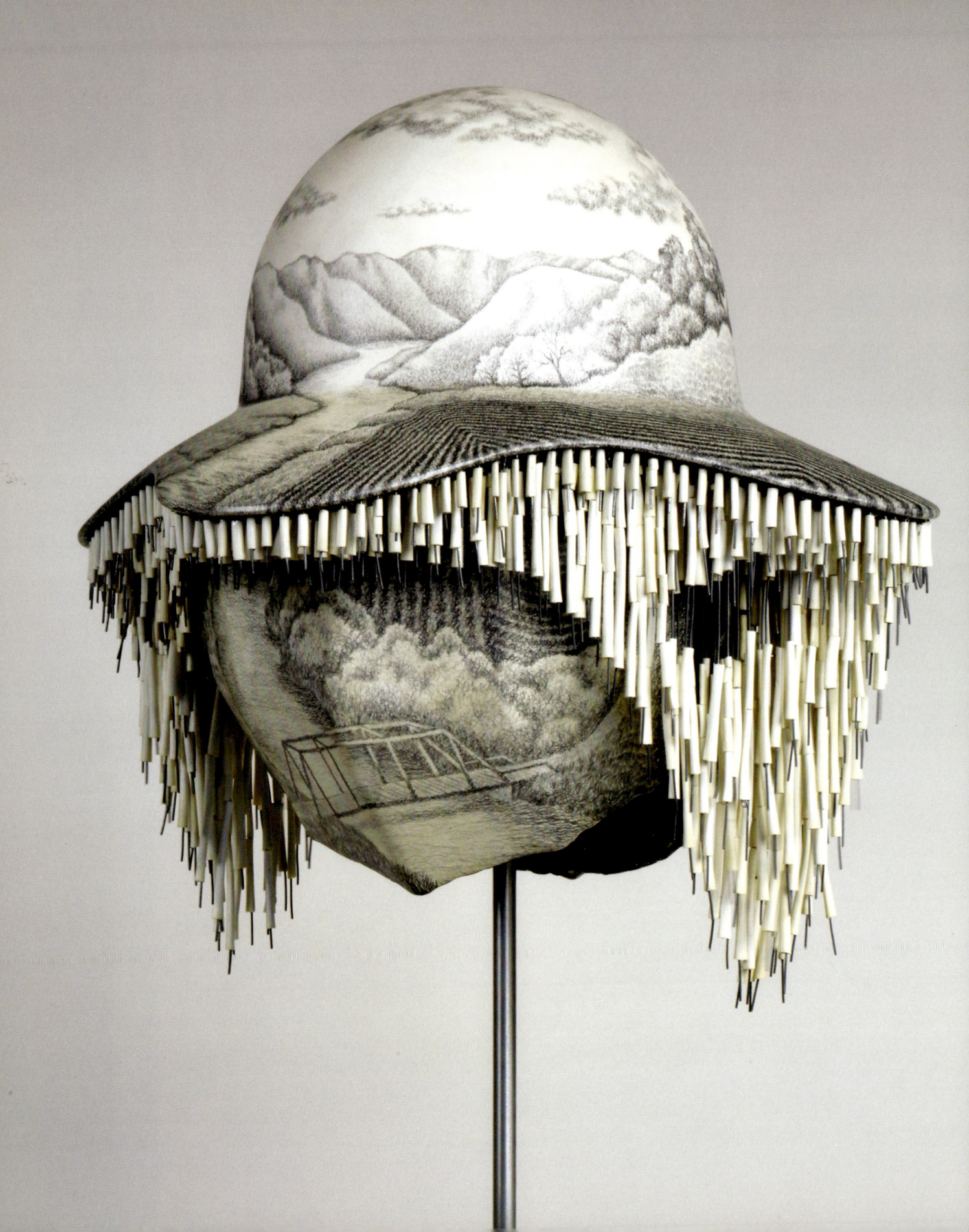

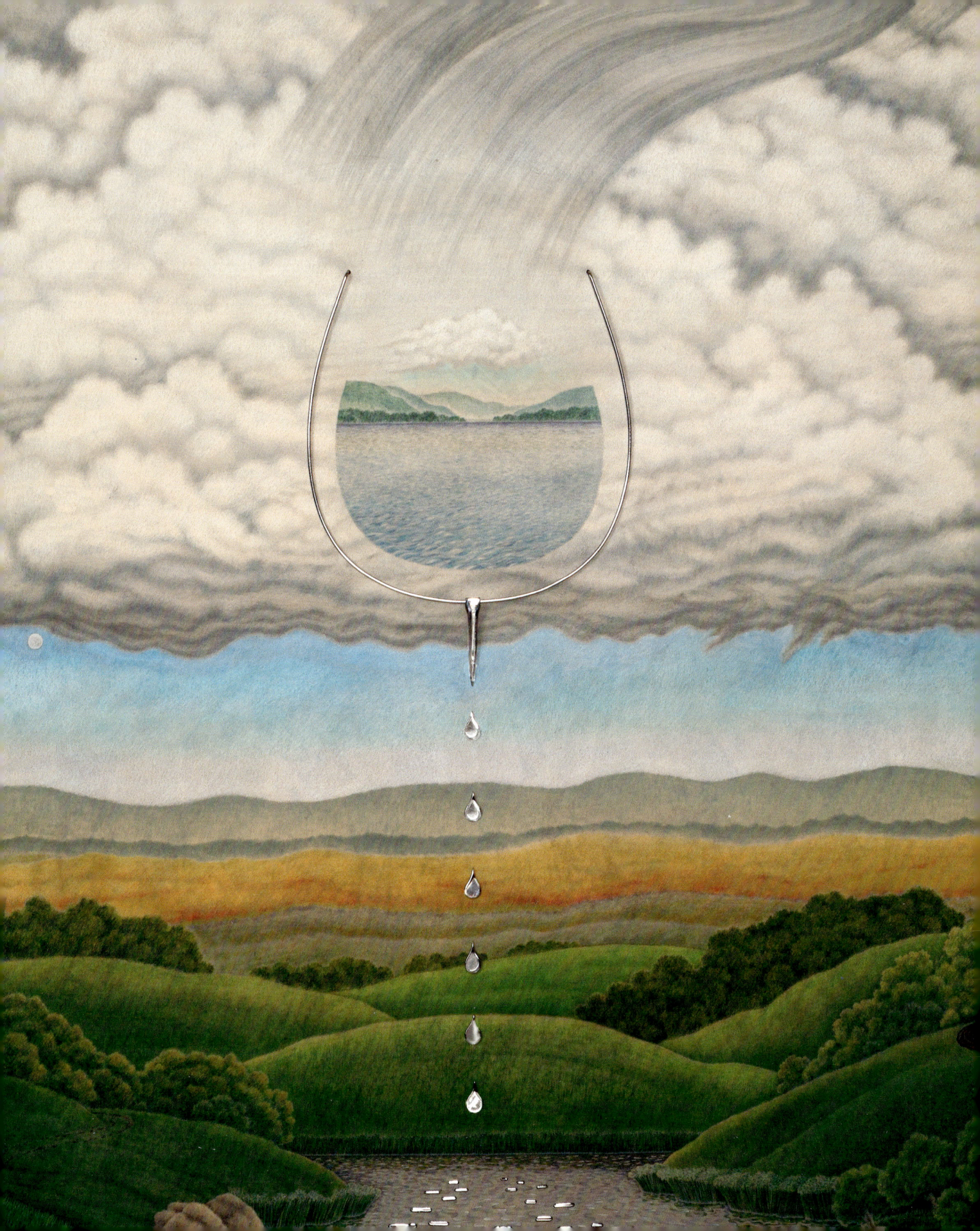

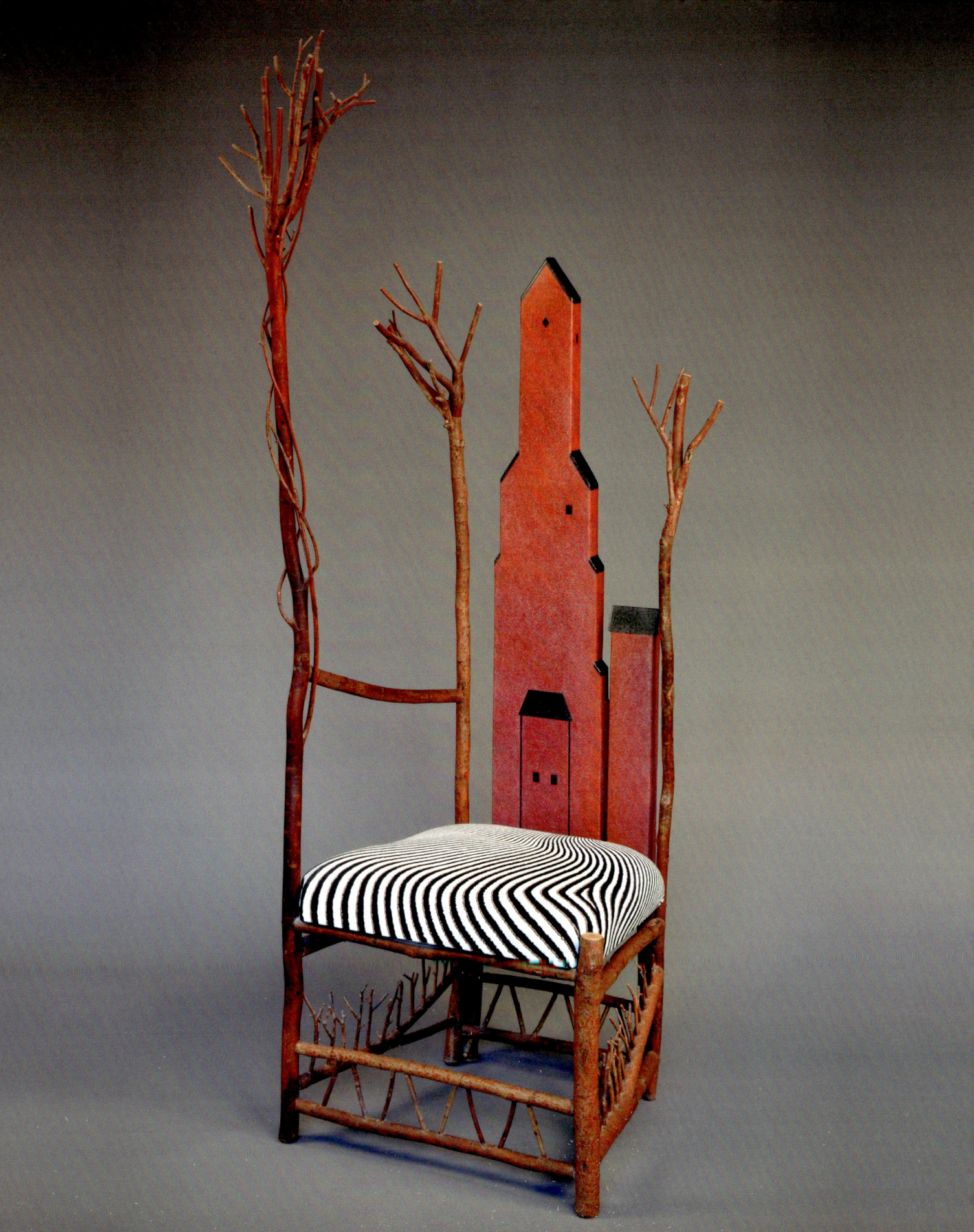

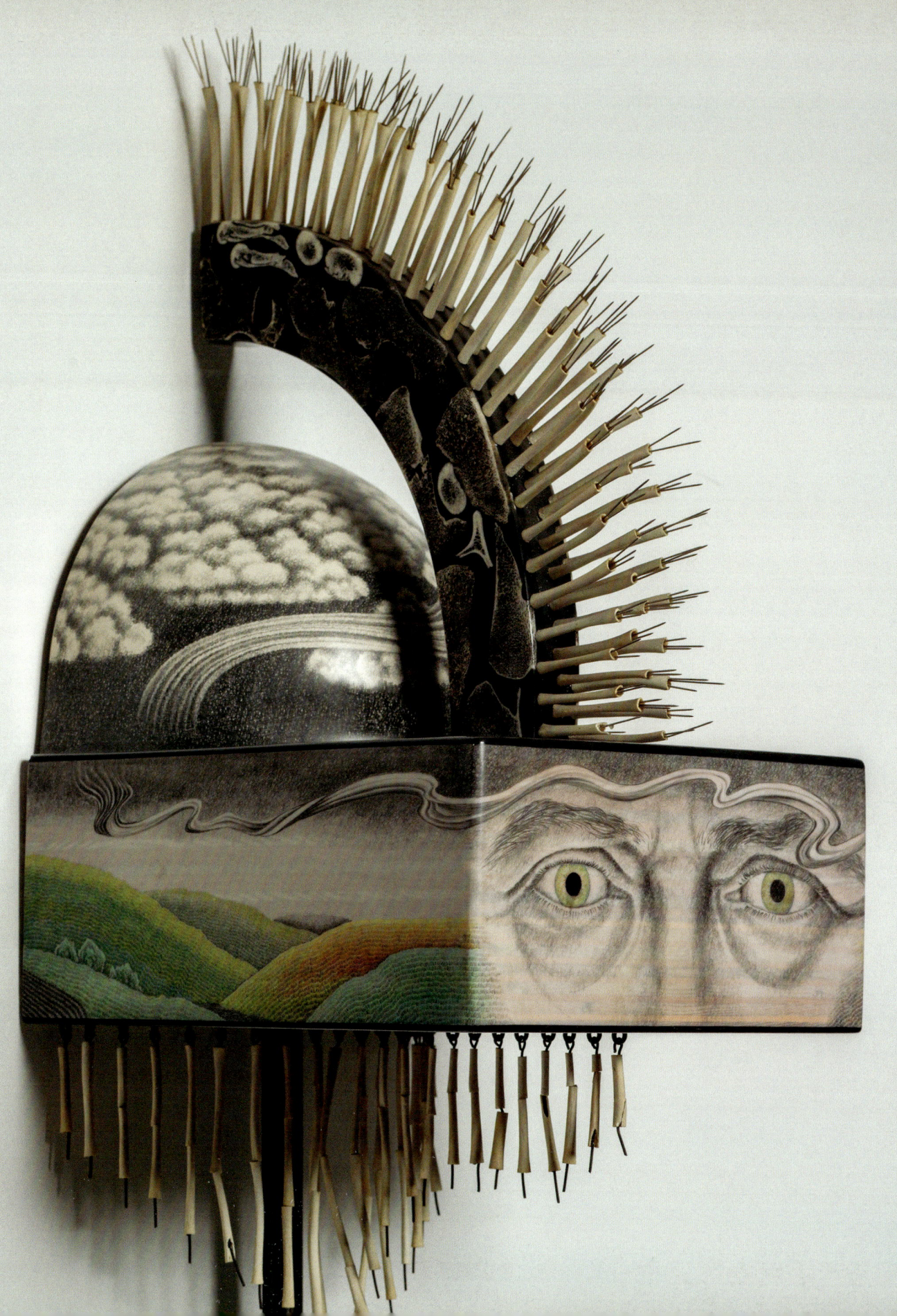

Don Proch: Masking and Mapping
© Patricia Bovey 2019

University of Manitoba Press
Winnipeg, Manitoba, Canada
Treaty 1 Territory
uofmpress.ca

Cataloguing data available from Library and Archives Canada
ISBN 978-0-88755-834-4 (PAPER)
ISBN 978-0-88755-569-5 (PDF)
ISBN 978-0-88755-567-1 (EPUB)

Cover and interior design by Frank Reimer

Excerpts from Robert Enright, "They Don't Make Horseshoe Nails
Like They Used To," *Border Crossings* 9, no. 2 (1990) are used with
permission of Robert Enright and *Border Crossings*, Winnipeg, Canada.

Printed in Canada by Friesens

University of Manitoba Press acknowledges the support of the Winnipeg
Foundation in the publication of this book.

Publication of this book has also been made possible by the generous support
of Susan Glass and Arni Thorsteinson, Arlene Wilson and Allan MacDonald,
David and Gursh Barnard, Dr. Neil Devitt, and a Winnipeg Friend.

The University of Manitoba Press acknowledges the financial support for its
publication program provided by the Government of Canada through the
Canada Book Fund, the Canada Council for the Arts, the Manitoba Department
of Sport, Culture, and Heritage, the Manitoba Arts Council, and the Manitoba
Book Publishing Tax Credit.

Funded by the Government of Canada   Canadä

Frontispiece: Don Proch, mid-1970s. Photo by Ernest Mayer.

Endsheets: (Front) Don Proch's Arthur Street Studio, Winnipeg, 2003–13.
Photo by Alan McTavish. (Back) Don Proch's Dufferin Street Studio,
Winnipeg, since 2013. Photo by Alan McTavish.

Images, pages vi–xi: *Velocipede* (detail), 1976; *Great Plains Mask*, 1986;
Chicken Bone Mask, 1978; *Prairie Waters* (detail), 2018; *Elevator Chair*,
1990; *Through the Artist's Eye Moon and Pine Bough* (detail), 1990.

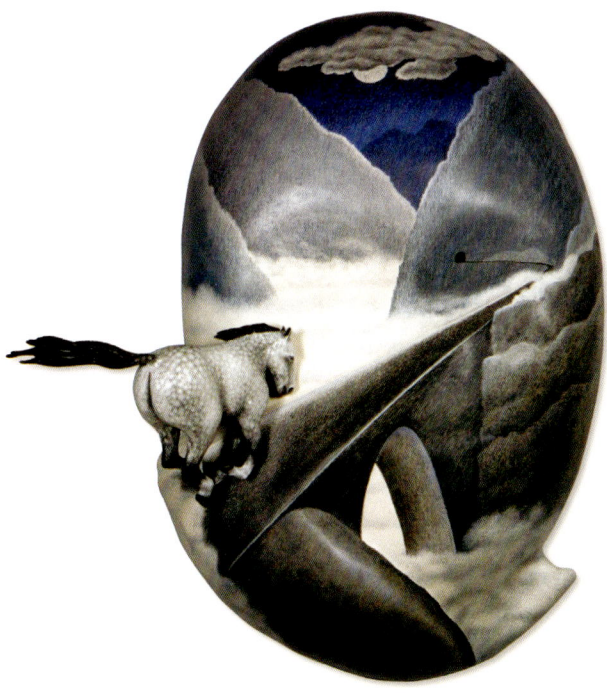

Contents

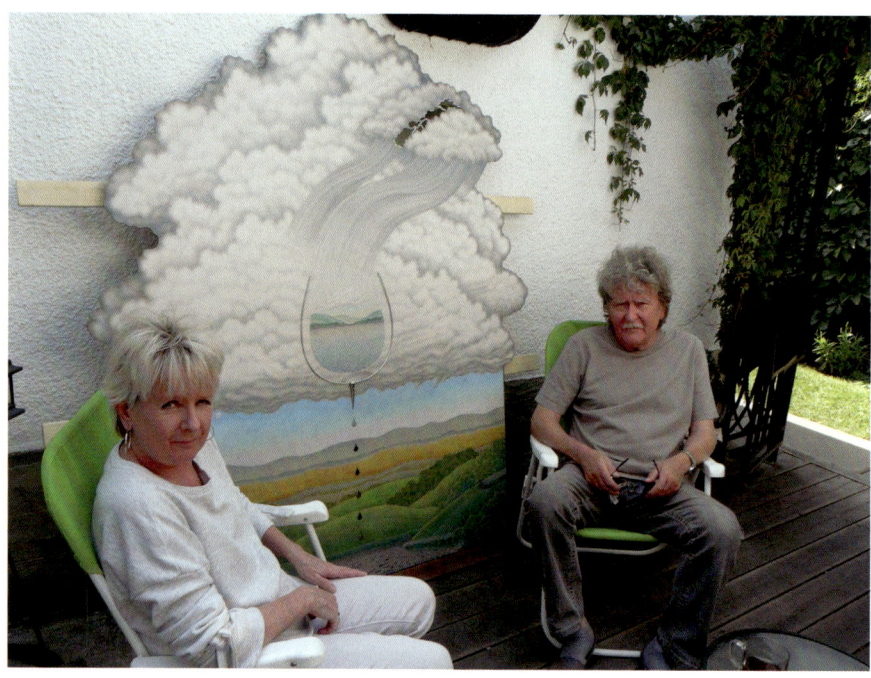

Debbie Parson and Don Proch in front of *Prairie Waters*, Magnus Avenue studio, Winnipeg, 2018.

ARTIST'S PREFACE

UNIVERSITY OF MANITOBA, day one: Ivan Eyre started his Basic Drawing class by stating that an understanding of drawing was the basis for exploring other paths in the visual arts. My interest in exploring drawing began in these classes and continues on. After receiving a Bachelor of Fine Arts and a Bachelor of Education, I worked as a high-school art teacher, during which time I continued drawing. After several years, a few shaped drawings led me to *Asessippi Tread*, an early three-dimensional drawing. In making that piece, I called on the expertise of others (a welder, chrome plater, and fabricator) to help make the 3-D drawing. At that point, The Ophthalmia Co. of Inglis, Asessippi, Manitoba, was created. Working toward the *Asessippi* exhibition at the Winnipeg Art Gallery, the Ophthalmia Co. membership grew as more interested people became involved. I gratefully acknowledge the ideas, opinions, suggestions, and work of the many contributors, including Len Anthony (printmaker), Steve Chachula (welder, Inglis, MB), Kelly Clark (pencilist), Bertie Duncan (wood carver of birds, Inglis, MB), Ted Howorth (printmaker), Bill Lobchuk (printmaker), Thomas Melnyk (pencilist, sander, Inglis, MB), Debbie Parson (design advisor, assistant), Nellie Proch (catalogue collator), Doug Proch (pencilist, sander), Don Proch Sr. (materials manager), Robert Wynnobel (chrome plating), Dan Teichman (fabricator, Henry Avenue Forge), Marsha Wineman (pencilist), and Robert Zetaruk (pencilist, sander, Inglis, MB).

In attempting to sum up my artistic approach and vision, I look to a moment even earlier, to what I believe was a time in my life that planted the seed for my making art: I was eight years old when George, son of Irene and George Anderson, moved to Inglis, Manitoba, from many northern Hudson's Bay Company store postings (Baker Lake, Pangnirtung, etc.). The Andersons brought with them a collection of exquisite Inuit art from the 1930s and 1940s. George and I were classmates and great friends. We often played with these magical objects that were prominent throughout their residence. There were bears, kayaks, seals, walrus, whales, drums, tools, hunting spears, fish, narwhals, sealskin-clad figures, hunters, and igloos, made from soapstone, bone, sinew, sealskin, wood, and ivory, with a variety of textures and natural colours all done in wondrous detail. This world-class art left a lasting impression on a young mind. The wonder for me was in who made this work, how, and why? My art is an attempt to portray that wonder in the land that I know.

—Don Proch, September 2018

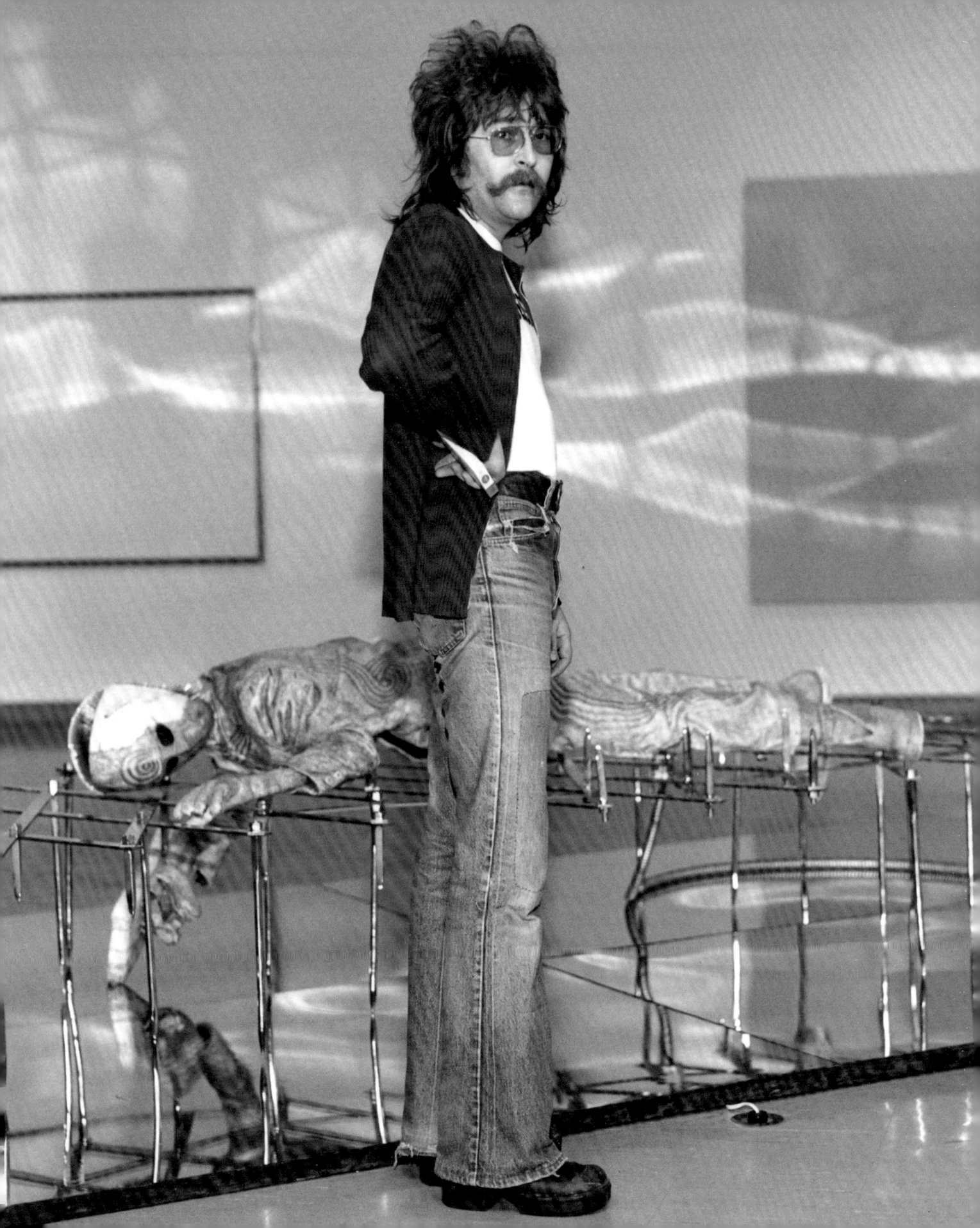

A 360° Multidimensional Voice

MANITOBA ARTIST DON PROCH has been heralded for his innovative and poignant works of art since he first emerged on Canada's art scene in 1970. He is both a prairie visionary, looking out for the future, and a prairie conscience, guarding the history and meaning of the landscape, its geology, people, and ways of life. Proch's masks, grain elevators, sculptures, installations, drawings, and prints evoke the prairie in all its dimensions, drawing viewers into his beautiful yet disquieting creative world. His messages are at once simple and direct though filled with complex and apprehensive premonitions. Illuminating the interrelationship between the land and humankind, Proch's art encourages respect for the histories and places of his youth. Using foreboding visual elements, Proch implores humanity to halt the current ecological devastation, and he challenges society to embrace the urgent need to stem climate change and steward the environment. His portrayals of rural icons and vanishing lifestyles steadfastly underline the need to secure rural sustainability.

Born in 1942 in Hamilton, Canada's steel town, this artist and environmentalist grew up in Manitoba's Asessippi Valley, first on his parents' and grandparents' farm and later in the small grain elevator town of Inglis.[1] Proch has never forgotten his roots or ancestral culture.

His visual approach to his art is unique, masking and mapping the prairie in both his two- and three-dimensional works. The national and international trajectory of his artistic career was meteoric, his acclaim rising quickly from the time of the first public presentation of his work in 1970. Over the years, Proch's art has been widely collected by public, private, and corporate collectors, some pieces having been purchased before they were completed. His art has been included in collections that hold the work of international artists like Andy Warhol, Dan Graham, Bruce Nauman, Robert Smithson, and Cy Twombly. Proch's secondary market is equally as active as his primary market.

The depth and substance of his art has made a difference to contemporary understandings, and has captivated all sectors of society. Critics, public institutions, academics, poets, writers, and anthropologists have engaged with his art over the decades. Evoking joy, humour, and serious thought, Proch's gift of visual expression has also aroused positive reactions and public actions on a number of civil realities. That is the mark of a truly successful artist.

1. Don Proch beside
   Pincushion Man, 1975.

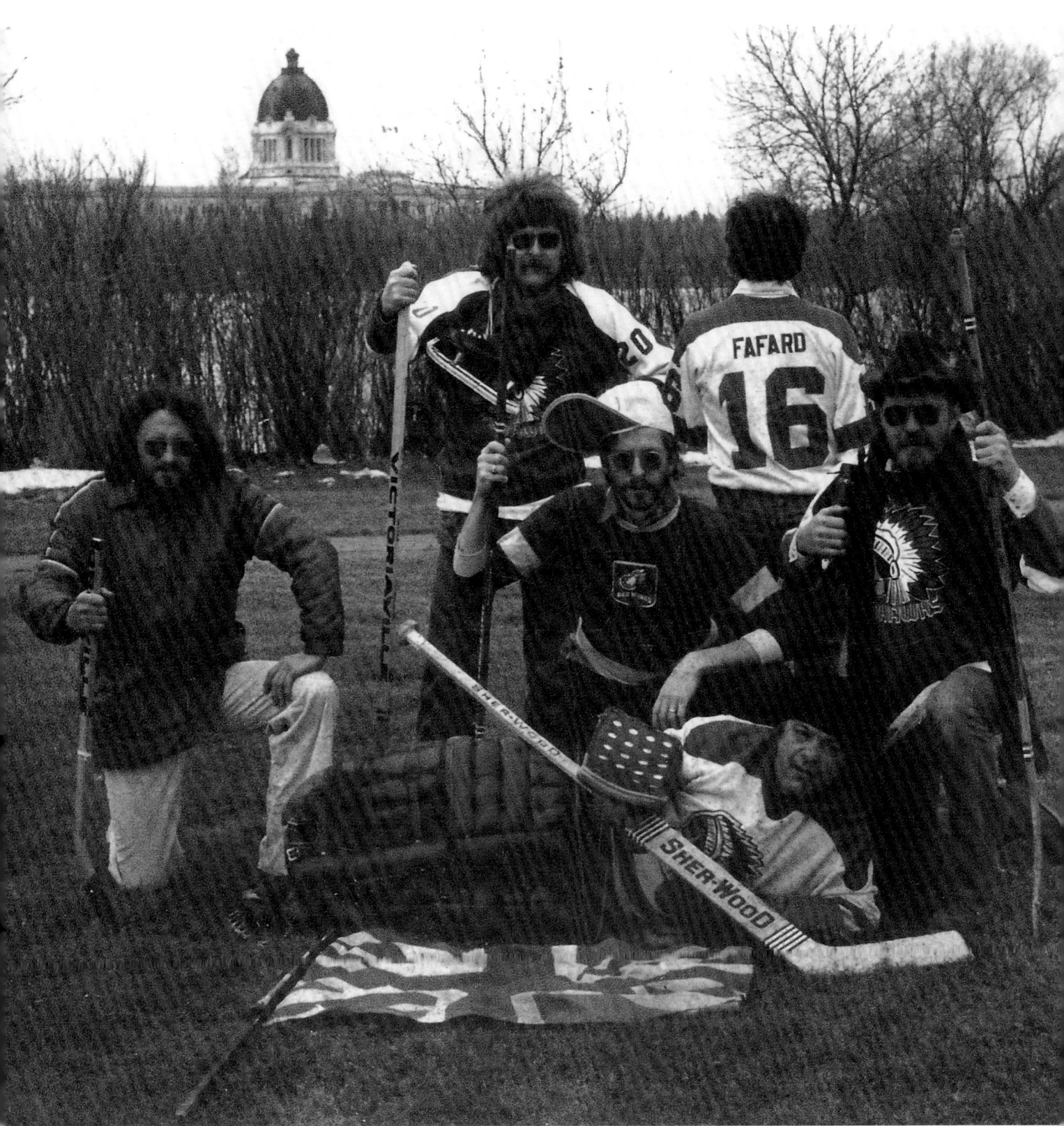

Farm to City: Quantum Transformations

ONE'S FAMILY AND EARLY experiences hold throughout a person's life. Some aspects of one's childhood provide positive memories and foundations; others recall situations and realities perhaps best forgotten. For many people, however, significant moments resurface later in life, consciously or subconsciously; and, in this, Don Proch is no exception. His family and early experiences affected his art directly, affording him continuing subject matter and feeding his quest for experimentation with innovative art-making materials. Always respecting his deep rural Canadian traditions, Proch was concerned simultaneously about the future and about the effects of the exodus in the 1960s from farm to city. That quantum societal shift spawned changing farming methods, created larger farms, and increased financial uncertainty for small farms.

In the art world at the time, there was an increasingly pressing need for fair and deserved recognition of Canadian artists. These conditions, societal and professional, coincided with Proch's artistic debut and inspired Proch to become part of an active movement in Winnipeg that radically changed Manitoba's art scene, its major institutions, private collectors, and commercial galleries. Of particular importance, the activities of this group of young Winnipeg artists heralded a new recognition of, and an appreciation for, the rights of individual artists.

The Artist's Path Defined: Inspirations from Childhood to 1970

In 1945, when Don Proch was three, the Proch family moved to Grandview, Manitoba, from Hamilton, Ontario, where Proch had been born. When he was eight, the family relocated to Manitoba's picturesque rural area of Inglis, Russell, and the Asessippi Valley. His Ukrainian immigrant farming family—parents Nastya (Nellie) and Don and grandparents Mary and George—introduced Don as child to their strong work ethic. The Prochs grew their own food, fixed broken farm equipment, built fences, and creatively improvised to meet their many

2. Hockey Game: Manitoba vs. Saskatchewan, c. 1975, in Regina. Back row, left to right: Don Proch, Joe Fafard. Middle row: Russ Yuristy, David Thauberger, Bill Lobchuk. Front: Tony Tascona.

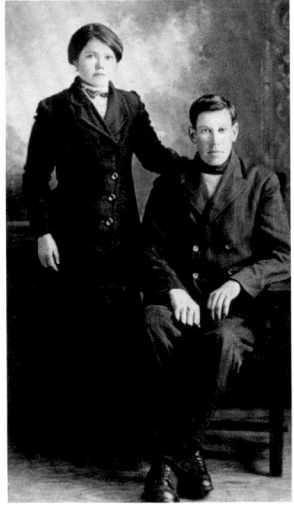
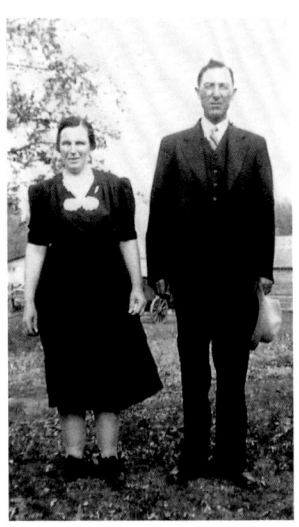
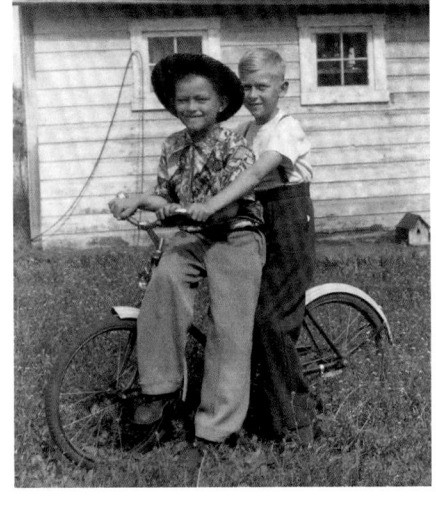
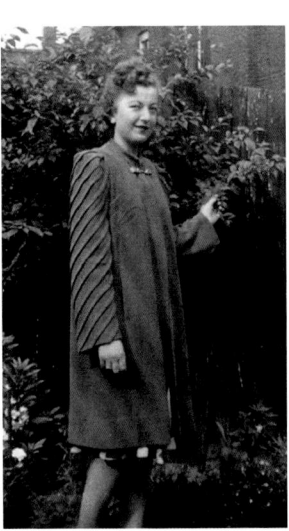
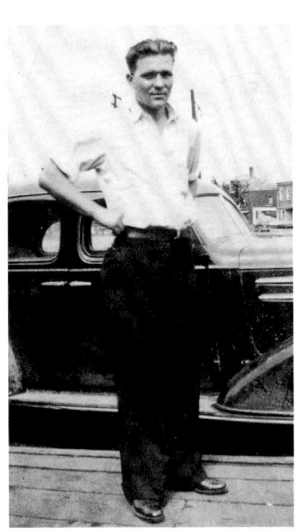

FROM TOP, LEFT TO RIGHT:

3. Don Proch's paternal grandparents and parents, Mary and George Proch.

4. Don Proch's maternal grandparents, Mary and Luke Burtnyk, Ethelbert, Manitoba.

5. Don Dudar and Don Proch, 1950.

6. Don Proch's mother, Nastya (Nellie) Proch, c. 1940.

7. Don Proch's father, Don Proch Sr., in the late 1930s in Hamilton.

other needs, reusing materials and reinventing various parts of machinery. Don's father, a steel worker in Hamilton before the family moved west, possessed much-needed skills for farming. Watching him at work was an early and meaningful inspiration to Don as a child. The skills that he learned in youth unquestionably assisted him later in his artistic career. The Prochs also celebrated Ukrainian festivals and held to traditions of the "old country," and these customs made a lasting mark on Don. All have been translated into his art.

One childhood Christmas in particular stands out for Proch. His mother had ordered six shiny balls from the Eaton's catalogue, and he was very excited when he saw them. That excitement was short-lived, however, as he was aghast and upset when he saw his mother purposefully break them.[2] He then watched transfixed as she transformed the broken bits into two dozen Christmas ornaments by gluing their tiny fragments onto whole eggs. She made the glue from the egg yolks. Amazed by this transformation into beautiful "magic decorations," Don was equally fascinated by the process of transition. That memory has stayed with him.[3] The transformation of old and new, and usual and unusual, has been a constant throughout his art-making career.

Before Don started school, his mother taught him the rudiments of math and how to read. He quickly advanced through high school and was the first in his family to attend university, the University of Manitoba, where he enrolled in engineering, switching to Fine Art in his second year. He had some knowledge of art and had demonstrated his

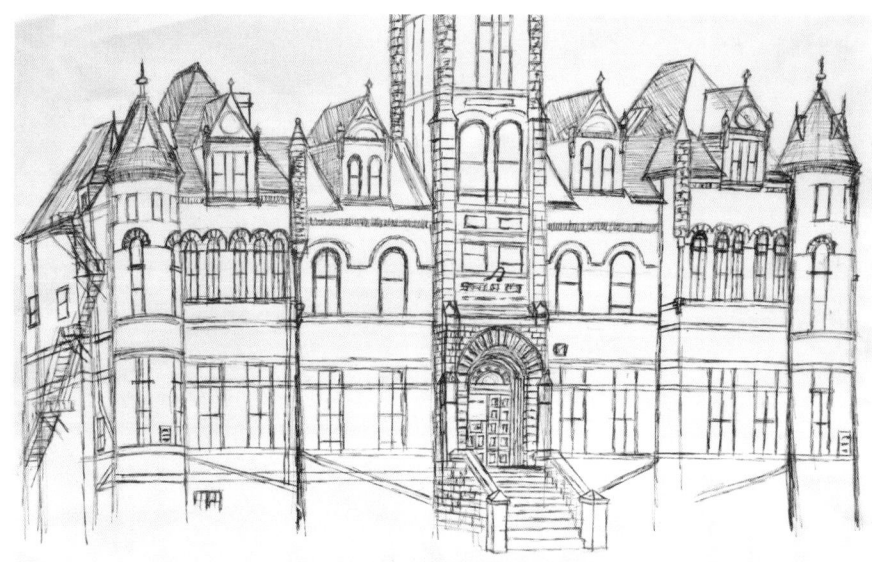

8. *School of Art*, 1961.

aptitude for art as a teenager in the art classes that he took in Inglis from Irene Anderson, an oil painter of landscapes and still lifes. He loved those classes and learned how to mix colours, prime canvases, and use various brushes.

Drawing, however, has been the focus in each stage of Don's multimedia and multifaceted art-making career. It is integral to both his two-dimensional and his three-dimensional work, and Proch says it is drawing that he likes most.[4] His 1961 pencil drawing *School of Art* reveals his drawing ability as a student. Details of the windows and roof lines, and precision in rendering angles and perspectives of the doorway and steps, are explicit. His cross-hatching of the roof foreshadows his later work, as does the evident dexterity with which Proch used both the point and the side of his pencil. His 1962 student pen-and-ink drawing *Dick Williams Print Studio, School of Art, University of Manitoba*, further developed his ability to capture detail. In this work, Proch conveys space and depth with parallel linear strokes—vertical for the walls, diagonal for the ceiling. The fluorescent lights above the press and work table are parallel with the pipes along the ceiling, effectively extending his spatial depictions. His portrayal of the figure over the press is as detailed as all else in the drawing.

Proch graduated with a Bachelor of Fine Art degree in 1964, and in 1967 he earned his Bachelor of Education degree. Years later, reflecting on his art school days, he said that "the University of Manitoba School of Art at this time was the school of George Swinton and the young Ivan Eyre . . . a strong influence."[5]

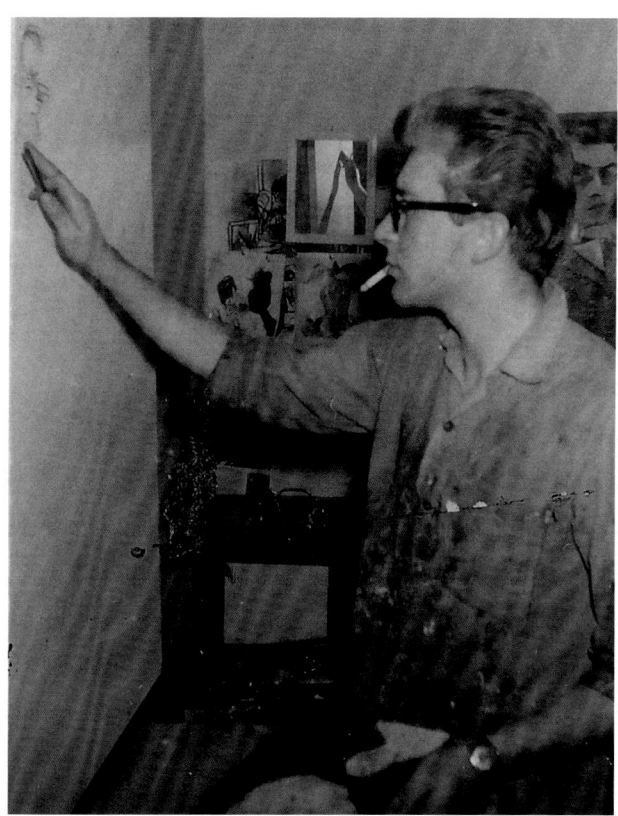

9. Don Proch, 1962, studio on Hargrave Street, Winnipeg.

5

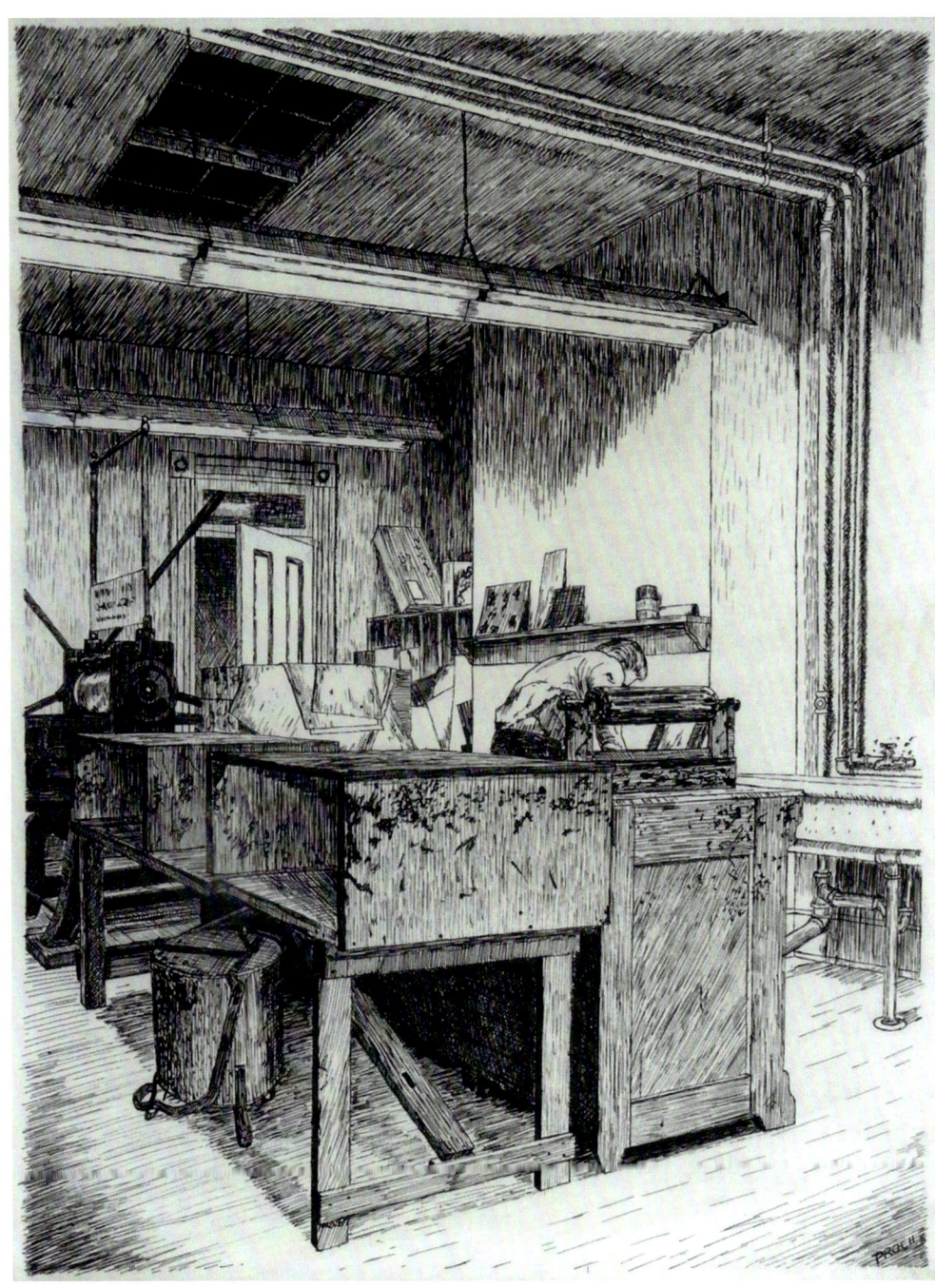

10. *Dick Williams' Print Studio, 1962.*

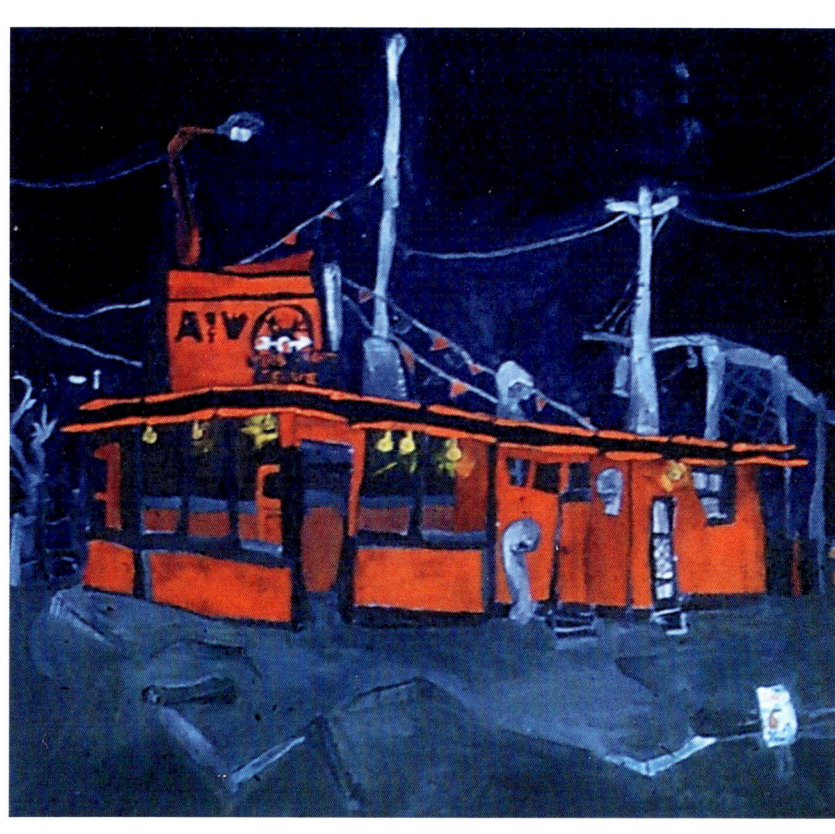

11. *A & W*, 1964, the last painting by Proch.

From the outset, Proch integrated his core messages into his landscapes. Architectural details, machinery, and places of work are combined in his prairiescapes, and the impact of human presence, evident early in his work, was sustained over the decades. A trio of paintings from 1964, his graduation year (*Black House on Black Hill*, *Lockport*, and *A & W*), done in oil on canvas, are examples of that interest. His nightscape *A & W* added a psychological and social dimension to his subject as he depicted the human impact of the drive-in but without including any figures. Since then, Proch has done relatively few works in which he depicts human figures, though many of the forms he draws on are those he has built of the human head and shoulders. He thus clearly puts the responsibility for place and the memory and psyche of the individual to the fore, situating the health of the land within the human realm, not the human being within the land. Proch was not satisfied with his 1964 paintings, his last, for he never returned to the medium. At the time, he felt that he needed to focus on drawing for a period, drawing being the foundation for painting. Indeed, the drawings and notes in his sketchbooks provide tremendous insights into his methods, inspirations, and evolving details throughout his career. The actual construction of each work was often noted in his sketchbook drawings too, and they are as critical to his process as is his attention to the surfaces.

Family roots, the farm, and the Asessippi Valley have been central themes throughout Proch's entire art-making career in his imagery and his materials, such as his use of binder twine, barbed wire, bones, and grasses. Proch, a very private person, admits that all his work has personal connections.[6] Although he says little about his work itself, his art is imbued with his memories of his background, revealing the values he learned in his youth. Skills in trapping, repairing machinery, and reusing materials were gained on the farm from his parents and grandfather. These means and values became important grounding for his later work. Full of his own perceptions of both past and present, his art confidently manifests his concerns and fears about the future of society. It is not surprising that Proch was simultaneously involved in the radical movements that transformed the Canadian and provincial art scenes.

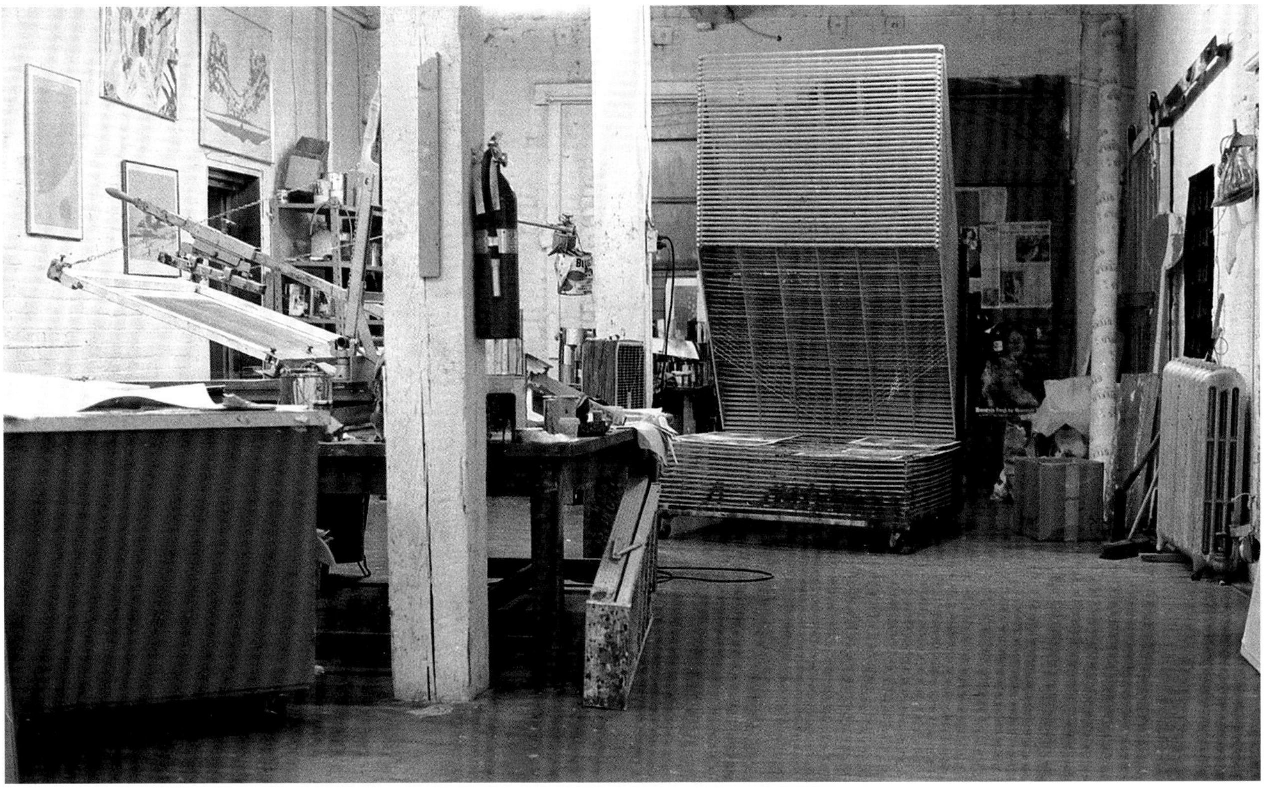

12. The Grand Western Canadian Screen Shop on Princess Street.

An Arts Milieu Transformed, 1968–1972

Proch and his colleagues worked during the era of centennials of the late 1960s and early 1970s—Canada's in 1967, Manitoba's in 1970, and Winnipeg's in 1974. Each of these milestones added to the impetus for a greater understanding of Canada's nationalism with its many diverse cultures and communities. Canada's multiculturalism policy was announced by Prime Minister Pierre Elliott Trudeau in 1971. At the same time, artists globally were challenged by the rapid development of new materials and technologies. Artists also responded to the speed with which international news spread. Issues of the Vietnam War were ever present. The result was a quantum shift in both the subjects and the means of creating art. Proch was at the forefront of this shift. He incorporated new technologies and materials, juxtaposing them with traditional means of making art. He consistently posed difficult questions facing contemporary society.

Throughout these heady and rapidly changing times, however, a more radical regionalism grew in Canadian art, its focus turning away from the international centres of New York and London. Proch gave a strong voice to the prairies and was at the centre of this new Canadian regionalism. He recognized first hand the impacts of the increasing numbers of deserted rural towns, and he viscerally expressed the dichotomies of nostalgia and the consequential harsh realities of change.

Historically, from the early 1860s on, Winnipeg had been a hub of new expression and artistic ideas. The city was the home of Canada's first civic art gallery with the founding in 1912 of the Winnipeg Art Gallery. In 1913, the Winnipeg School of Art was established, the first formal art school in western Canada. By the 1960s, when Proch and his colleagues went to Winnipeg to study art, the 1951 merger of the Winnipeg School of Art with the University of Manitoba was well established, and it was granting both diplomas and degrees in Fine Art.

When Proch and his colleagues graduated from the University of Manitoba, the Manitoban and Canadian artistic scenes were on the verge of a significant paradigm shift. The artistic milieu of the mid-1960s was as it had been for decades. The Winnipeg Art Gallery was relatively small and still housed in part of the Winnipeg Civic Auditorium, built in 1932. No artists' fees were paid for exhibitions or for copyright. Collectors bought art from a variety of sources: from commercial galleries, directly from artists, or at cocktail parties from dealers from various Canadian centres who presented a specific artist's work. However, that scene was about to undergo a dramatic change with the arrival of these "country boys," as they were dubbed by Bill Lobchuk, artist and fellow student with Proch.

Having come to the big city from his small rural community, Proch decided to stay after graduation. So, too, did a number of his fellow students. Proch would return to Russell, Inglis, and the Asessippi Valley only to visit family and to re-experience the space and light of the prairie. Like Proch, many in his fine art class were from rural communities, and they too had strong personalities and big visions. It was a group that included Don Proch, Bill Lobchuk, E.J. (Ted) Howorth, and Joe Fafard. All of them, singly and collectively, have made significant artistic and political contributions to the overall Canadian art scene. Together, they were the core of the Grand Western Canadian Screen Shop, founded in 1968 by Bill Lobchuk. Along with master printer Len Anthony, and Saskatchewan artists David Thauberger and Vic Cicansky, the Screen Shop under Lobchuk's leadership transformed how art was made and its inherent message. Their aim was to make original art accessible financially, increase its availability, and reach wider audiences by depicting relatable subject matter. They enhanced the human essence in their art, portraying everyday prairie places and activities in prints such as Proch's country dwelling *Woodsmoke* (1977) or his curling themes *Granite I* and *Granite II* (1979). Theirs was the communal art-making process of printmaking. As Lobchuk commented, "prints are like social art. You can do it yourself and/or collaborate. They are for a market of

people who may, or do, appreciate art but cannot afford paintings. It has a democratic involvement, for as multiples many can have them. Prints challenge the rarefied notion of art, in the creating, the looking, owning, and engaging."[7]

Their impact was immediate. By the early 1970s, the Grand Western Canadian Screen Shop was flourishing in an intoxicating social and artistic milieu in which printmaking now vied with painting and sculpture as a primary art-making method. To art historian Angela Davis, "printmaking became the 'rebellious' technique in a socially rebellious time."[8] Lobchuk reminisced that, with their prints, they collectively succeeded in "breaking the barriers of the 'hierarchy' in the traditional art world. Prints had become a legitimate art form in contemporary Canadian art and widely recognized as such."[9]

Canada was thriving economically, and societal traditions were being tested in the 1960s and early 1970s. It was an era of renewed feminism, political debate, and exponential growth of galleries, artist-run spaces, cooperatives, art publications, and funding programs. Underlining the democracy of prints, Davis opined that, in "a period of experimentation and social encounter, both in art and everyday life, the Screen Shop was the place where art, technology and communication could meet. The print is uniquely capable of becoming . . . an inexpensive bridge to an understanding of the wealth of visual expression in Canadian art. . . . This was the aspect of printmaking that would make the new art form so important."[10]

The Screen Shop became a vibrant social centre in Winnipeg, where members of the entire arts community congregated on Friday nights, often pouring out onto the sidewalk. As Lobchuk noted, "we clicked. People were speaking the same language and heading in the same direction from similar experiences in art and life. It was the prairie and about the prairie. We understood that." He added that "we were all country boys in the city."[11] Regionalism reigned in Winnipeg.

The Screen Shop also created unique group projects and developed two special portfolios, in 1978 and 1980, respectively. Winnipeg's Bill Lobchuk, Don Proch, and

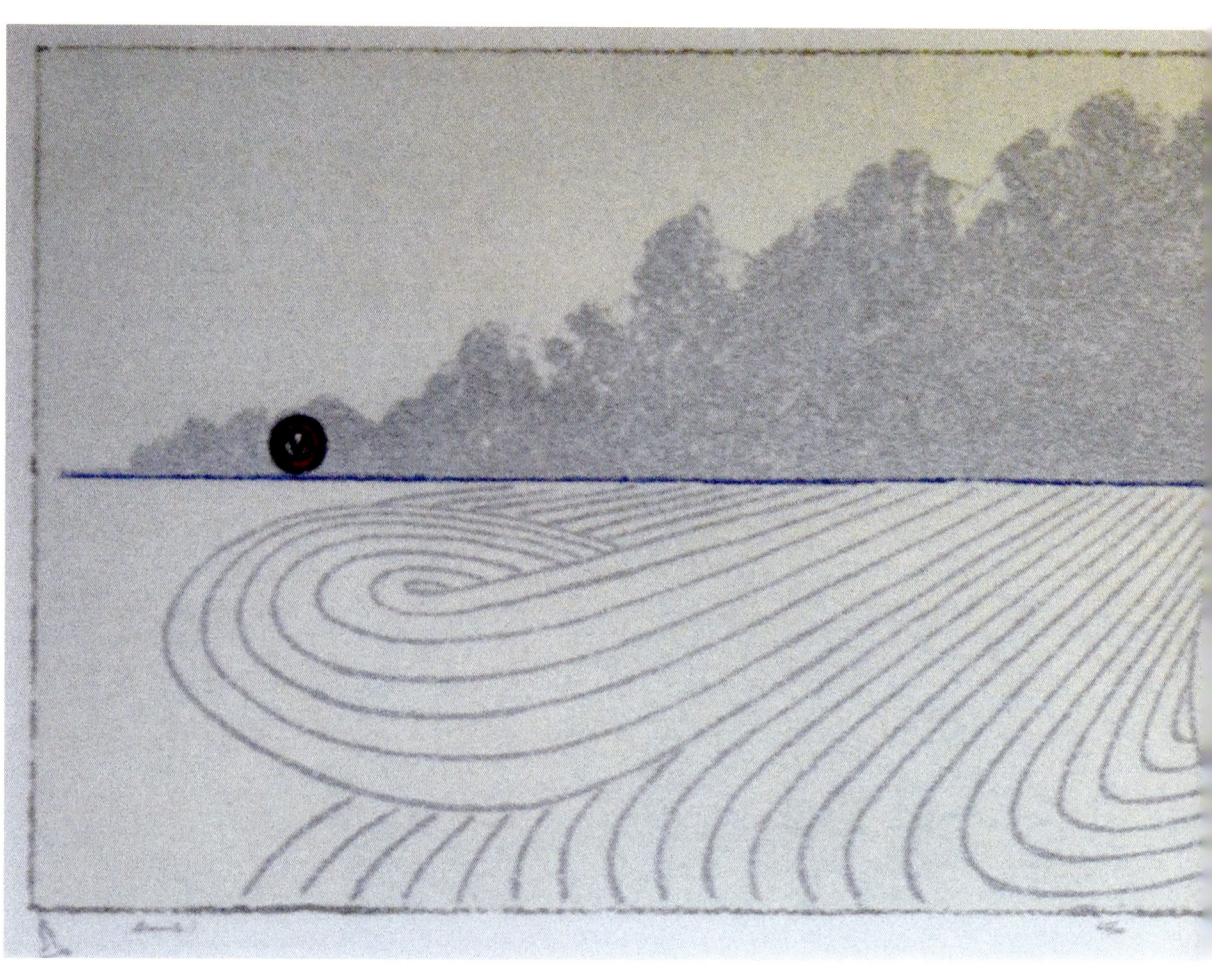

13. *Granite I*, 1979.

Tony Tascona, and Regina's Joe Fafard, David Thauberger, and Russell Yuristy were in the first portfolio, and they were joined by Winnipeg's Chris Finn and Regina's Vic Cicansky for the second. These two print series were the highlights of their concerted efforts to reach "a wider market and more collectors. We wanted to prove that we could produce and market our own work. The first, an edition of seventy-five, was great. We reached our goal (to sell enough sets to cover the cost of production) and were in profit mode before production was completed. We subsequently sold the entire edition. We felt heady! So we conceived of doing a second, inviting two more artists, and doing an edition of 150. Egos got in the way, and we made our costs but no more!"[12]

For Proch, the Screen Shop was, importantly, "one of the ways to get artists moving across the country, and when they came to Winnipeg to print we found out what was going on elsewhere."[13] The Screen Shop undertook a number of joint projects with St. Michael's Print Studio in Newfoundland, with Pierre Ayot from Graff Studio in Montreal, and with Open Studio in Toronto. Proch went to Montreal to print at Graff, and artists from Western Front in Vancouver came to Winnipeg. Newly available grants from the Canada Council for the Arts were critical in enabling these exchanges. The new sense of connection with national colleagues was paralleled by their growing sense of the celebration of regionalism. Simultaneously,

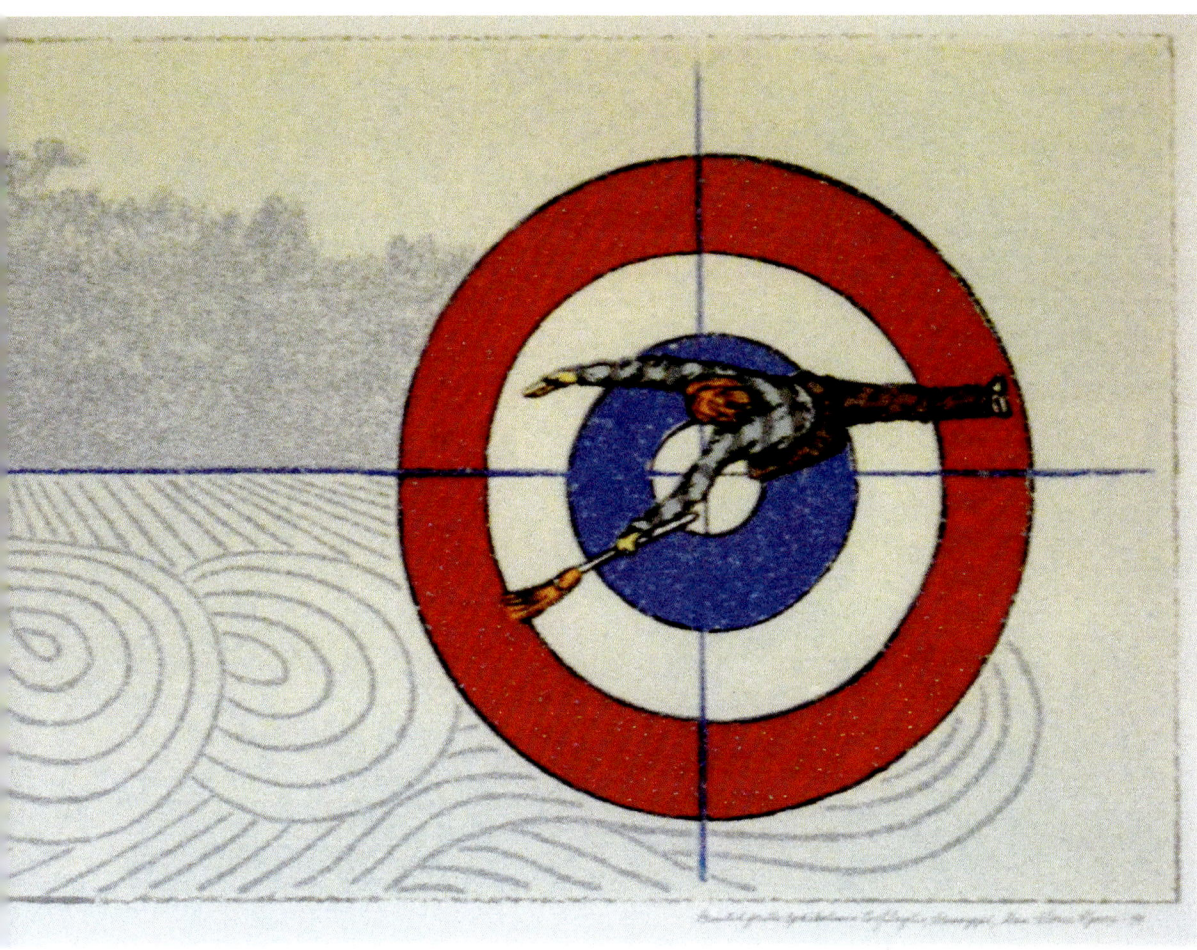

an increased recognition of Aboriginal art was evident in the early 1970s with the founding of the Indigenous Group of Seven. Both Jackson Beardy and Daphne Odjig made prints at the Screen Shop. Beardy also travelled to Paris in 1978 as part of the Screen Shop exhibition at the Canadian Cultural Centre.

Other critical developments also marked Canada's artistic milieu at this time. The most significant was the impact through the 1960s and 1970s of the Canada Council for the Arts, founded in 1957 following years of lobbying by artists and organizations after the Kingston Conference in 1941. A truly positive impetus for art and artists, the Canada Council supported touring exhibitions across Canada and artist exchanges and residencies, enabling artists to travel and develop relationships with colleagues in other parts of the country.

Winnipeg artists, including Proch and his Screen Shop colleagues, were actively involved in national and provincial advocacy for artists' rights, recognition, and intellectual property. In 1968, London, Ontario, artists Jack Chambers, Tony Urquhart, and Kim Ondaatje had founded CARFAC (Canadian Artists Representation, Front des Artistes Canadiens) to enshrine artists' intellectual rights. In 1970, Lobchuk, Howorth, Proch, and others of their Winnipeg colleagues were involved in CARFAC's work, spearheading CARFAC's initiatives in Manitoba and western Canada. Proch was integral to the group's discussions, though perhaps more as an observing

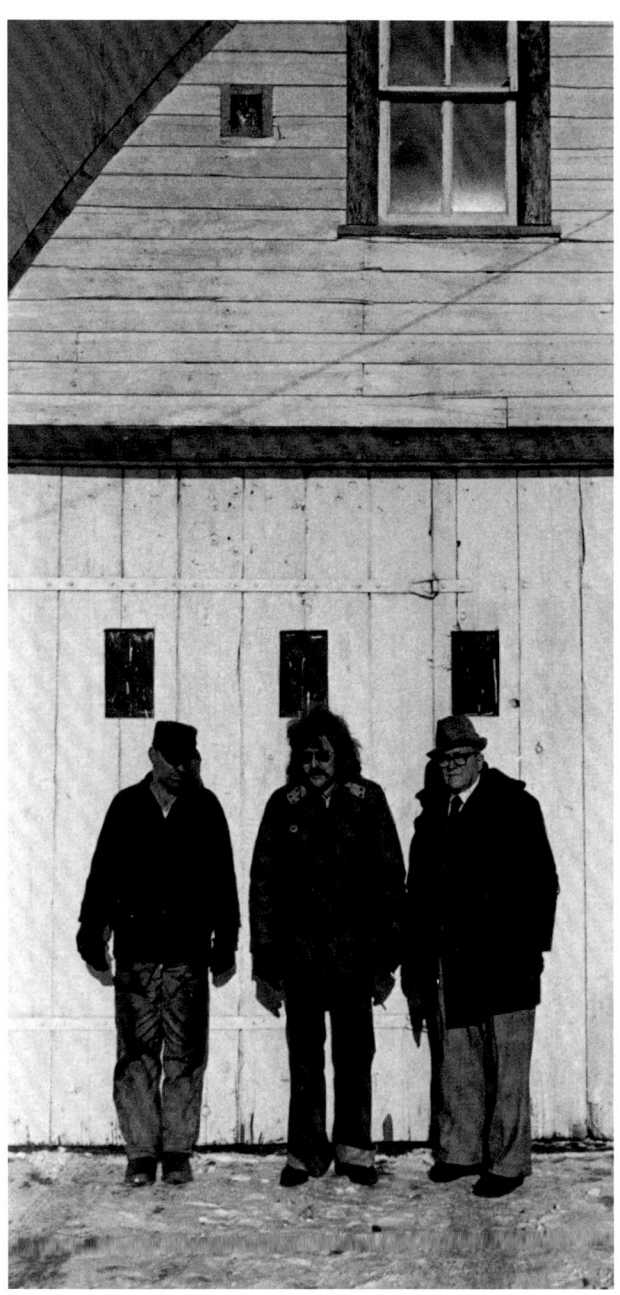

14. Stewart MacPherson (left), Don Proch, and Don Proch Sr. (right), at Stewart's Shop, Roseisle, Manitoba, 1978.

participant and reflector than as a leader. He recalled that the first meetings of the Winnipeg CARFAC group were held at the Union Hall on Portage Avenue. Lobchuk became CARFAC national director in 1972, and "we moved the national headquarters from Edmonton to Winnipeg as we did not want it to be in Toronto."[14] Collectively demanding that artists' copyright rights be recognized by galleries and publishers, the Winnipeg group picketed the new Winnipeg Art Gallery and overturned the nominations to its board of governors to secure artists' places on it. Their actions in 1971 and 1972 brought high visibility to their cause. Success was realized in 1975 when the payment of exhibition fees by galleries, based on CARFAC's minimum copyright fee schedule, became mandatory. That year the Canada Council made the payment of artists' fees to living Canadian artists a key requirement of eligibility for program assistance grants to public art galleries.

Despite the successful advocacy for many artists' economic and recognition rights, the group did not realize all of its goals. There was still no federal or provincial legislation on the status of artists. The Copyright Act applicable to the visual arts remained that from the 1920s; the new act came into effect only on 8 June 1988. Also, the Cultural Property Import Export Act designating works of art of national significance was not proclaimed until 1982.

Newly initiated artist-run centres were another important development on the national arts scene in the 1970s. Winnipeg's Plug In was the first, founded in 1972, followed shortly by Open Space in Victoria and soon after by others across the country. Many artists involved in the Grand Western Canadian Screen Shop were involved in Plug In's founding with the centre's inaugural curators Doug Sigurdson and Suzanne Gillies. Proch attended some of Plug In's early meetings, as did other Screen Shop artists, including Bill Lobchuk, Tony Tascona, Bruce Head, Winston Leathers, Ted Howorth, and the Winnipeg Art Gallery Curator of Contemporary Art, Philip Fry. The mandate of artist-run centres was the presentation of contemporary art. At the outset the centres were free from the bureaucracy of the older, larger collecting institutions. A special funding stream for artist-run centres was established at the Canada Council. The Council marked another visual arts milestone with its establishment in 1972 of the Canada Council Art Bank. The Art Bank bought work from contemporary artists, including Proch, for its new rental program to government departments and offices. This program proved to be an important financial and profile support for artists. It also increased public awareness and understanding of the significance of contemporary Canadian art.

Closer to home for Proch and his colleagues were the new and equally impactful provincial supports for the arts. The Manitoba Arts Council, the province's arm's-length arts funding body, was established by legislation in 1965 "to promote the study, enjoyment, production and performance of works in the arts." The Manitoba Arts Council, however, was not actually incorporated until 1967, Canada's centennial year. Once running, its initial funding was directed to organizations for the presentation of contemporary Manitoba art, resulting in artists having more exhibitions with accompanying publications. In 1973, when the Screen Shop reached its fifth anniversary, the first visual arts awards were granted to individual visual artists.

University of Manitoba professor of English Ken Hughes was particularly influential as a member of the Manitoba Arts Council, being its chair for a short time in the 1970s, and as a collector of art. Hughes also made a number of purchases of the works of Screen Shop artists for the new art collection at St. John's College. Further, in 1982, he wrote *Manitoba Art Monographs*, featuring six artists who he thought had great promise and whose work, in his view, "spoke of the prairie": Don Proch, Bill Lobchuk, Ted Howorth, Esther Warkov, Kelly Clark, and Tony Tascona, the senior artist of that group. All but Warkov were associated with the Screen Shop.

In assessing the quantum positive shifts in Canada's art scene in the 1960s and early 1970s, Winnipeg's role as a key centre of national and provincial grassroots action is widely recognized. This Winnipeg group of emerging artists raised awareness of artists and contemporary art while making many advances on the national scene and transforming the visual arts environment in Manitoba. Their endeavours unquestionably did much to revolutionize Winnipeg's arts' establishment and the Winnipeg Art Gallery's approaches to, and relationships with, contemporary artists, and changed how other public and commercial galleries represented artists. Democratizing the process of art making and its affordability for collectors radically changed the broader Winnipeg art scene and its institutions.

Despite his engagement during these heady years of advocacy, demonstrations, societal changes, and national, provincial, and civic centennials, Proch steadfastly maintained his focus on art making and his burgeoning career. His priority was the creation of work for his upcoming 1972 solo exhibition *The Legend of Asessippi* at the new Winnipeg Art Gallery. Proch investigated new materials, ideas, and innovative approaches to art making, and his experiments at the Screen Shop, his unique installations, and his stand-alone works defined what were to become the constants in his art. Proch was never swayed by new fads or waves, eschewing influences of others and current trends. Always staying true to his core concerns, he never bowed to conceptual or performance art, abstract art or geometric abstraction, computer manipulation, film, or photography. His was a self-developed, deliberate, and unique visual language.

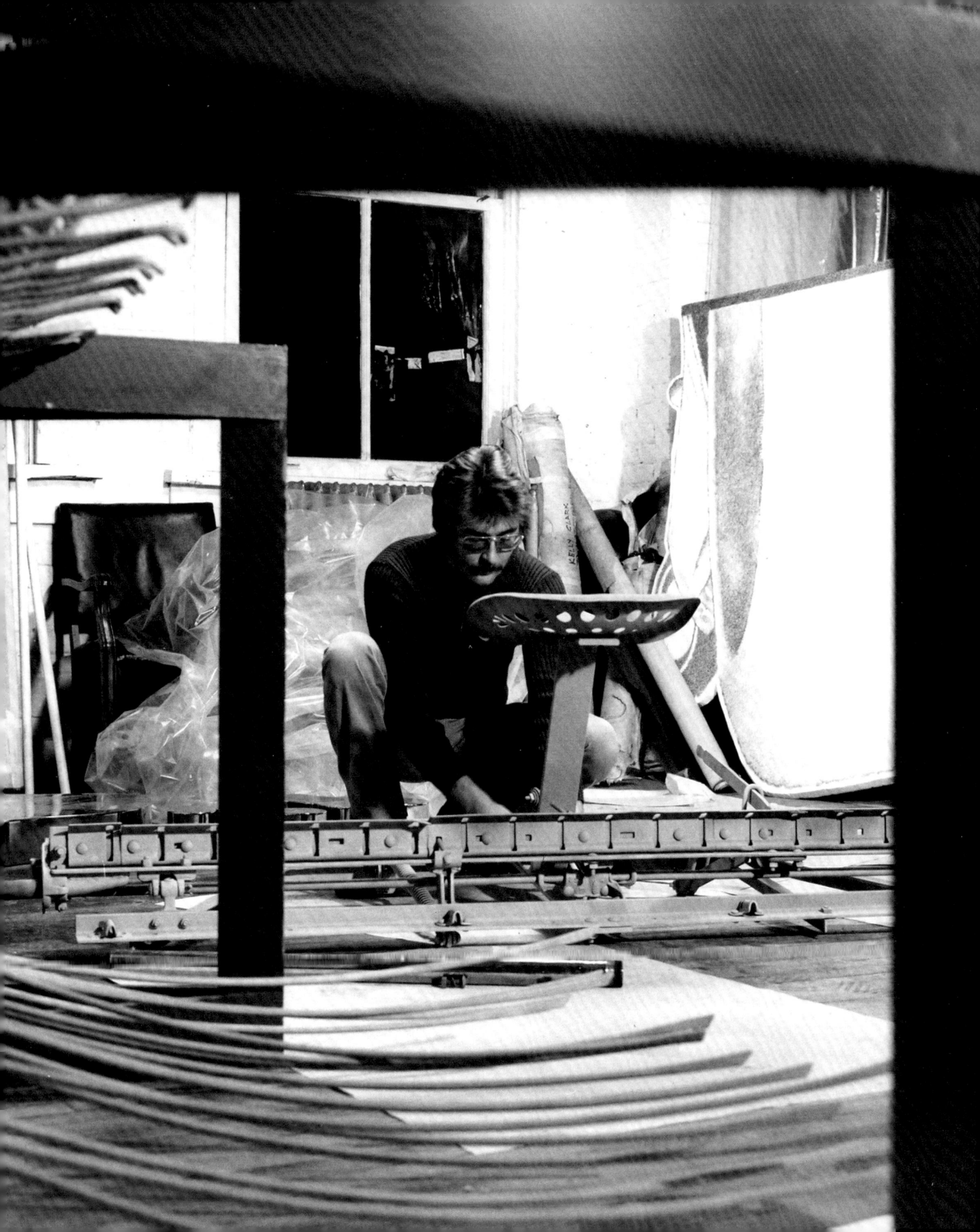

Preoccupations and Experimentation

GRAIN ELEVATORS, those vanishing prairie icons, have been focal points of Don Proch's art from the beginning. Proch knew elevators especially well having grown up in a farming community and as a result of his job in his youth at the building storage annex of the local elevator. His first painting was of an elevator, done when he was a student of Irene Anderson. In this small 1954 oil on canvas, *Paterson Elevator*, the elevator situated on the east side of the town of Inglis takes prominence in the middle of the prairie landscape. The horizon line is at the mid-point, with the clear blue sky topped by several fluffy clouds in formations that became the precursor to his later stylized clouds. The houses and outbuildings in front of the elevator are painted with the precision that would increase as his career progressed. The colours are pure, and his care of application is obvious, further traits that would characterize his work over the subsequent decades. In 1968, Proch returned to the subject with his ceramic tile mural *Inglis Elevators East View*, in which he set the last remaining group of five elevators in Canada behind a wheat field, a location now recognized as a national historic site. Later, in the 1980s and 1990s, grain elevators became the subject of his large sculptural *Elevator Series*, and his interest in them as vanishing prairie icons returned in his masks of the 2010s, including *Typeface Mask* of 2016. Here, a tiny elevator is set in the eye of the mask, in front of a full moon, as if it is looking at and seeing a vanishing past.

Consistency in message, substance, and exploration over the decades has marked Proch's evolving and unique creative visual language. As climate change and ecological concerns have accelerated, so too has the foreboding quality in his art, shown by the heightening contrasts within each work between the natural prairie landscape and the escalating harm from chemicals in the environment.

In writing about Proch's understanding of the history of the Asessippi region, Adele Freedman noted that "the colonizers melted from the land, leaving their buildings and farm implements as crumbling monuments to their spirit. For Proch, who as a kid bicycled down the highway to Asessippi, it is a spiritual place and the Asessippi leftovers are relics. He works the old wood,

15

15. Don Proch assembling *Motria's Hair*, 1971, at his studio on Princess Street.

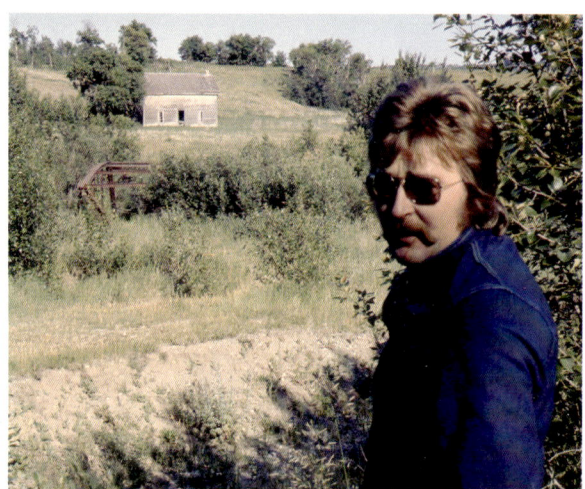

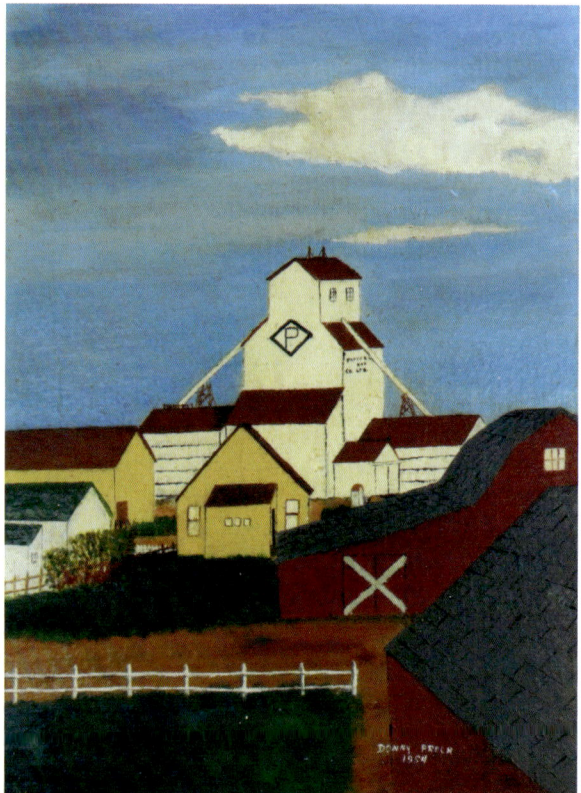

machinery, and bones of the Asessippi into his art."[15] His respect for and knowledge of Indigenous Plains cultures are also clearly articulated in his masks and sculptures that refer to traditional Indigenous materials such as porcupine quills and as seen in *Pincushion Man*, which relates to early Indigenous histories with the bison.

Interestingly, save for his childhood family memories, Proch was not involved in Manitoba's Ukrainian community. He attended one Ukrainian artists' conference, in Thunder Bay in the early 1970s, before creating *Motria's Hair* in 1972. Writers and the academic community in Ukraine, however, are rightly proud of this artist of Ukrainian heritage and have included his work in publications and exhibitions. Pride and interest in Proch's prairie roots are evident in the 1991 issue of the *Kyiv Journal*, which describes the Asessippi region and Proch's esteem for Canada's Indigenous history:

> As an adolescent, he observed that everything grows from the earth, the earth feeds us, and her bountiful layer/surface [that which produces] is so small/thin/shallow and so fragile. . . . His desire to think through and comprehend his internal link with his native earth evolved into a calling. For this reason he sought visible media through which to convey the silent grace/blessing of the earth. Indeed, his understanding of nature as relevant to all which exists in her, as the continuity of life and the eternal cycle/rotation, this unites him with the worldview and artistic symbols of the original residents of the land. . . .[16]

These perceptions are a poignant summary of the essence of Proch's oeuvre. It is clear that by the end of the 1950s his interests were established, and by the end of the 1960s they were evolving into a unique visual and visceral exploration and presentation. Thereafter they have been systematically developed through his various series and interests, which span decades, his masks, grain elevators, prints, and woodblocks, all with overarching links of message and drawing between series.

16. Don Proch in the Asessippi Valley, c. 1978.

17. *Paterson Elevator*, 1954, Proch's first painting.

18. (OPPOSITE) *Asessippi Tread*, 1970.

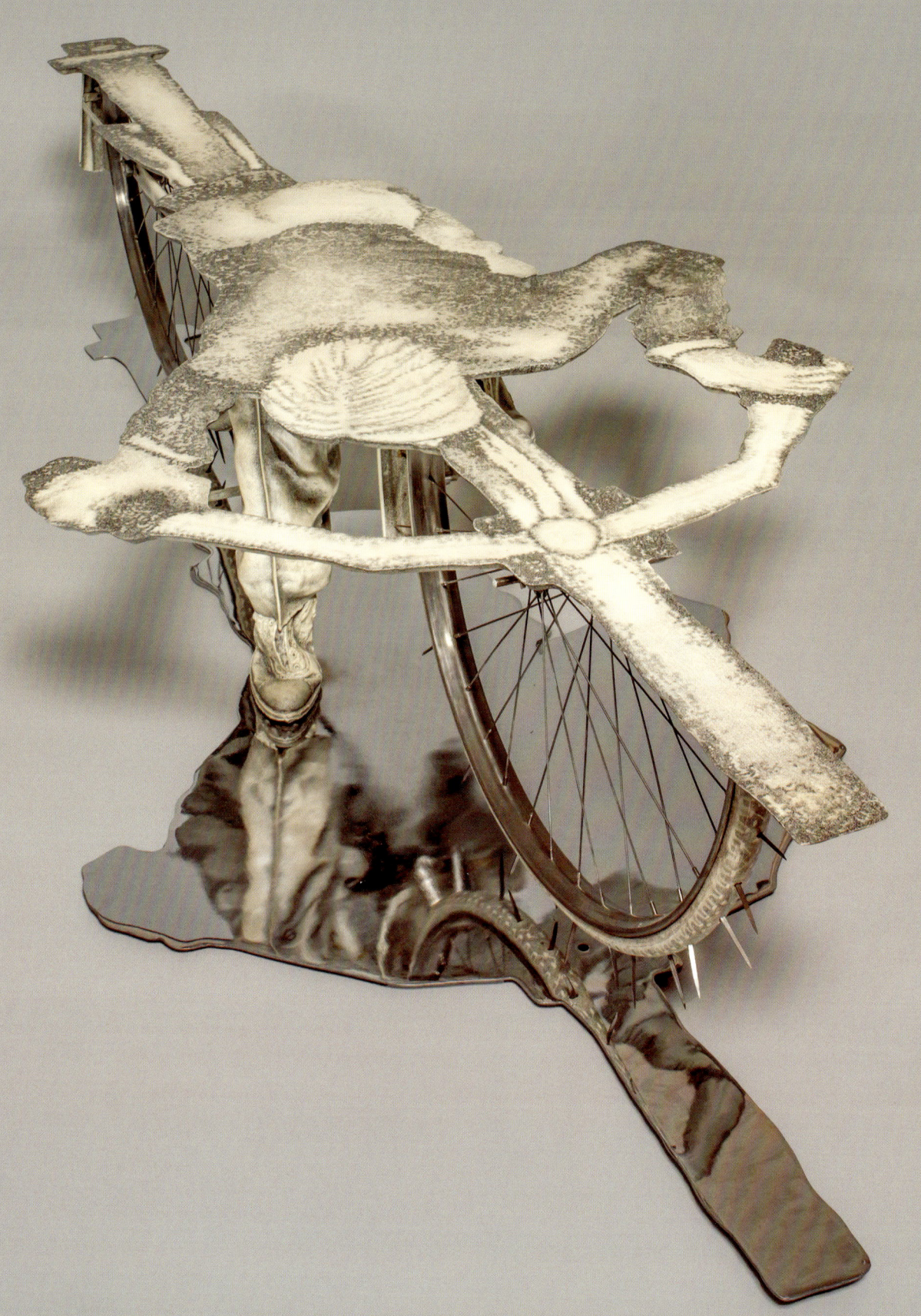

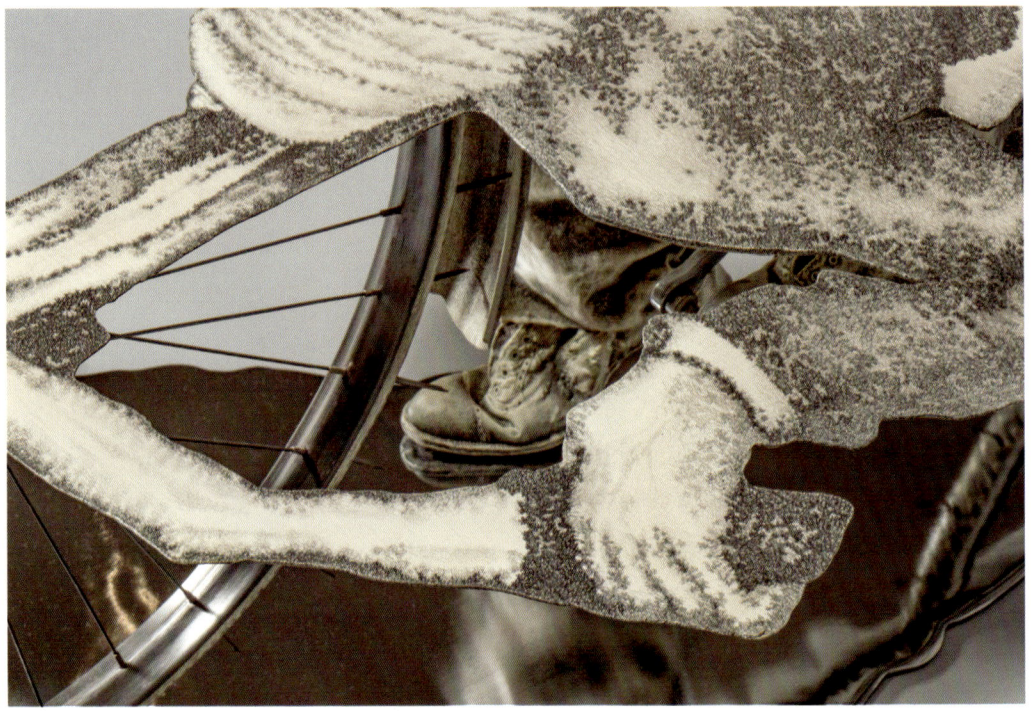

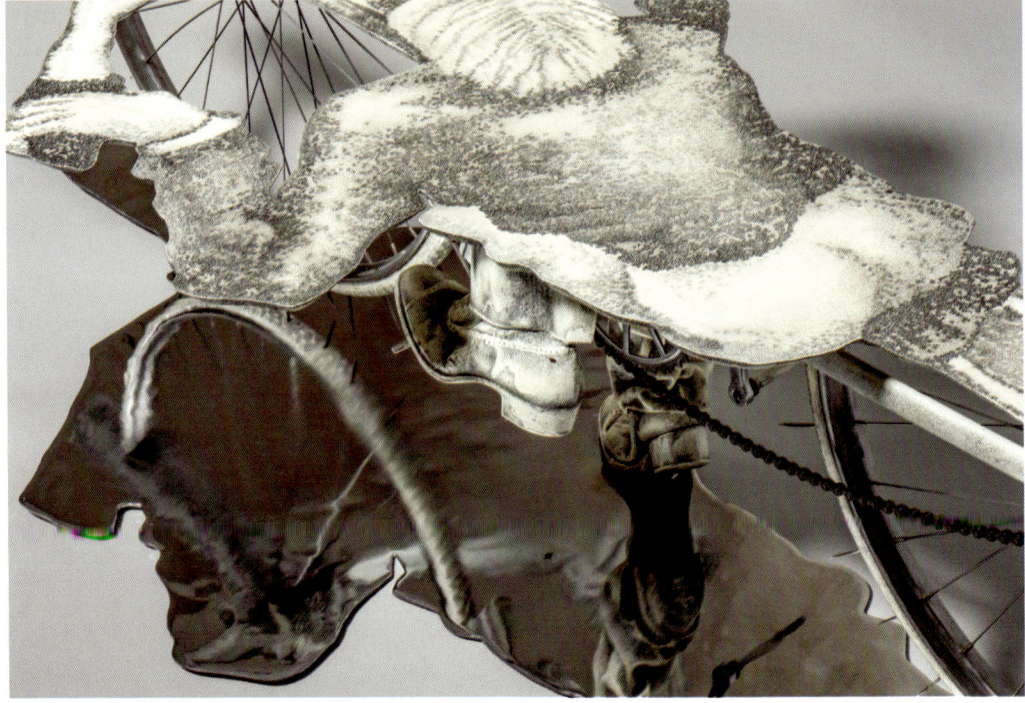

19 and 20. *Asessippi Tread* (detail), 1970.

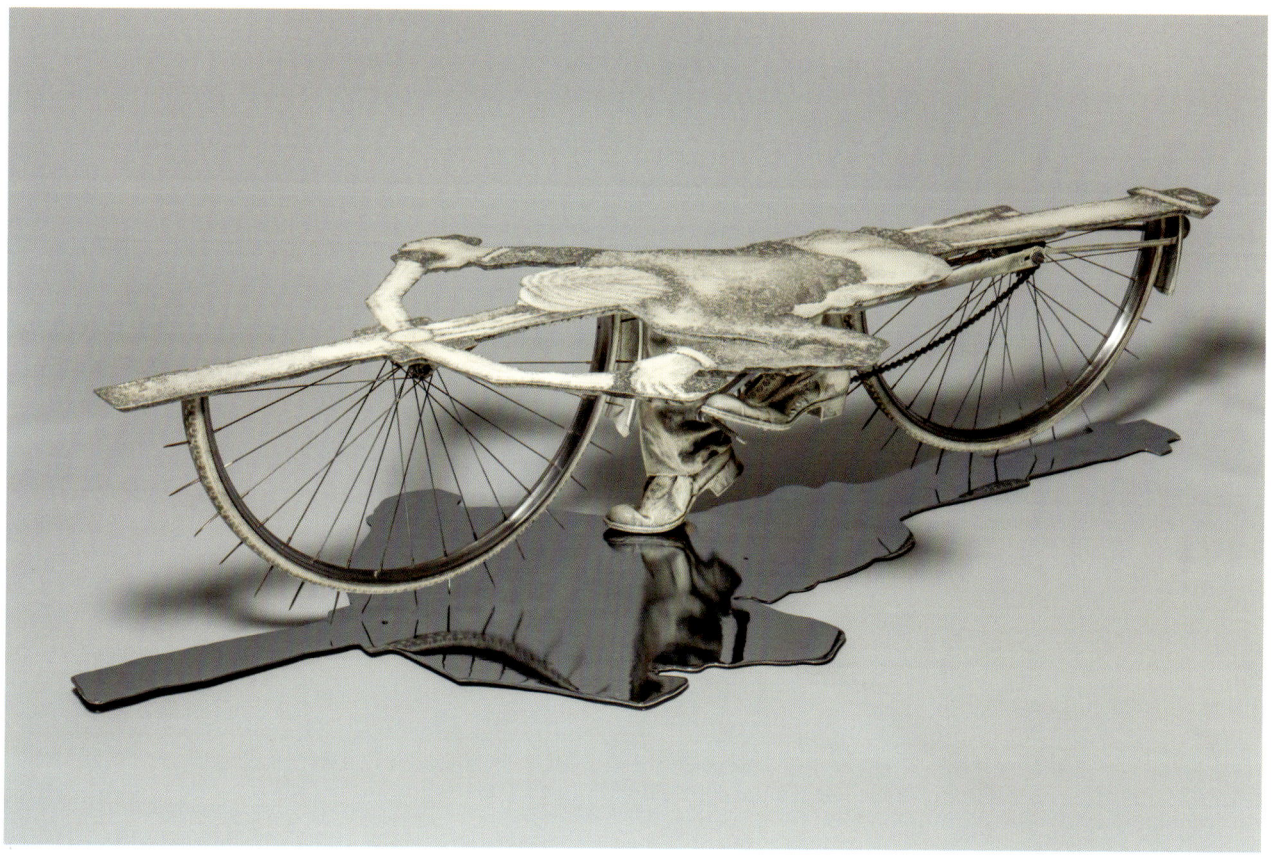

21. *Asessippi Tread* (side view), 1970.

A Career Defined:
Bicycles and Velocipedes, 1970–1980

Asessippi Tread (1970), his breakthrough work, vaulted Proch onto the national stage. It was accepted into the Twelfth Winnipeg Show in 1970, the Winnipeg Art Gallery's renowned biennial national juried exhibition. The juror that year was Brydon Smith, Curator of Contemporary Art at the National Gallery of Canada. Winner of the Purchase Prize, *Asessippi Tread* was immediately recognized as an important sculpture by an emerging Manitoba artist and was bought for the Winnipeg Art Gallery's collection. The Winnipeg Art Gallery also invited Proch to present his first solo show, *The Legend of Asessippi*, two years later. His approach to art making and the scope of his work, correlating rural and urban, were new, and *The*

Legend of Asessippi was revolutionary. Including prints, sculptures, and large-scale farm implements, such as the hayrake in *Motria's Hair*, the exhibit was a complex and comprehensive project that had to be completed in a relatively short time. Proch invited a number of artists, friends, and family members to be his collaborators, forming the Ophthalmia Company of Inglis, Asessippi, Manitoba. With two exhibitions at the Winnipeg Art Gallery, *The Legend of Asessippi* in 1972 and another, *Asessippi Clouds*, in 1975, his place in Canadian art was confirmed, and his career was launched on the national stage. In 1980, he was given a solo exhibition at the National Gallery of Canada.

Proch's first international foray was in 1973 when he was part of the *Trajectories* exhibition at the Musée d'art moderne de la ville de Paris. Four pieces in this Paris

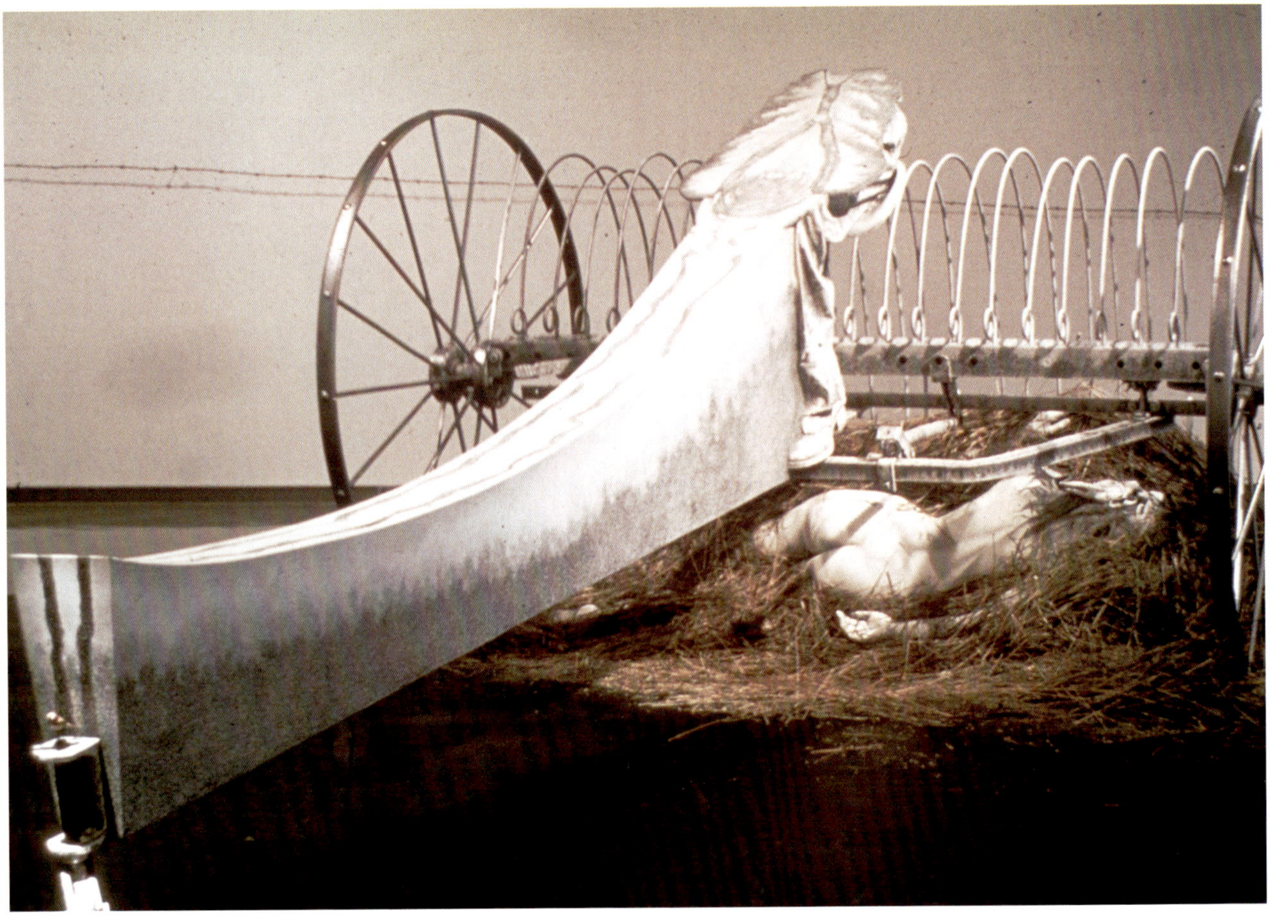

22. *Motria's Hair*, 1972.

exhibition included two from his 1972 solo exhibition at the Winnipeg Art Gallery: *Motria's Hair* and *Mud Puddle Crossroads*. As Proch said of the Paris exhibition, "it was an extension of the Opthamalia Company's activities, and we tried to put it together again." In 1978, he showed in Paris for a second time. This exhibition, with the Grand Western Canadian Screen Shop, was at the Canadian Cultural Centre. Four artists, along with their wives, went to Europe for this exhibition: Ted Howorth, Bill Lobchuk, Len Anthony, and Don Proch. The group first went to Portugal and Spain and were joined in Paris by Jackson Beardy, who had travelled separately. These trips were important to Proch, who reflected on the significance of international opportunities: "The work in the Canadian show was as good as anywhere that we had seen, reaffirming that we were on the right track. The reaction to the Canadian Cultural Centre exhibition was overwhelming, and people were impressed by the quality of our work. Exhibitions like this are pretty helpful in giving artists confidence in what they are doing so we are not groping in the dark. It is certainly worth the time and effort to pursue that."[17]

Since the 1970s, Proch's art has been shown and published in a number of countries, including his ancestral Ukraine. His rich exhibition record includes representation in exhibitions at major Canadian and international institutions, such as the Musée d'art contemporain in Montreal, the National Gallery of Canada, Canada House London, the Canadian Cultural Centre in Brussels, the

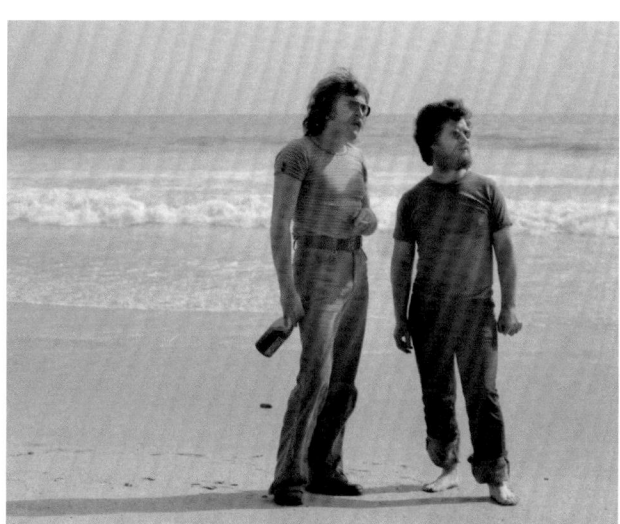

23. Don Proch and Glen Tinley on the coast of Portugal.

Ukrainian Institute of Modern Art in Chicago, the University of the Pacific Gallery, Stockton, California, and large and small galleries across Canada.

After earning his education degree, Proch taught high-school art for three years, a period in which he spent a considerable amount of time thinking about his art and the issues to which he wanted to give voice. Always reflective about art and society, he commented about the work that he did after graduation: "I was nowhere. . . . My stuff was hard, stark." The rather tortured element in his early work resurfaced in some of his prints of the 1970s, but "as far as I'm concerned my life started in 1970. . . . The floodgates opened for me in 1970—from *Asessippi Tread* I jumped to current technologies—this piece was a big leap."[18]

From 1964 to 1970, Proch embraced fast-paced experimentation with materials, ideas, and iconography, which became the essence of his 1970s installations and two- and three-dimesional work. All foreshadowed future significant developments. Proch translated his childhood experiences speeding down the Asessippi Valley on his bicycle, and later on motorcycles, into his prints and his sculptures. Through the 1970s, bicycles and motorcycles were juxtaposed with old farm equipment, expressing the rural and contrasting farm and urban lifestyles.

Asessippi Tread and the Twelfth Winnipeg Show, 1970

Through the 1960s, the Winnipeg Show, the biennial national juried exhibition, was one of two major regular contemporary exhibitions in Canada; the other was the Montreal Spring Show. Jurors for Winnipeg's biennial were senior national and international curators and gallery directors, and this biennial exhibition always brought new artists and new work to the fore. It established the careers of many artists, giving them critical national stature with their inclusion. Importantly, too, these juried shows gave artists the opportunity to meet colleagues from other parts of the country and to see their work while raising their profiles and expanding audiences for contemporary art in Canada. The Twelfth Winnipeg Show was no exception. Proch's *Asessippi Tread* was the highlight of the exhibition and marked a pivotal point in his career.

Like Proch's later works, *Asessippi Tread*, which measured 42.5 x 84.5 x 197 centimetres, was made of fibreglass, wood, and steel. A bicycle with half wheels had spokes of sharp horseshoe nails piercing through the tires. The torso and arms of the flattened figure of the crouched rider were the surface for Proch's intricate silverpoint drawing. The figure has one booted foot on a pedal and the other on the ground. The work sits on a reflective pad mirroring the shape of the bicycle and the figure of the rider, simultaneously offering the audience a view from below as well as from above. The sense of speed is palpable, evoked by the position of the figure as if hurtling downhill, recalling Proch's youth when he sped down the hills in the Asessippi Valley on his bike. The impact of this work was immediate. Adele Freedman noted that "Proch draws people in as though his graphite pencil were a magic wand."[19] Philip Fry, the Winnipeg Art Gallery curator of contemporary art, who gave Proch his first solo exhibition two years later, wrote about the significance of *Asessippi Tread*: "What he came up with was the idea of drawing on three-dimensional surfaces, 'prairie space drawings.' . . . With *Asessippi Tread*, Proch knew he had made a breakthrough. There was the technical sculpture but there also was a creative rupture from what had come before."[20]

21

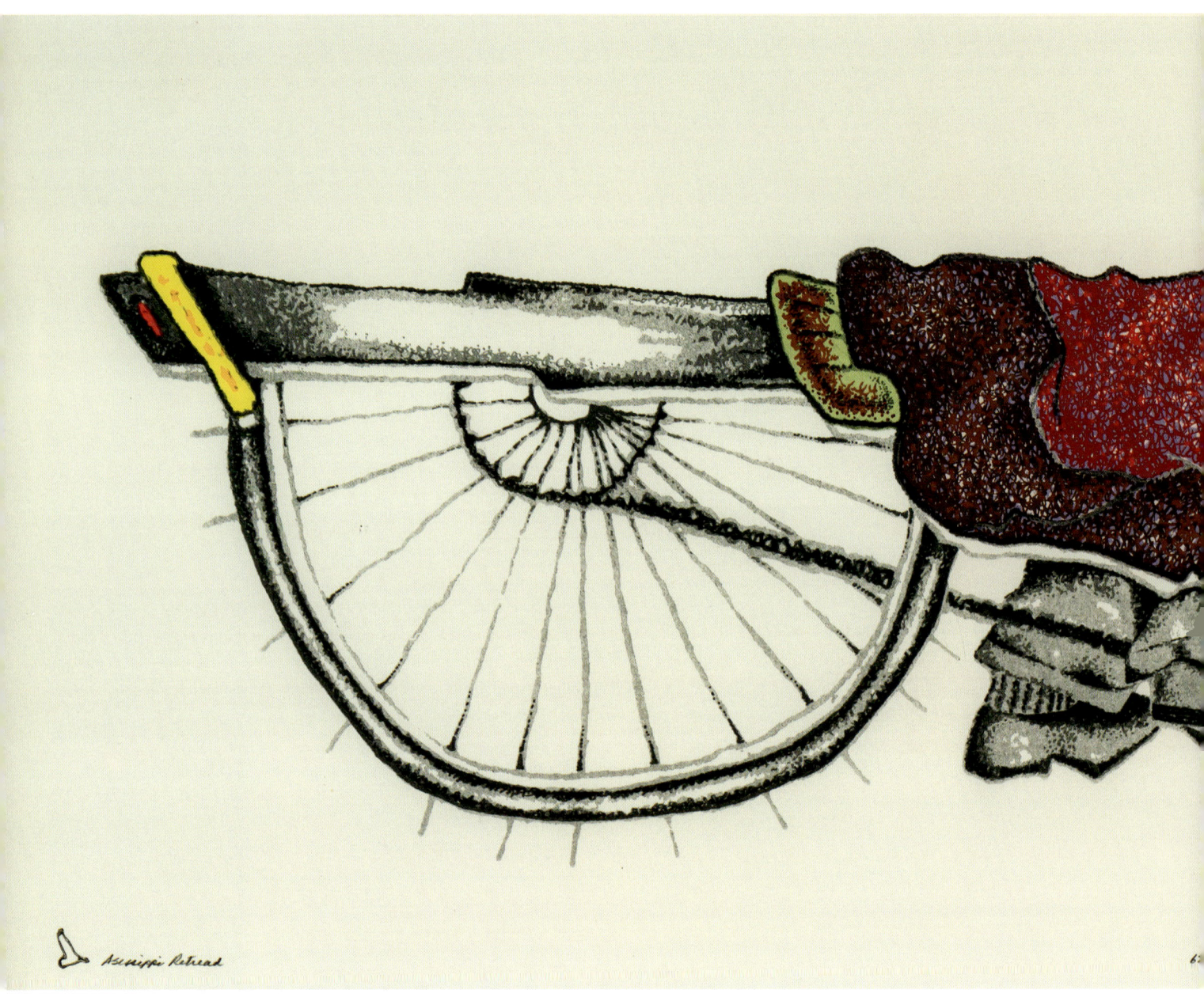

24. *Asessippi Retread*, 1978.

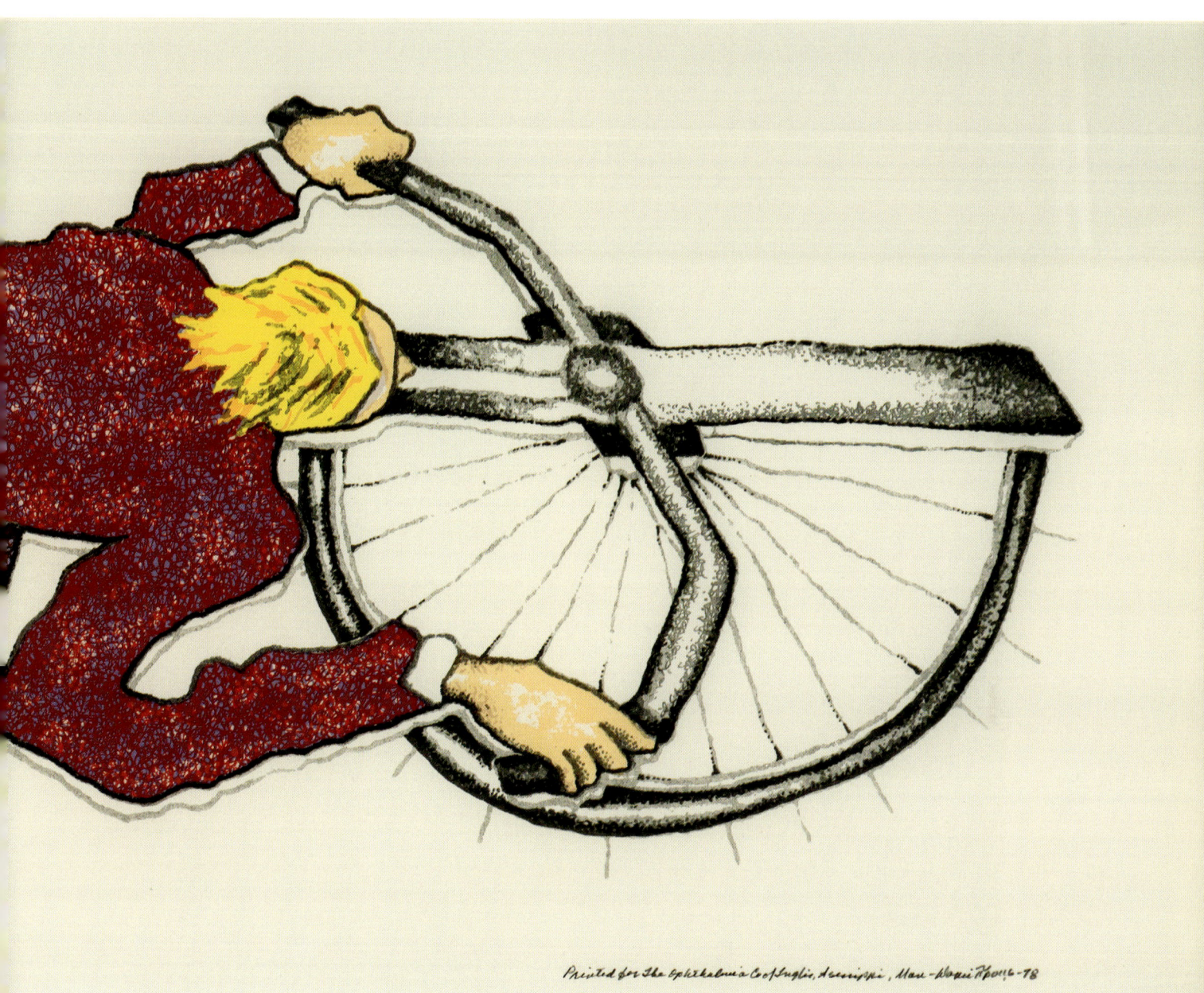

Printed for The Ophthalmia Co. of Inglis, Mississippi, Mau-Nami Ppong -78

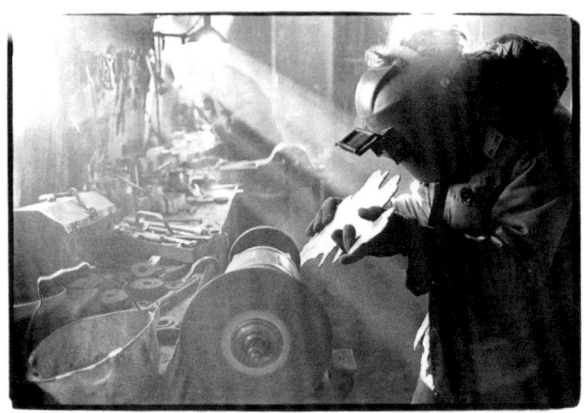

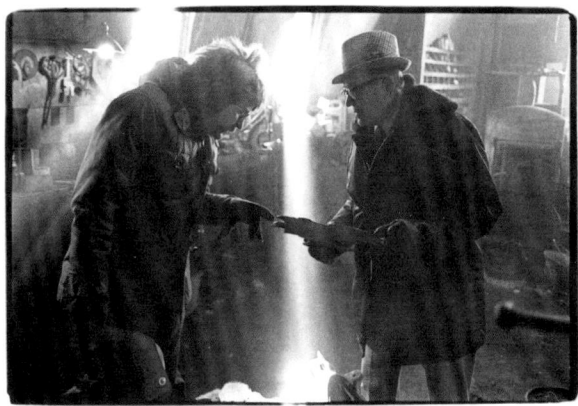

25 and 26. Don Proch and Don Proch Sr. working on *Velocipede* in the workshop, 1976.

27. (OPPOSITE) *Velocipede*, 1976.

Velocipedes

Important to Proch, bicycles emerged as the subject of other sculptures and prints in the 1970s, including his 1976 sculpture *Velocipede* and his 1978 silkscreen *Asessippi Retread*. The coloured print shows the same figure crouched over the bicycle as the one in the 1970 sculpture *Asessippi Tread*. As in the three-dimensional work, the spokes pierce the tires.

In *Velocipede*, Proch used materials that he would continue to use through the following decades: silverpoint, coloured pencil and graphite, chromed nickel, stainless

steel, and fibreglass. Two figures ride the bicycle, and like *Asessippi Tread* the work is reflected in its shiny metal mirror-like base. The riders wear helmets covered with drawings of clouds, executed in Proch's typical stylized form, with the prairie landscape in silverpoint, coloured pencil, and graphite. Furrow patterns continue from the helmet and down the front of the first rider's shirt. There is only one foot on the pedal—that of the front rider. The front rider's other leg and both legs of the back figure are truncated, their pant legs cut off mid-calf by the mirrored surface on which they rest.

Proch's rider theme soon expanded to include both motorcycle riders and farm equipment, highlighting his interest in urban-rural juxtapositions with the confluence of farm and city vehicles within a single piece. This juxtaposition unquestionably reflects his dual country and city lives, nostalgia and the present, and memory and current reality. The dichotomies between city and country were to become a key and evolving preoccupation.

Asessippi Laser Racer (1975) is a work in point. The helmeted laser racer rides a motorcycle, a Honda 350, and as in Proch's earlier works the rider is fully covered with his precise black-and-white drawing of clouds. In the gallery installation, clouds hung from the ceiling, and the rider had a dirt road before him. His speed was anticipated; his route was suggested. The flat dirt road and the cumulus clouds reveal a summer day on the open prairie. Freedman comments that Proch's art "is a stunning working out of primitivism and futurism. In his big, raunchy pieces of motorbikes and cyclists hurling themselves into nowhere and his enchanting masks in which inwardness and outwardness merge in silver-point fantasy, Proch expresses all the shock and mystery of his experience."[21] The work unfortunately no longer exists, its motorcycle, electrical cables, and laser units having been stolen from a storage area.

Proch's motorcycle helmets were soon to become masks and later hats. Just as his shift from helmets to masks evolved, so too did his penchant for using the mask as an object to conceal as well as to reveal.

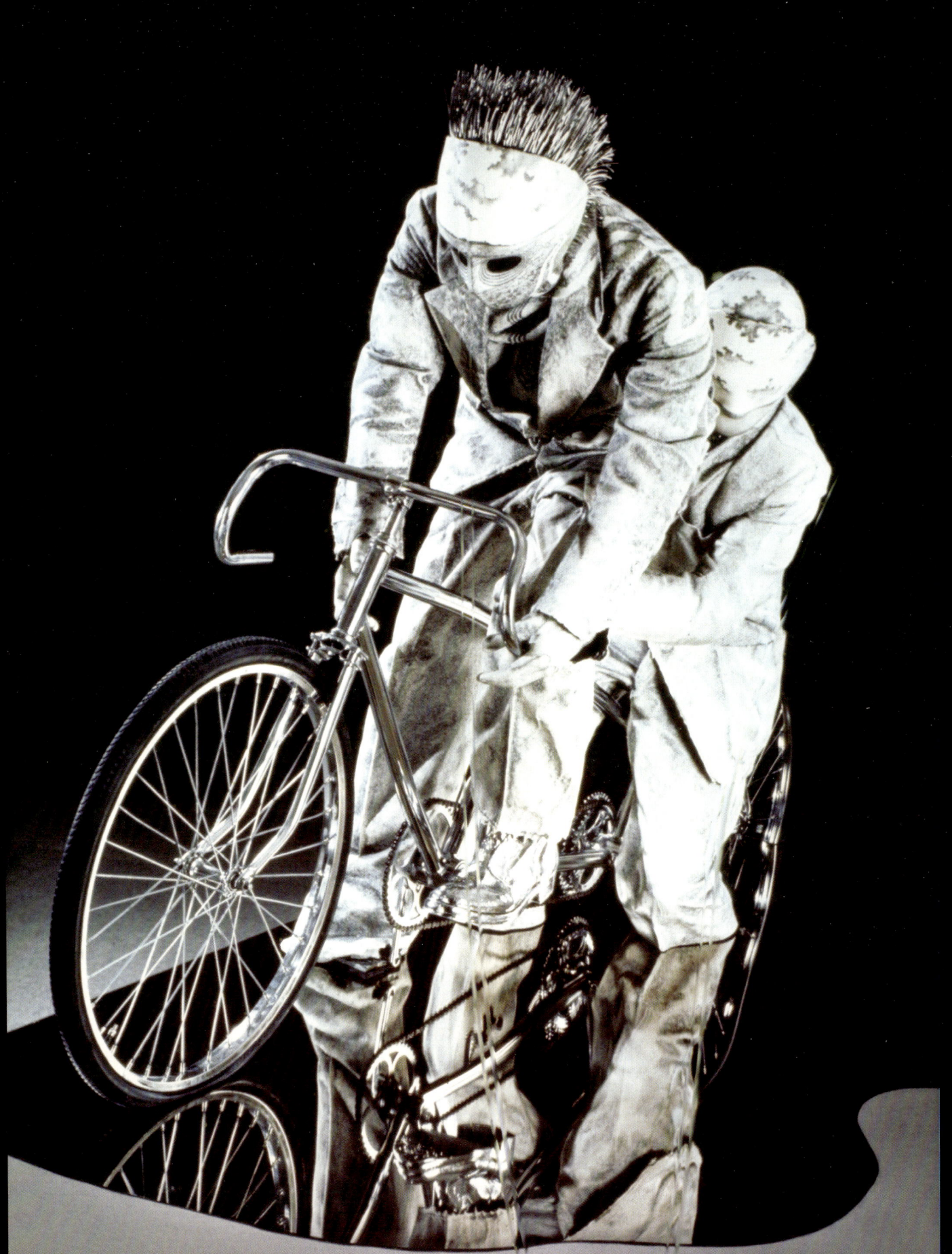

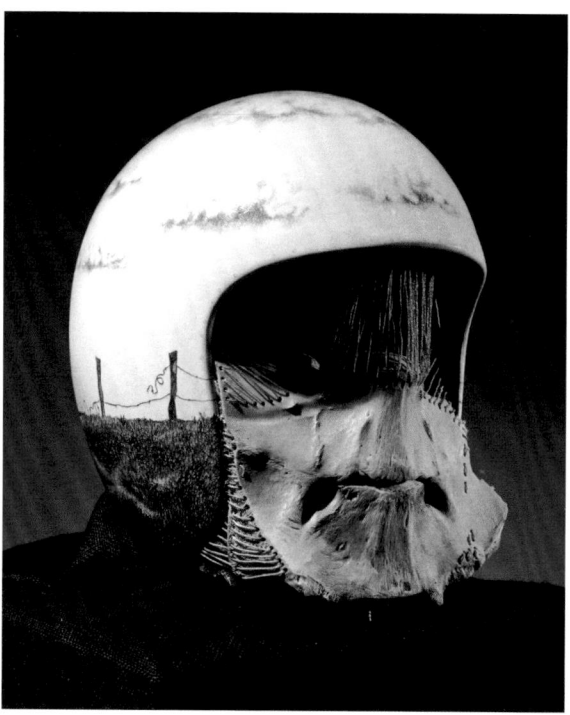

28. *Legend of Asessippi* Exhibition Installation, 1972.

The Legend of Asessippi, 1972

Building on the success of *Asessippi Tread*, Proch's first solo installation at the Winnipeg Art Gallery in 1972 opened soon after his meteoric rise to artistic acclaim. A complex installation, *The Legend of Asessippi* was conceived and realized in a short time. Proch in fact admitted that he had harboured some doubts about being able to complete enough work for such a major presentation in the two years from invitation to installation. He therefore organized a collective of artists, friends, and relatives to assist him, the Ophthalmia Company of Inglis, Asessippi, Manitoba. Ophthalmia was the name deliberately chosen since it means "eye inflammation." His goal for this installation was to challenge perceptions. Proch wanted to extend the ability of individual viewers, and society as a whole, to see. Proch rarely speaks of his personal life, but he has talked about family and personal issues regarding eyesight, his grandfather having lost an eye in a farm accident and Proch himself having worn glasses since he was eight years

old. Thus, the Ophthalmia Company juxtaposes personal and societal, past and present, and rural and urban.

Those whom Proch invited to be part of his company had specific skills, such as welding, which he felt he lacked himself. In her article "The Magic Masks of Asessippi: Don Proch Is the Shaman of Prairie Art," Freedman describes the company's dedication "to a way of seeing the prairies, and that way of seeing was focused through the eyes and mind of Proch. . . . They worked steadily for a year, photographing, recording, videotaping, printing. Headquarters was the Grand Western Screen Shop, in Winnipeg's factory district, where Proch had his studio. By August Proch was working a twenty-two-hour day. 'I love to push myself down to the edge. That's when I do my best work.'"[22]

Proch's father, a skilled carpenter, helped with building and sanding. Bertie Duncan, a friend who lived on a farm near Inglis, carved little hummingbirds out of caragana branches, one to be featured later in Proch's *Hummingbird Watching Mask* (1974). "I really liked birds and I liked him and he gave me birds to use in my pieces," said Proch.[23]

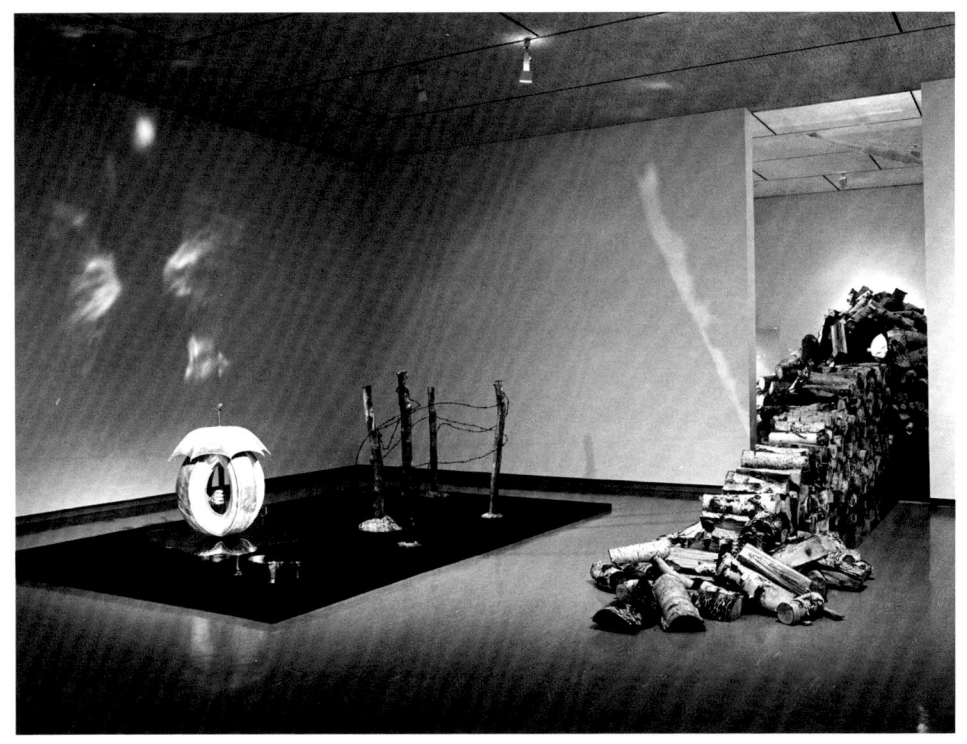

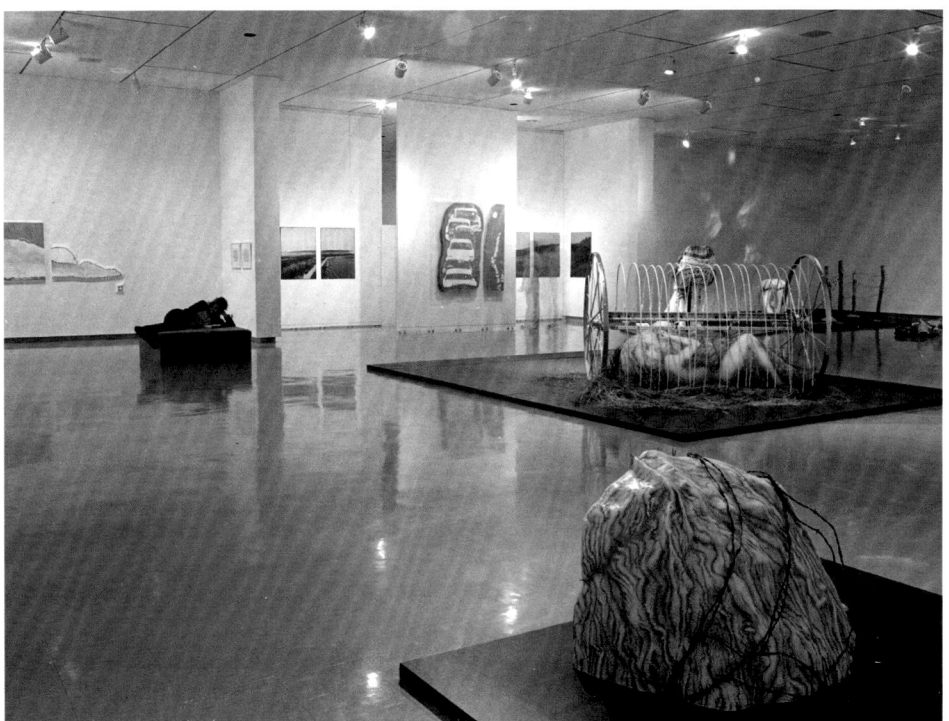

29 and 30. *Legend of Asessippi* Exhibition Installation, 1972.

27

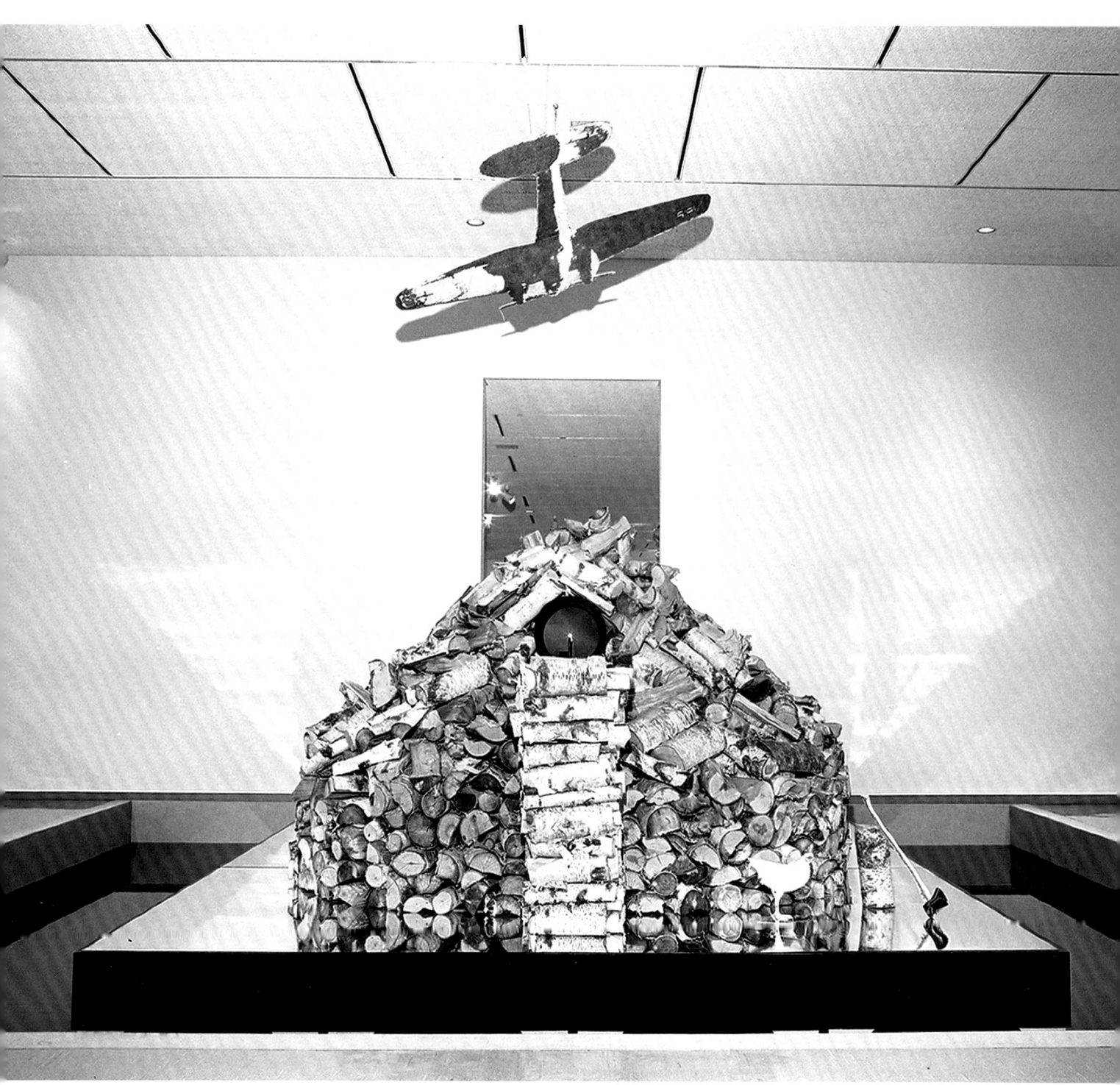

31. *Chicken Block*, 1972.

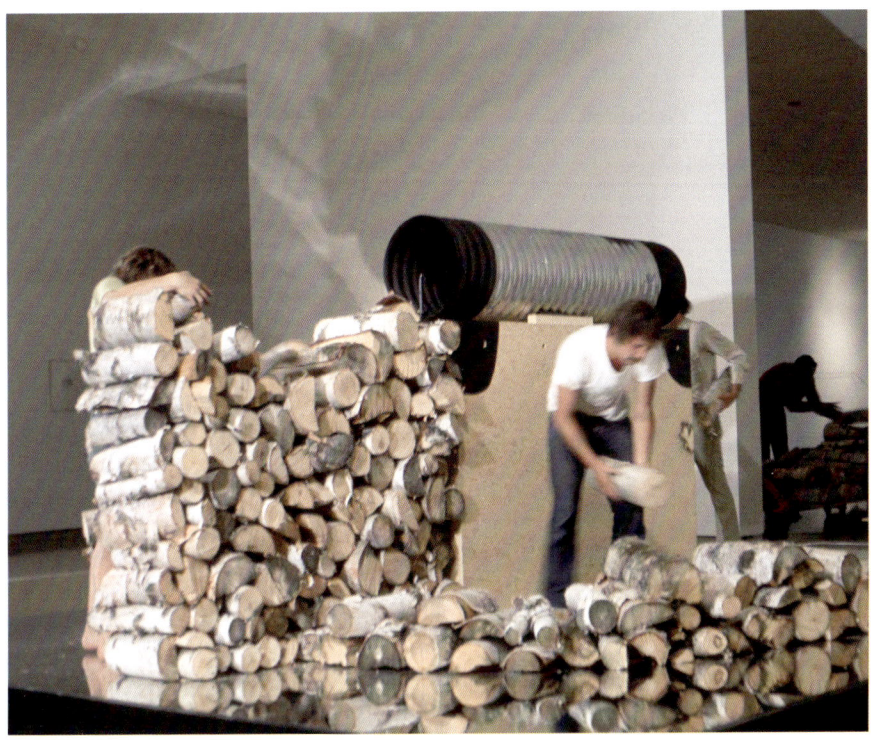

32. Constructing *Chicken Block*.

Steve Chachula, the town blacksmith, welded all of the pieces to be chromed. As Proch said, "I spent many hours in his shop watching him work at his forge."[24]

Proch dedicated the 1972 *Legend of Asessippi* installation to prairie farmers' experiences of the land: "It was rugged and stark and it wasn't the kind of imagery that art critics or people at the Art Gallery were used to. I really didn't care. That's the way the work came out. The concepts came from a rural, environmental situation that most people in Winnipeg weren't familiar with. . . . The camaraderie [of the Ophthalmia Company] made it a support group. . . . The entire company worked with a remarkable kind of intensity."[25]

The installation comprised twenty-three stand-alone works, including drawings, silkscreen prints, assemblages using discarded farm equipment, and bicycles. Together they fused to create the overall legend, all transformed into poignant messages of past lifestyles foreshadowing the future. Each part related to the others. *Motria's Hair* and *Chicken Block* were two focal works in the show.

Robert Enright reflected on this self-defined "primitive realist": "Proch's visual world was one he not only made, but also one he and fellow artists actually lived in. . . . The art was simultaneously beautiful and ugly, enchanting and grotesque; it was landscape and figure, drawing and sculpture; its character was illusory and realistic, crude and obsessively refined, spectrally old and aggressive 'Pop'; it co-existed in two and three dimensions; it was astonishing in all directions."[26]

Motria's Hair (1972), one of the most disturbing works in the installation, a drawing on fibreglass and carved wood, included mown hay and chromed steel. The figure was placed within a hayrake. As Proch commented,

29

to me the female figure is the embodiment of the whole cycle of life and growing. I was trying to feminize prairie space. I think one word that I always associated with the piece—not when I was doing the drawings for it but when I saw the structure—was fragility. That's how the front of the piece developed with the little wheel and the bird sitting on it. Motria was the name of a girl whom I met at a Ukrainian Arts Conference in Thunder Bay and when I started doing the drawings I had this memory of riding the hayrake on grandfather's lap, sort of in between his legs. He was driving the horses with his arms around me. It was one of those beautiful fall days with a bluish haze in the air and we were just rolling up bunches of hay.[27]

Proch's use of materials and farm equipment in this installation elicited great interest, for it related not only to the cycle of growth but also to the changing ways that human beings have used and affected that cycle:

> The motif of ecological unwellness, danger of the earth, echoes through many of the artist's works. Especially clear is the portrayal of unprotected nature in 'Motria's Hair' (1972). . . . There are used horse rakes, straw, upon which lies a sculpture of a nude woman, which again personifies Earth. Created quite naturalistically, the composition impresses [the viewer] with the natural relationship of its objects, their semantic aberrations. Because indeed one can call a woman's hair straw. And her name indicates the national 'I' [identity] of the artist, that far from Ukraine he is in his way protecting our beautiful earth, nature, life . . . since his native mother earth is present in almost all of his works, even though he has left the prairies long ago and lives in urban surroundings.[28]

Multi-layered in nature, *The Legend of Asessippi* changed the ways of art making, the definition of what constituted an exhibition, and audience interaction with art. Further, since there had never been a show like it at the Winnipeg Art Gallery, critics could not write about it as they had about earlier exhibitions. Proch had catapulted the art world into new arenas. The *Winnipeg Free Press* art critic and University of Manitoba architecture professor John Graham reflected on its impact:

> Though Mr. Proch and company have chosen to try to capture and express the inner spirit of a particular place which still bears the scars of a former intrusion, this is not an exercise in maudlin nostalgia. . . . It is an investigation into the nature of an environment and the interaction of the agencies which operate within it. . . . They have attempted, by translation into expressive images in new contexts, to give more universality of meaning to what they have recorded. . . .
>
> Much of the inner meaning of the work depends for its clarity upon the ability of the observer to identify with the rural scene in the prairie context, with its ambiguous confrontation of earth and sky, and the elemental struggle to wrest a living against the will or spirit of the land. For the true urbanite, this may be a difficult experience to appreciate, just as it must also be for the conventional gallery goer who expects to see 'fine art.' . . .
>
> In trying to evoke the inner spirit which gives the prairies and Asessippi in particular their special power and impact upon the undertakings made by man, Mr. Proch has imbued the landscape elements with human qualities, combining the animism of primitive man and socio-religious analogies with anthropomorphic mutations of the tools or artifacts evolved to aid survival.[29]

33. (OPPOSITE) Don, and Steve Chachula of Inglis, Manitoba, working towards Don's 1972 WAG exhibition, *The Legend of Asessippi*.

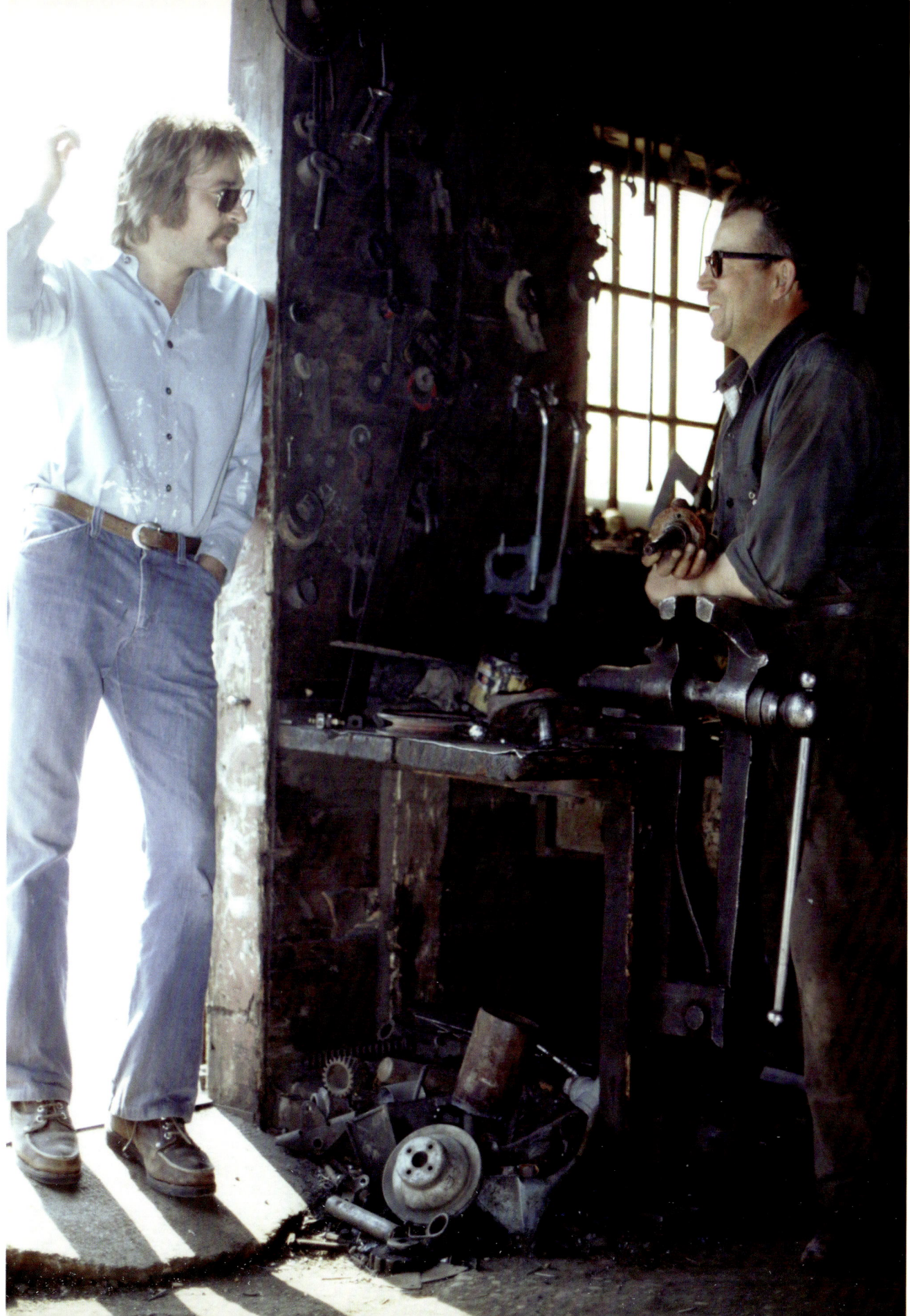

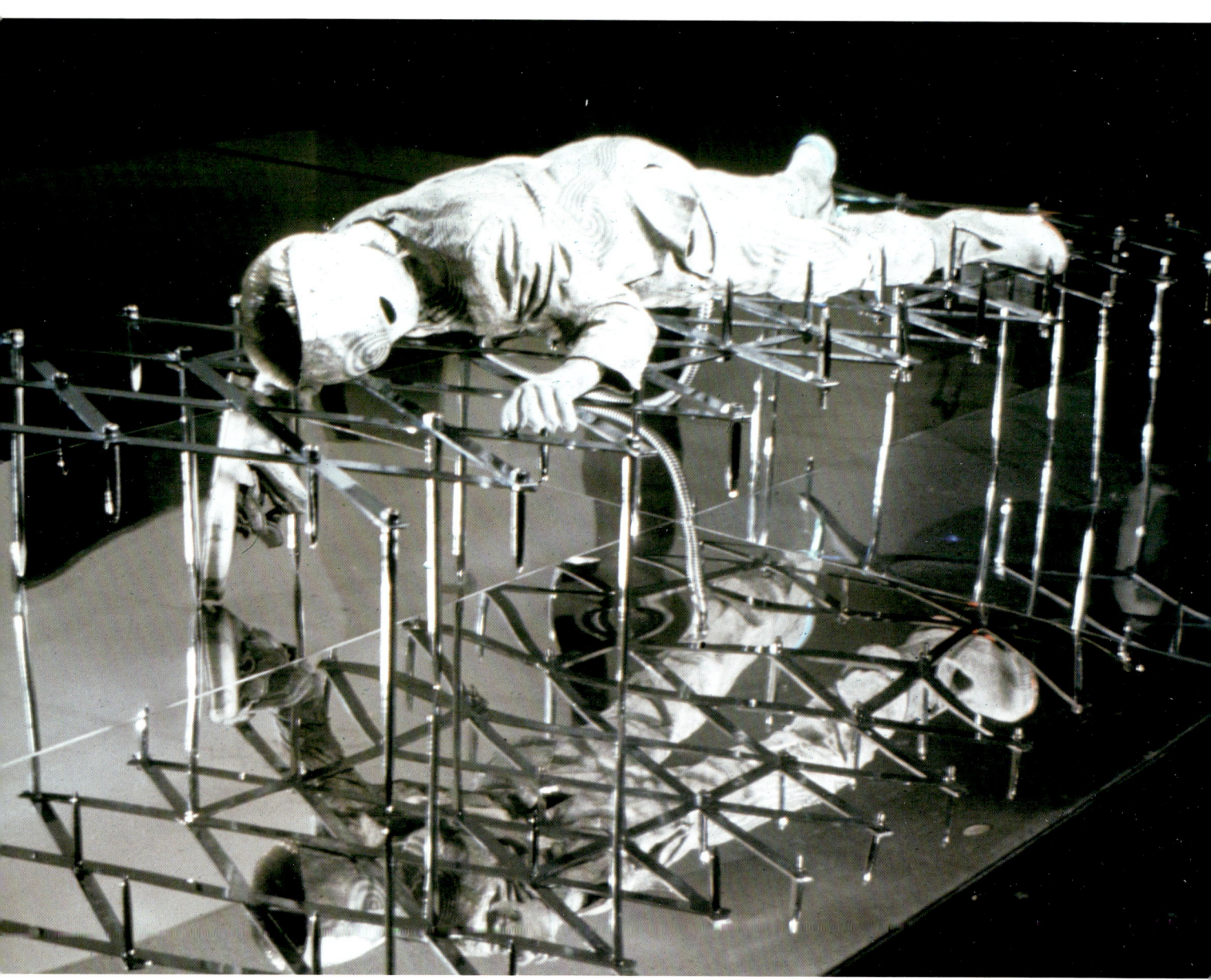

34. *Pincushion Man (Wearing Brushcut, Listening for Buffalo Mask)*, 1975.

Pincushion Man, 1975

Pincushion Man (Wearing Brushcut—Listening for Buffalo Mask) (1975), included in *Asessippi Clouds*, is another of Proch's seminal works, and as with all his major works the details recorded in his preliminary sketches are critical and informative. This particularly important, large sculpture, measuring 2.4 x 4.9 x 0.8 metres, again includes drawing on fibreglass and both past and new technologies, including chromed steel and electric neon elements. Like most of Proch's work, its roots are complex, harkening back, of course, to his childhood on the farm. The traditional farm equipment contrasts with the polished chrome, electric elements, and contemporary city garb of the figure lying on his stomach on a modified chrome set of farm harrows. The neon lights in the soles of the boots, red for the left and blue for the right, Proch says, were inspired by Elton John's "Bennie and the Jets," which refers to "electric boots, a mohair suit."[30] As in *Asessippi Tread*, the reflection in the chrome base allows us to see the front of the figure as we experience his back. Proch also incorporated a number of symbols into this work that he was to use frequently in later works, such as horseshoes, the prairie symbol of fertility:

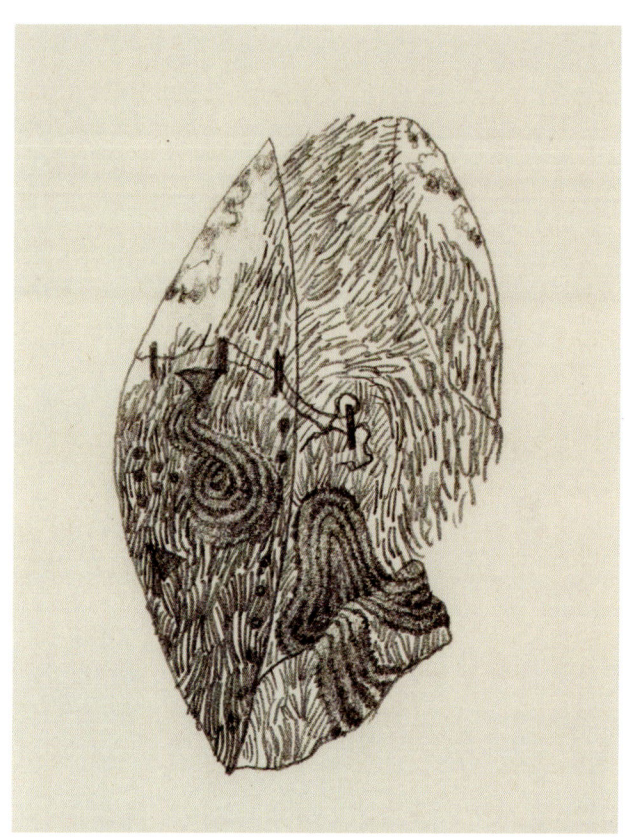

> I have this open horseshoe and this raincloud imagery which have the shape and fragility of an exquisite water tumbler. Then the open horseshoe becomes a point where the water drains out. Below the horseshoe nail are chrome droplets that flow down into another landscape and the water droplets from the stem of the glass, and the horizon and the landscape underneath become the base of the glass that holds the whole thing up. It's a balancing act and a very delicate environmental metaphor. We would all be better off the way we were before all this chemical, anti-environmental crap. The only way we are going to survive is to get back to respecting the land.[31]

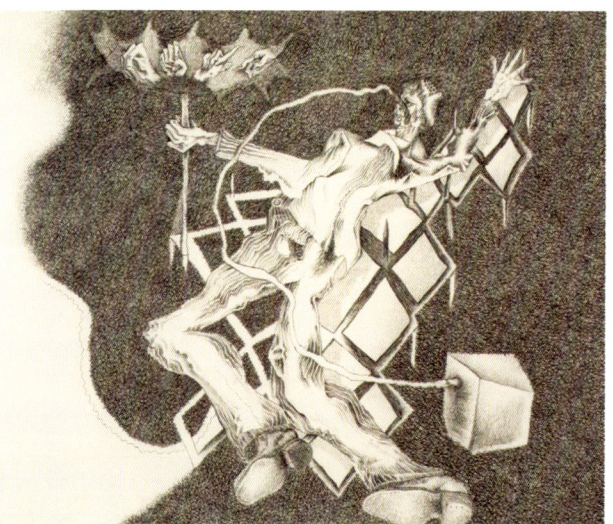

35 and 36. Studies for *Pincushion Man*, 1975.

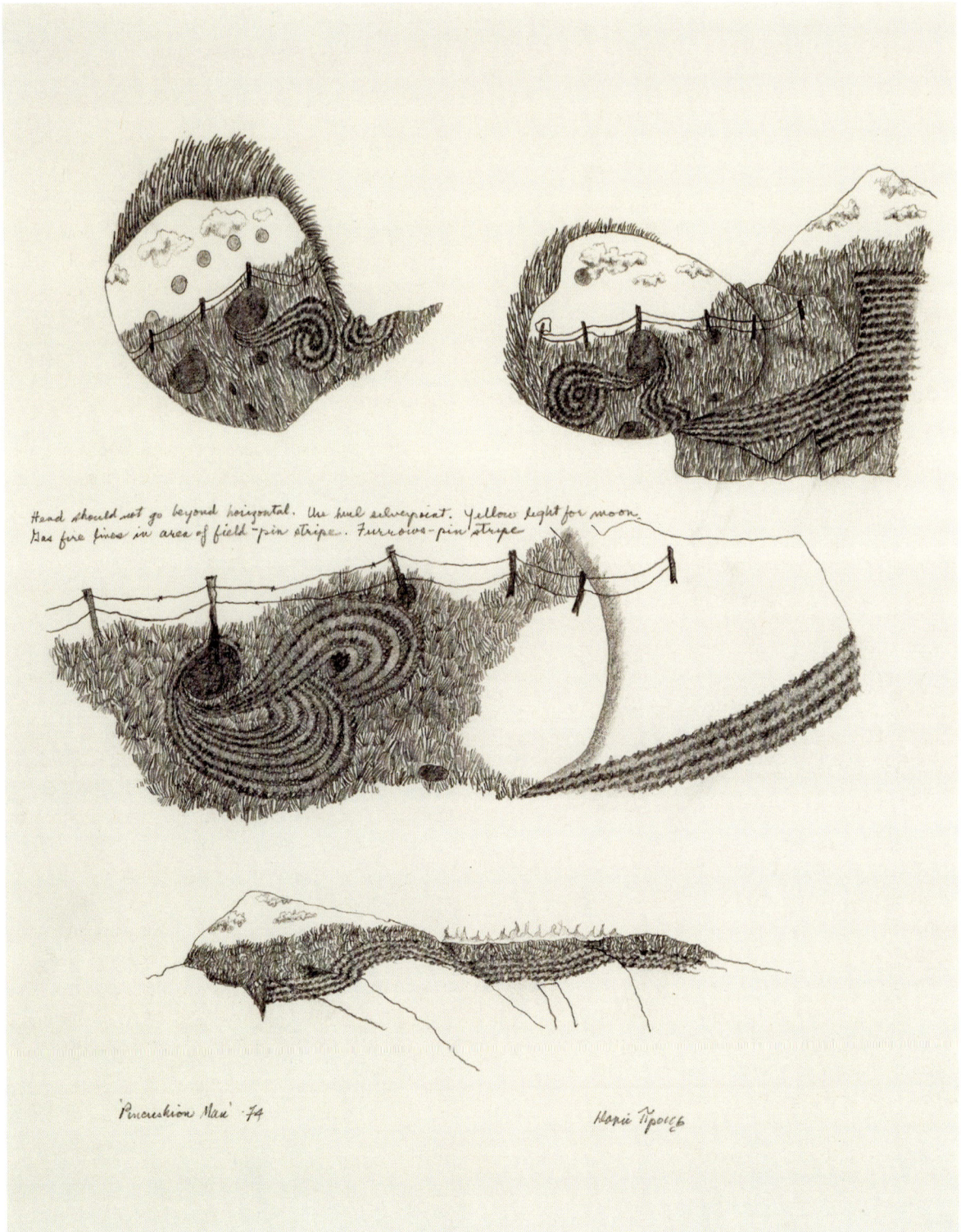

Head should not go beyond horizontal. Use kuel silverpoint. Yellow light for moon.
Gas fire fines in area of field - pin stripe. Furrows - pin stripe.

'Pincushion Man' '74

Honii Tipoiçb

34

37. Studies for *Pincushion Man*, 1974.

In *Pincushion Man* Proch drew cultivated furrows in the shape of a horseshoe on the right boot. The horseshoe also appears later in his 1996 landscapes *Blackbird with Horseshoe Nail* and *Yellowheaded Blackbird with Horseshoe Nail.* In both these 1996 works, Proch repeated the "U" of the horseshoe in a manner far less jarring than that of the 1970s, but in these later works oil drips from the horseshoe. He realized that the jagged elements in *Pincushion Man* are perceived by many viewers as violent. For Proch, these jagged elements equate fragility. In *Pincushion Man*, the violent-fragile juxtaposition is at its most visceral where the steel points meet the mirror, the moment when reflection encounters reality. Proch commented on fragility thus: "I think people who work the land probably understand that fragility more than anybody. More than I do. They live with it every day. What I know about it I probably learned living on a very small, poor farm where almost every move that parents and grandparents made was a survival thing. Everything was considered, nothing wasted. . . . It's the same reason I decided to call the company Ophthalmia. I wanted to make people aware of the harshness of living on the land."[32]

Patricia Vervoort's insights on this work are particularly keen:

> The juxtapositions of the real and referential, the present and the past, the two- and three-dimensional, the mask, the head, all combine to emphasize the ambiguities which characterize Proch's view of man and the prairie landscape. Is the *Pincushion Man* indeed listening or is he dead? The title suggests the latter, whereas the subtitle indicates he's alive and listening for buffalo. The impact of *Pincushion Man* is intensified by its life-size scale and the message of the hardships of survival both in the past and in the rural present on the Canadian prairie.

As these sculpted fragments of the prairie landscape demonstrate, the land is neither flat nor pretty. It is a particular environment seen from many angles simultaneously, from above and below, in vast vistas and close-up detail, the landscape is both fragmented and mapped. The placement of these drawings on masks, heads, and human figures binds together the human and natural worlds, they can't be separated nor easily interpreted.[33]

Proch had several specific intentions in creating this work with its three-dimensional landscape drawn on the back and arms of the figure and the furrows along the body, circling to form a "P." He wanted to encourage viewers to get as close as possible to the land and natural environment. He wanted people to look, to see, and to discover the prairies. "I wanted to make people aware of the harshness of living on the land."[34]

Pincushion Man also looks back to pre-contact times, before European immigration to the prairies, and honours the traditional livelihood of Métis and Indigenous peoples. The figure, his arm hanging below the harrows, holds a shield on which Proch has drawn a landscape. His ear is to the ground, as if he is listening for bison. Vervoort notes that "the pose and shield are reminiscent of Native hunters in Manitoba a hundred years ago and their technique for locating buffalo herds."[35]

Complex depths of meaning in this work, like its multi-layered creation, again balance societal nostalgia, past histories, and continuing yet far from positive relationships with Canada's First Nations. The visual and intellectual impacts of this work were evident both locally and universally.

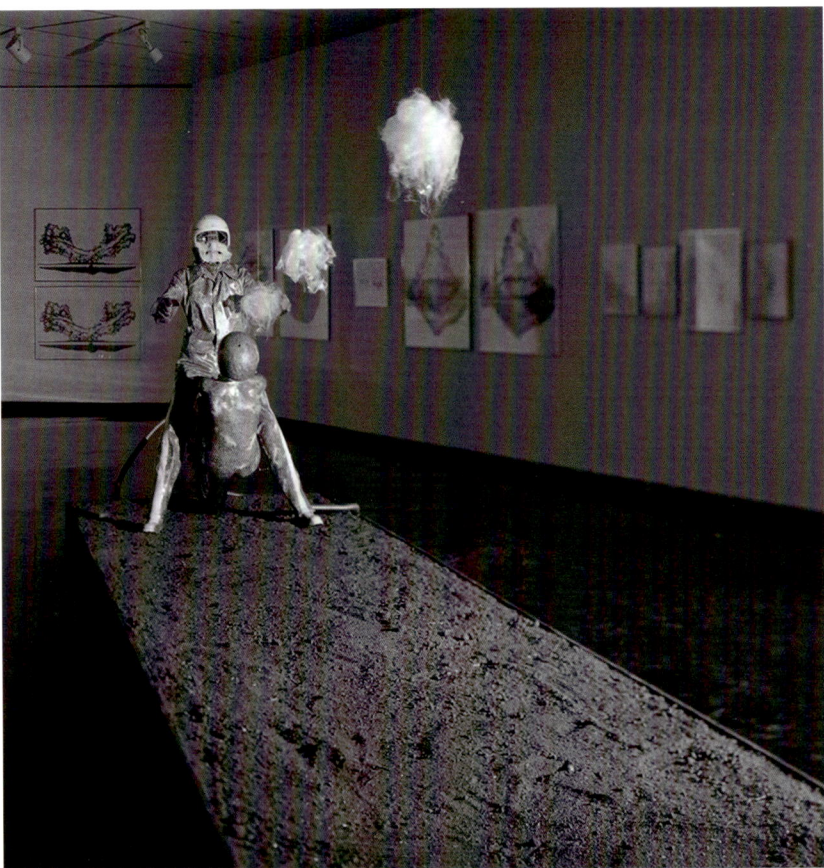

38. *Asessippi Laser Racer*, 1975.

Asessippi Clouds, 1975

Asessippi Clouds, Proch's second solo Winnipeg Art Gallery exhibition, was held in 1975. This exhibition, like the previous one, included drawings, silkscreen prints, and assemblages, along with his major pieces *Pincushion Man* and *Asessippi Laser Racer*, both dating from 1975. Proch also included motorcycle riders and some of his early masks, which he had started making in 1974. Once again his juxtapositions of real and imagined, past and future, convey a narrative based upon both truth and conjecture. Clouds, formed in his signature stylistic shapes, hung from the gallery's ceiling. As in all of Proch's work, this installation included the beautiful, the elegant, and a jarring disquiet.

The review in the *Winnipeg Free Press* noted that, "in his sculpture, he takes recognizable objects and modifies and transforms them into new configurations . . . the motorcycle crowd and the farmer . . . and represents the difficulty of those living an essentially closed way of life in adapting to the complexities of rural life. . . . Rather than trying to represent the prairies, the works in the exhibition present basic prairie values—what it is like to live on the prairies—and explore themes based on the reciprocal opposition of man and the land."[36] However, for Proch, "the 1972 exhibition had more of a whole feeling," achieving more than the sum of its parts than the 1975 *Asessippi Clouds* accomplished.[37]

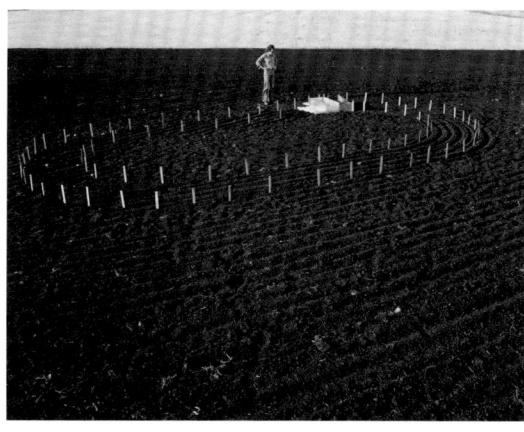
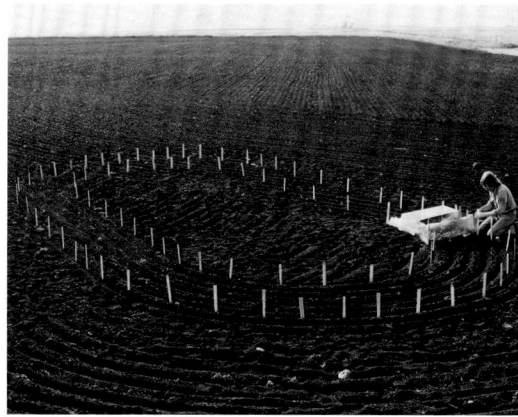
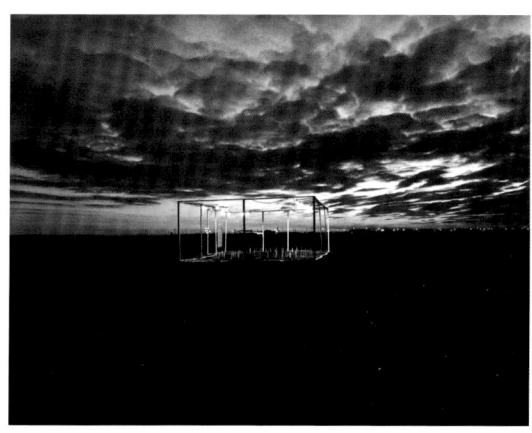
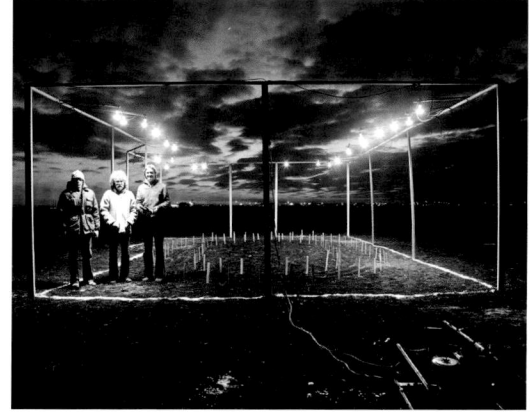

39–42. *Field, In Situ*, 1980.

Field and *Pluralities*:
National Gallery of Canada, 1980

Proch was invited to be part of the 1980 *Pluralities* exhibition at the National Gallery of Canada. His installation was taken from his outdoor on-site exhibition *Field*, created in a field west of Headingley, Manitoba, where the prairie is absolutely flat. Photographer Ernest Mayer photo-documented it weekly "as it was rising from the field. I was able to capture the wonderful atmosphere. In Ottawa, we put it into a sterile space; the cost was losing the essence of the process. I especially liked photographing it at night with the lights strung around the site."[38] Again, leading the way, the development of this on-site exhibition was the first major eco-installation in Canada. Proch said of this project that it "developed in

a way we were not expecting at the time. The important aspect was what happened in the field where the furrows were cast. *That* was the exhibition. The National Gallery was not the piece. The framework of the gallery being out on the prairie gave it the drama. Indoors we lost that. Ernie Mayer photographed it outdoors with a security guard. Did that translate in the gallery? Was it too difficult for the viewer to follow?"[39]

These fields became a fundamental macro-element in Proch's work, the furrows his "mapping" of the prairie. Subsequently, furrows appeared frequently on his masks, elevators, and sculptures; here as micro-details they are his "masking" of the prairies.

43. (PAGES 38–39) *Field, In Situ*, 1980.

44. (PAGES 40–41) *Field*, National Gallery of Canada Installation, 1980.

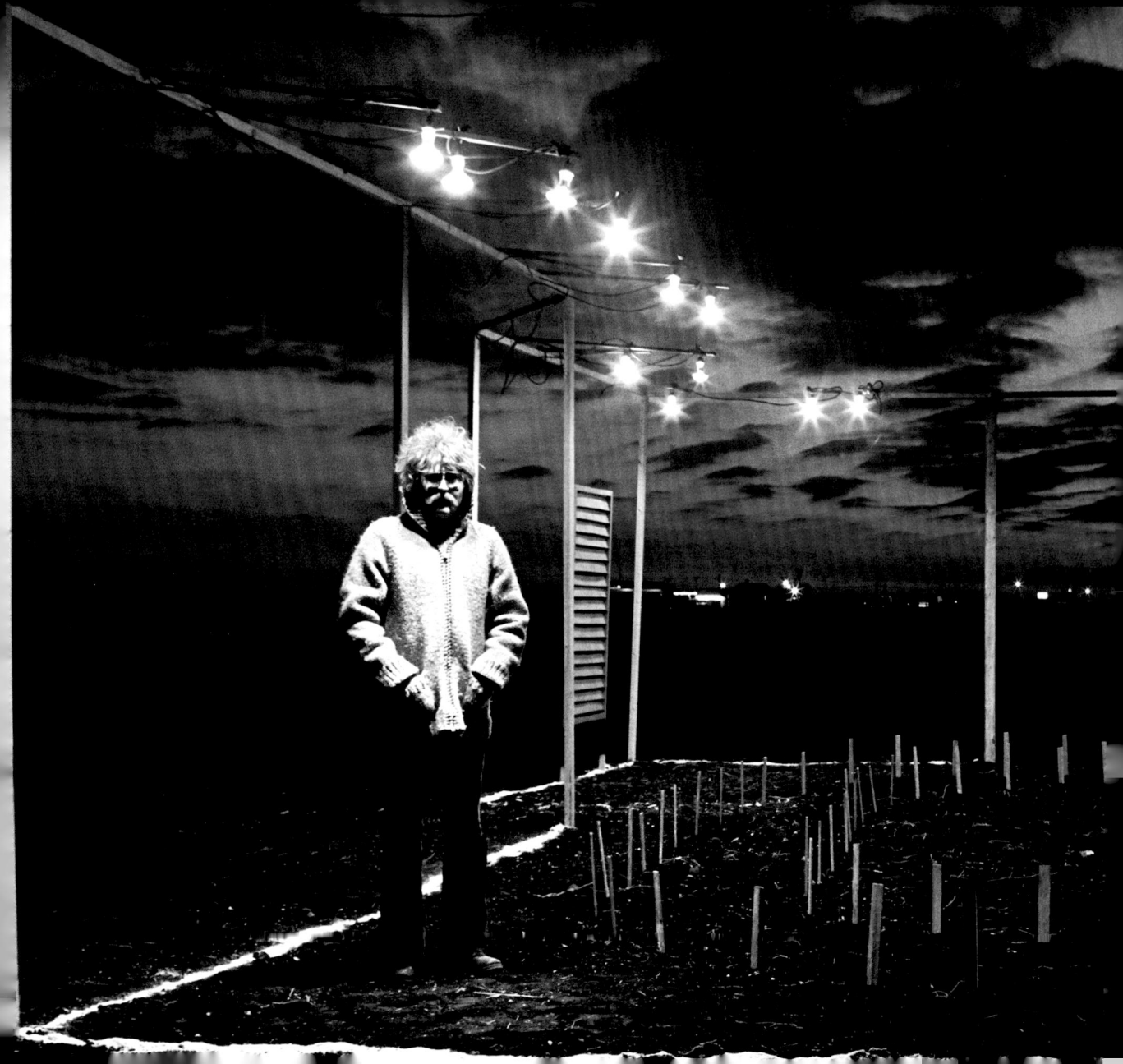

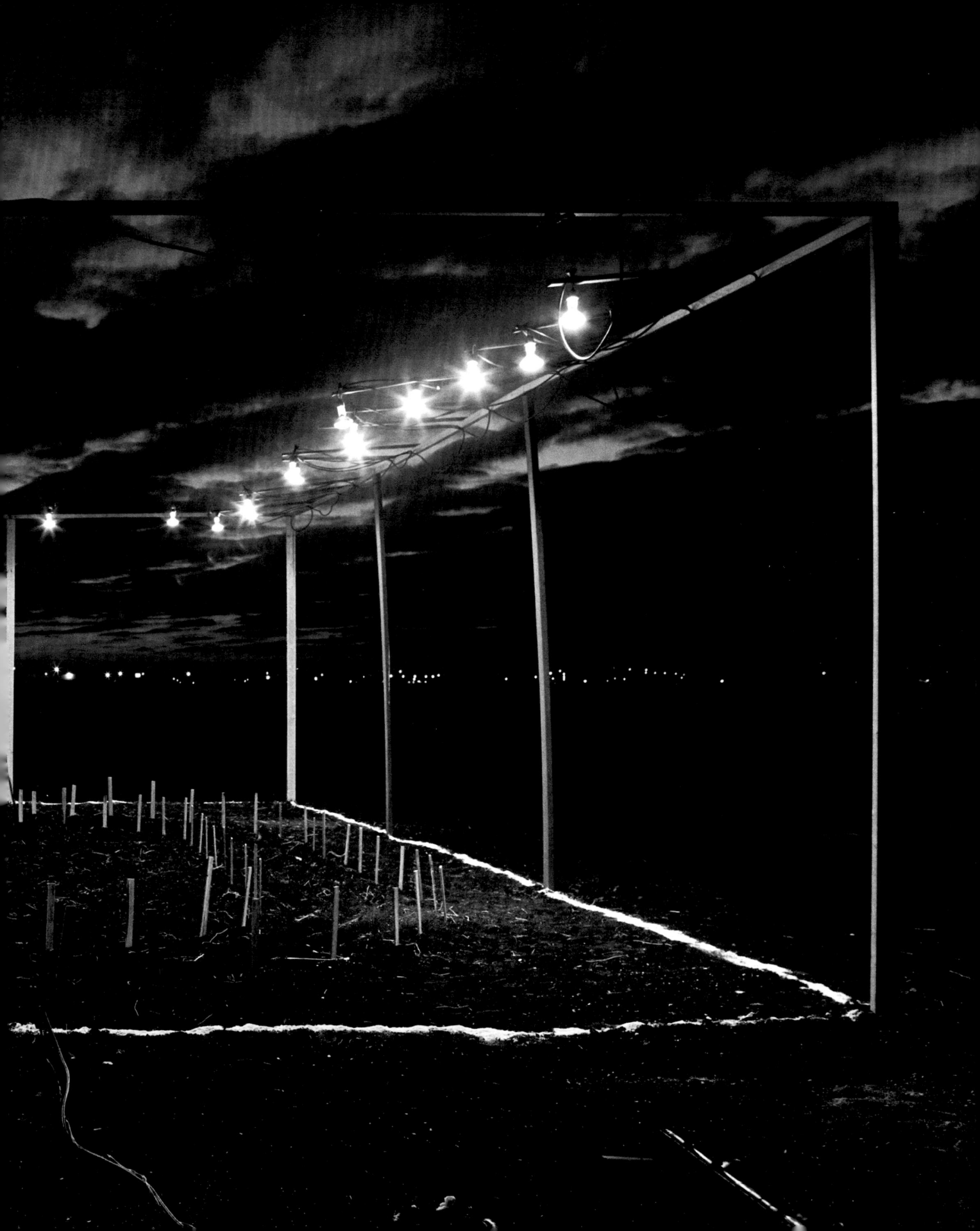

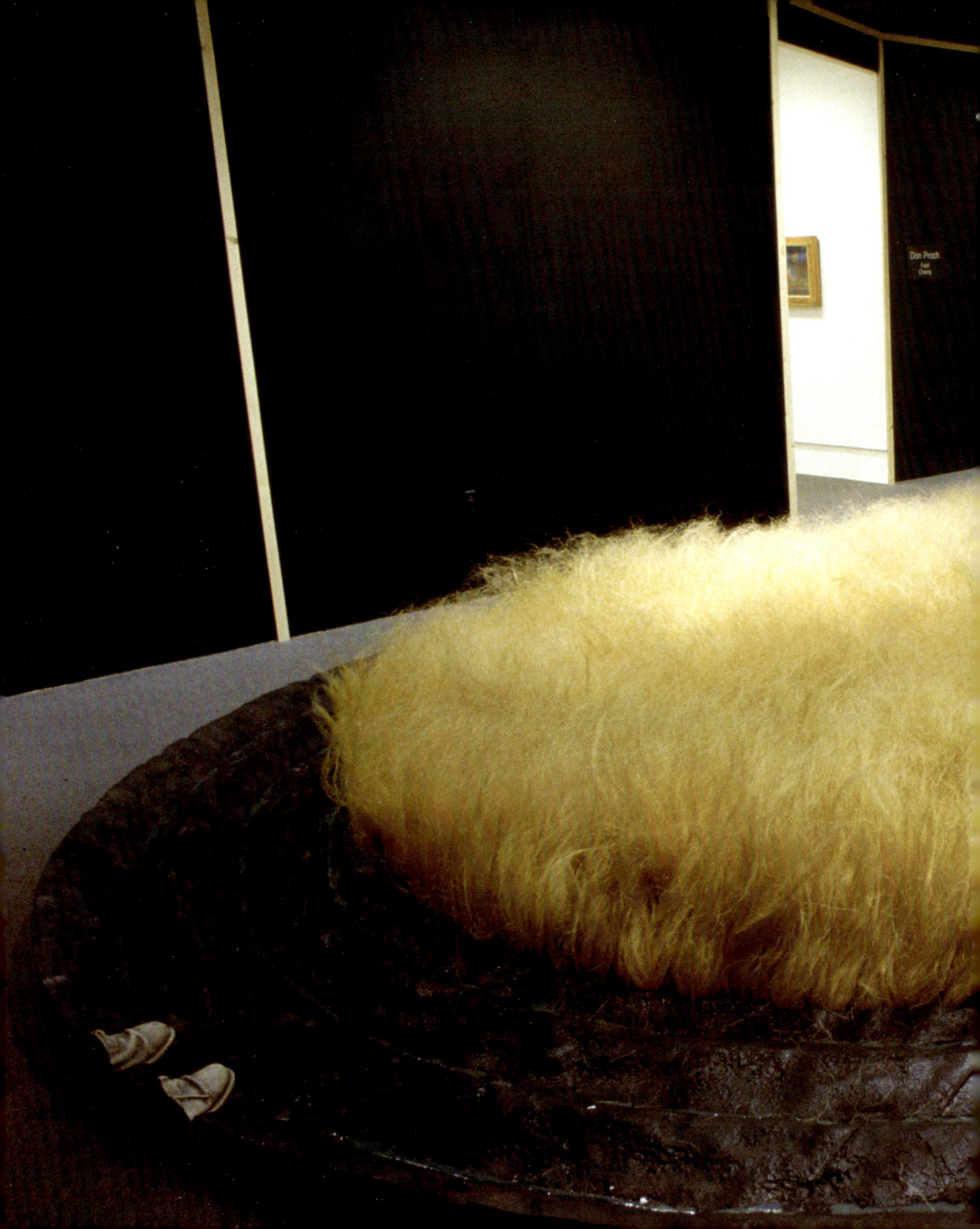

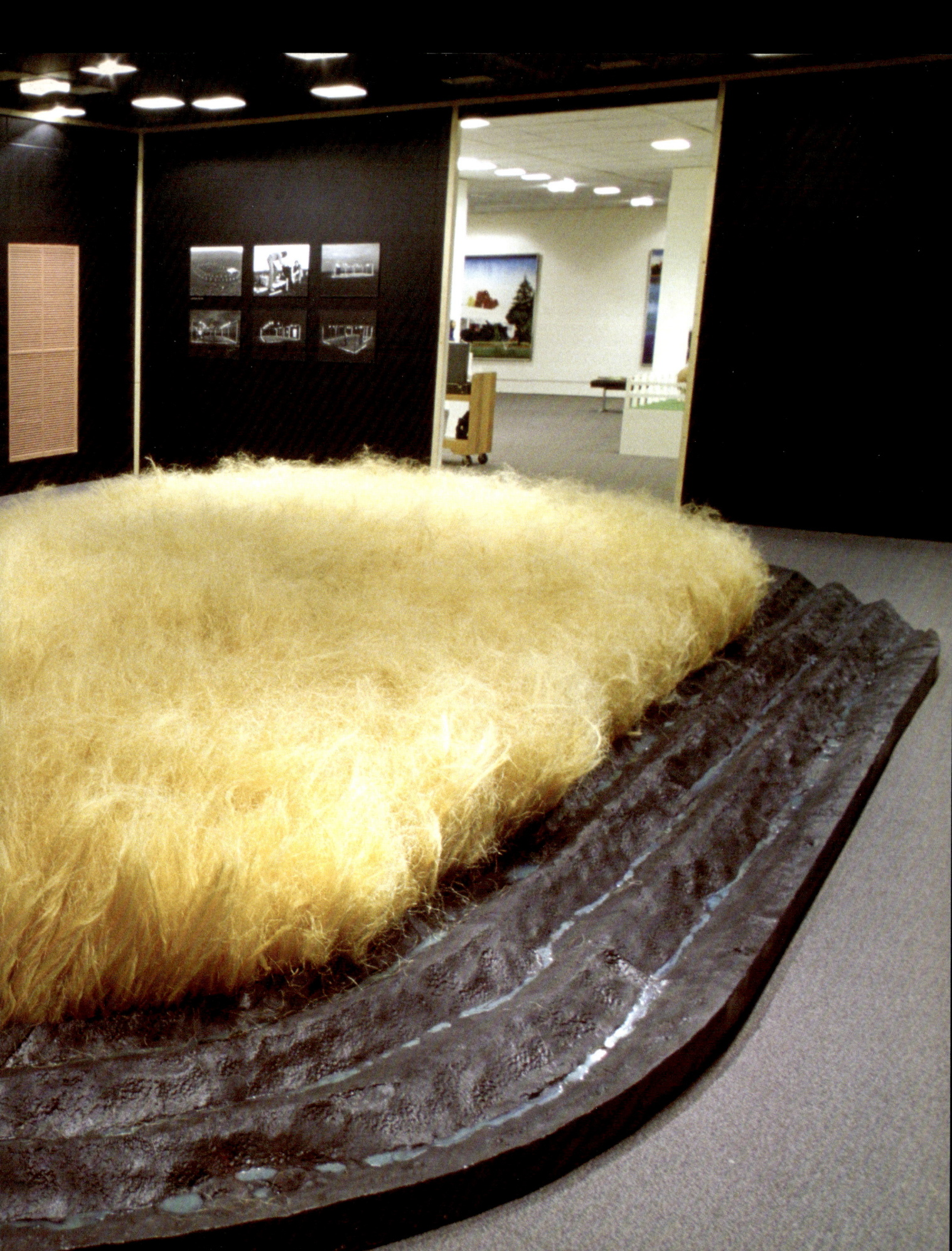

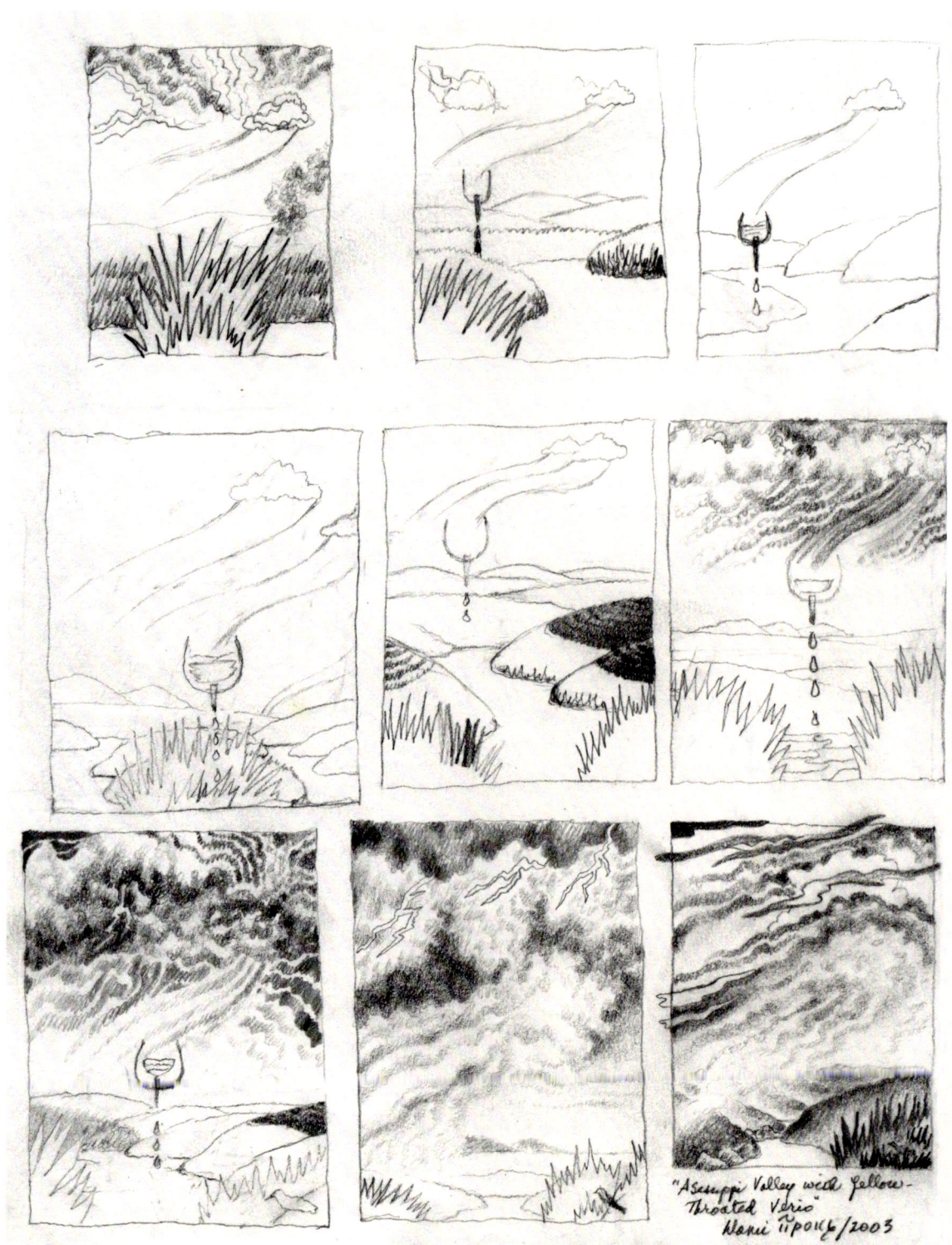

42

45. Sketches for *Asessippi Valley with Yellow-Throated Vireo*, 2003.

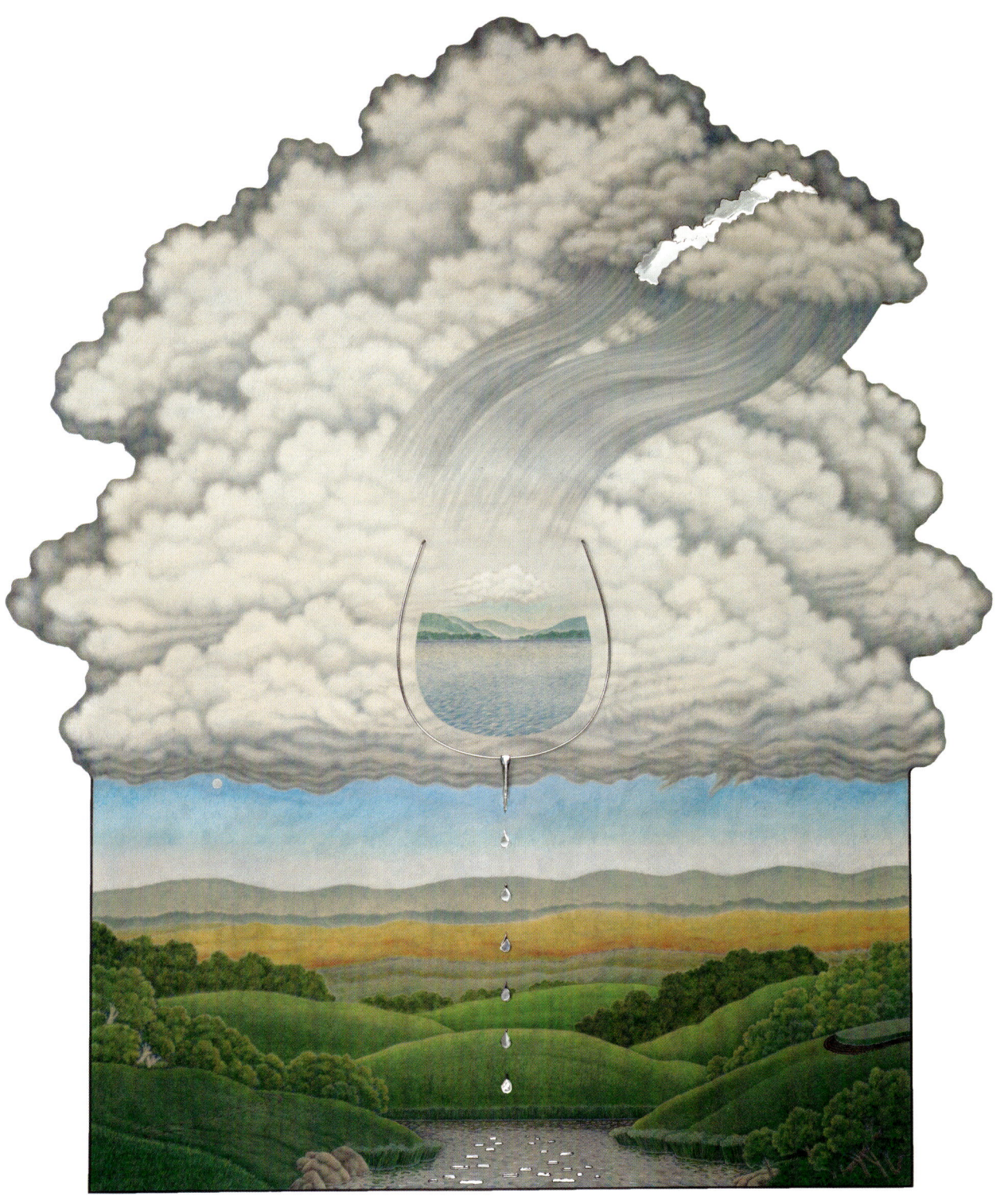

43

46. *Prairie Waters*, 2018.

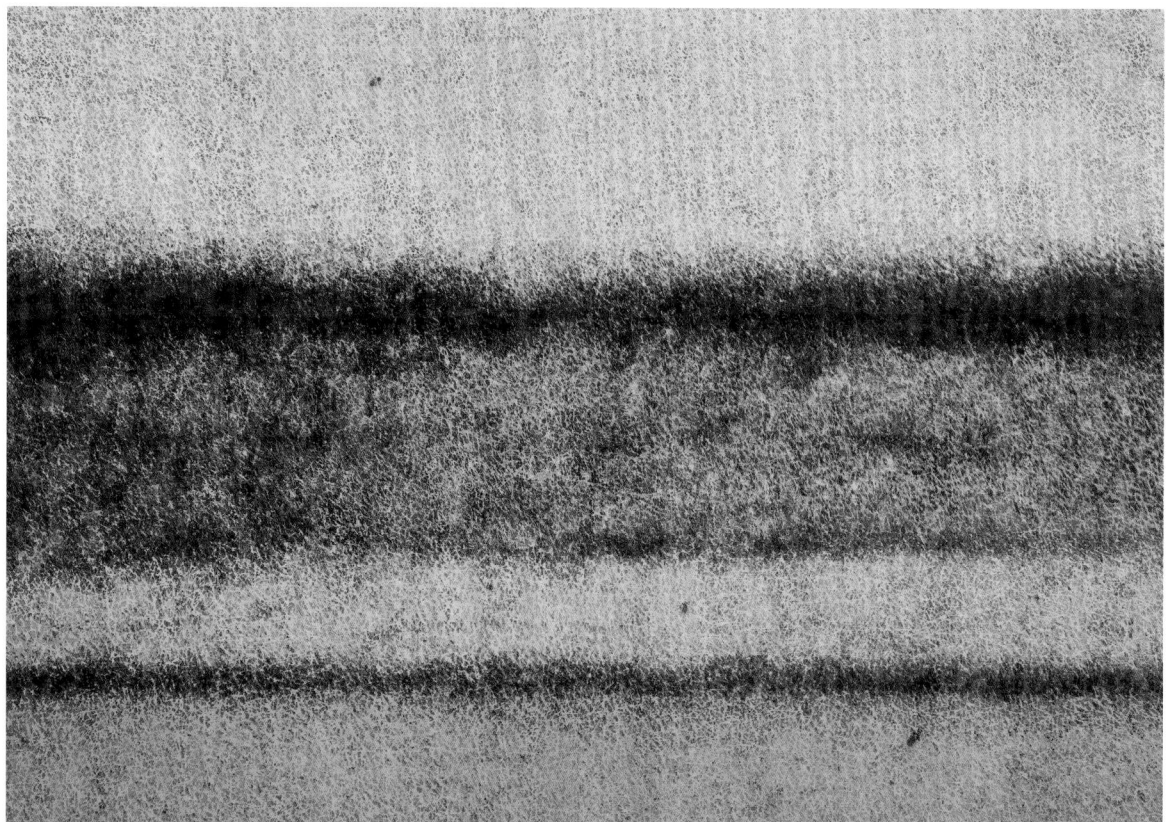

47. *Horizon Detail*, 1974.

Silkscreens and Colour

Proch's prints of the 1970s, done at the Grand Western Canadian Screen Shop, serve as anchors for many of the artist's creative thoughts. Through his prints, Proch developed much of his iconography and the various characteristic elements that extend to other works as well as some of the prints having direct iconographical links to his masks.

Printed in collaboration with print master Len Anthony and E.J. (Ted) Howorth at the Screen Shop, Proch's prints done between 1974 and 1981 were primarily black and white. They were small editions of only two to four pulls each. Proch did do a few, however, such as *Three Furrows* (1974) and *Woodsmoke* (1977), in colour as well as black and white. After his two solo exhibitions at the Winnipeg Art Gallery, he reintroduced colour into his art for the first time since his student days. At the same time, a softer aspect of the prairie landscape appeared in his prints. Curvilinear flowing lines became furrows, a stylistic element characteristic of much of his work from the mid-1970s forward.

Proch always stretched the properties of the materials he used. While at the Screen Shop, he undertook many labour-intensive experiments in order to achieve his desired effects. In turn, these expanded the traditional boundaries and properties of printmaking. Proch sought to achieve the effects and sensibilities of an original drawing in some of his prints. To obtain the subtle gradations of grey he wanted in the black-and-white version of *Horizon Detail* (1974), he used roller-bearing graphite, acquired from a local automotive machine shop, mixed with bronzing varnish. This yielded a quality almost indistinguishable from his drawings. It was, as he said, "a liquid drawing."[40] Bill Lobchuk recounted that Don Proch and David Thauberger presented specific technical

44

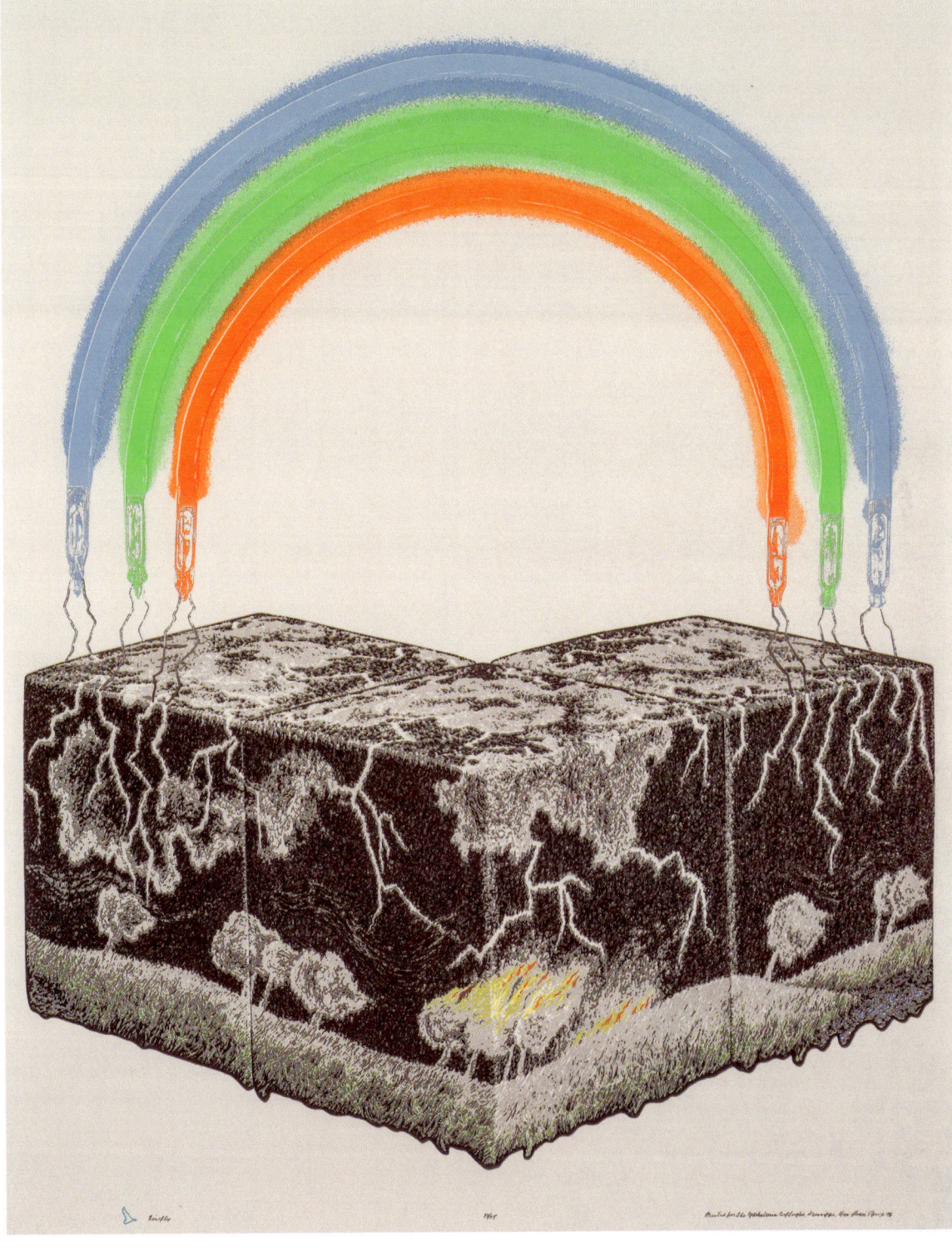

48. *Fire Fly*, 1978.

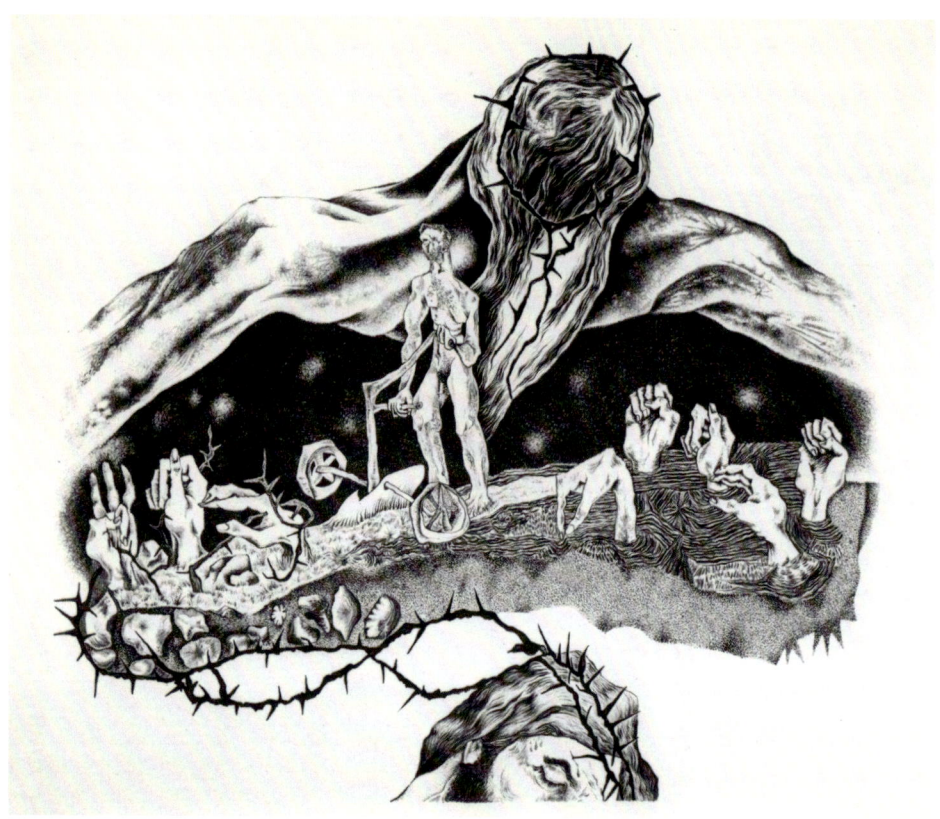

49. *Walking Plow*, 1972.

challenges for the Screen Shop.[41] In addition to achieving the sense in his print of an actual drawing, Proch also wanted to work in a scale that was too large for commercial printers. Thauberger, for his part, desired to print on velvet and to use flocking in some works. Both artists credit Anthony for his technical knowledge and skill in solving these artistic challenges.

Proch was a master of balancing black and white and colour to achieve maximum psychological effects of serenity and drama. *Fire Fly* (1978), for example, primarily a black-and-white print, had one area of bronze in the landscape itself. Proch reserved his use of colour in this piece solely for the electric neon rainbow, thus creating an effect that heightened the dramatic impact of the print. The rainbow in this lightning storm is the source of natural, and dangerous, electrical charges that strike the ground, spark lightning and here ignited the trees he depicted.

Proch also experimented by introducing new technology in this work. He had Ernest Mayer photograph three-dimensional neon tubes and Proch then transported the photographs directly into the print. He thereby achieved another technical advance, introducing three-dimensional objects into a two-dimensional print. It was an achievement about which he still talks.

Proch incorporated his personal iconography of jagged slivers for lightning, images that recur in his masks and *Elevator Series* from the late 1970s onwards. His increasing use of personally devised symbols intensified his obvious links between prints and masks. Proch does not compartmentalize his messages by medium but moves from one means of expression to another, each building his unique visual philosophy. The geology of the Asessippi region, depicted in *Fire Fly*, is yet another image that surfaces in many of his two- and three-dimensional pieces.

46

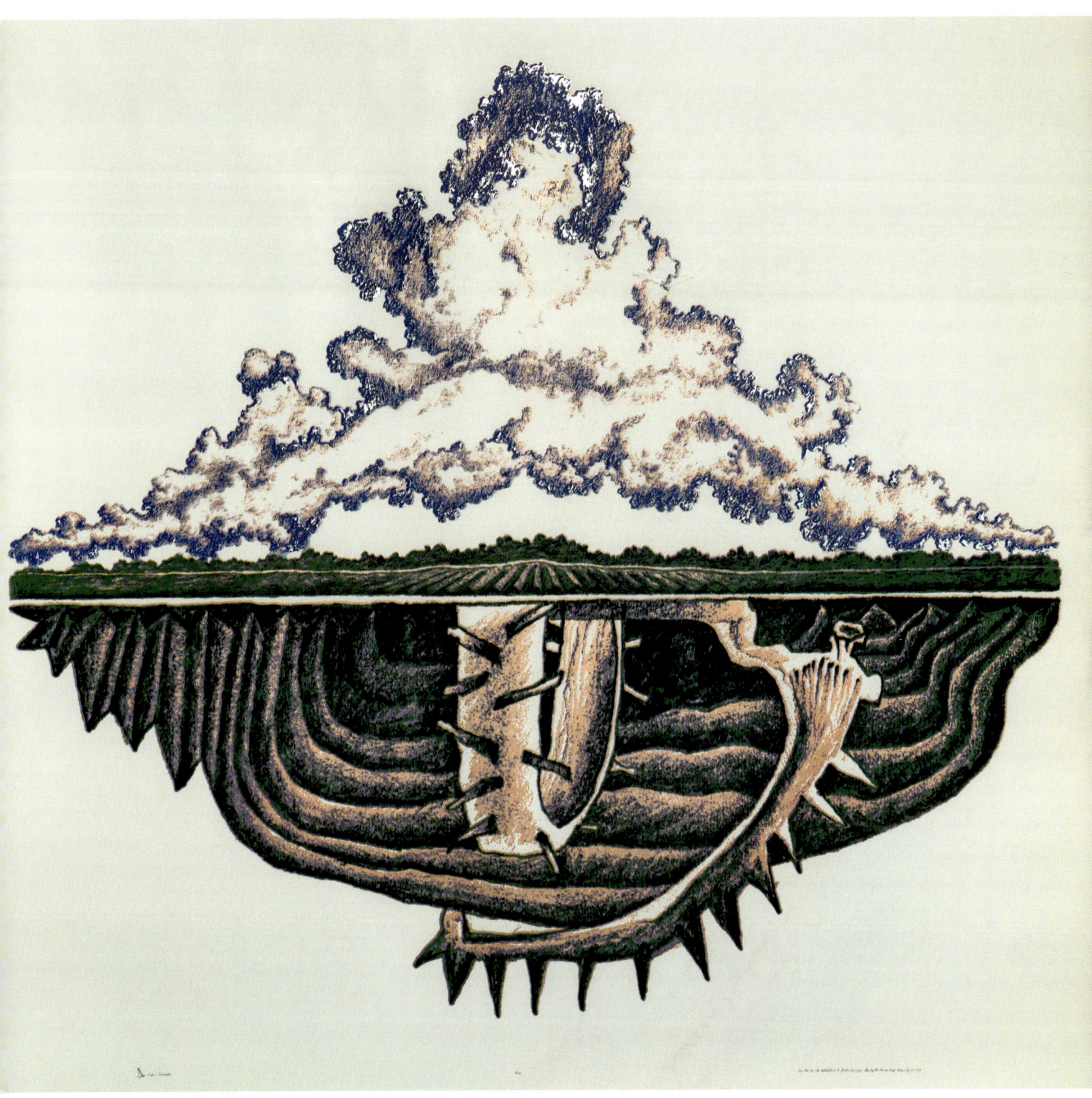

50. *Luke's Cultivator*, 1974.

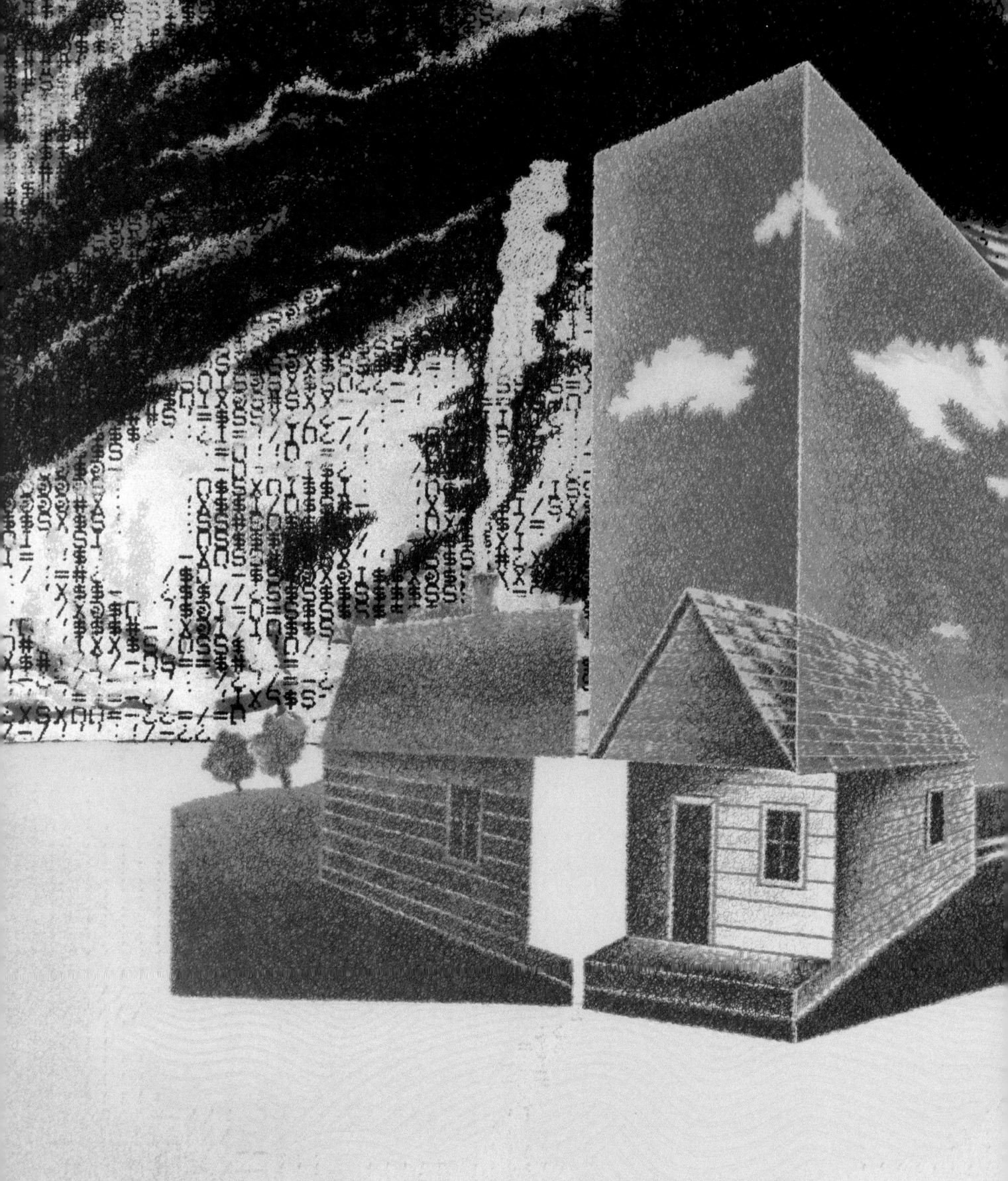

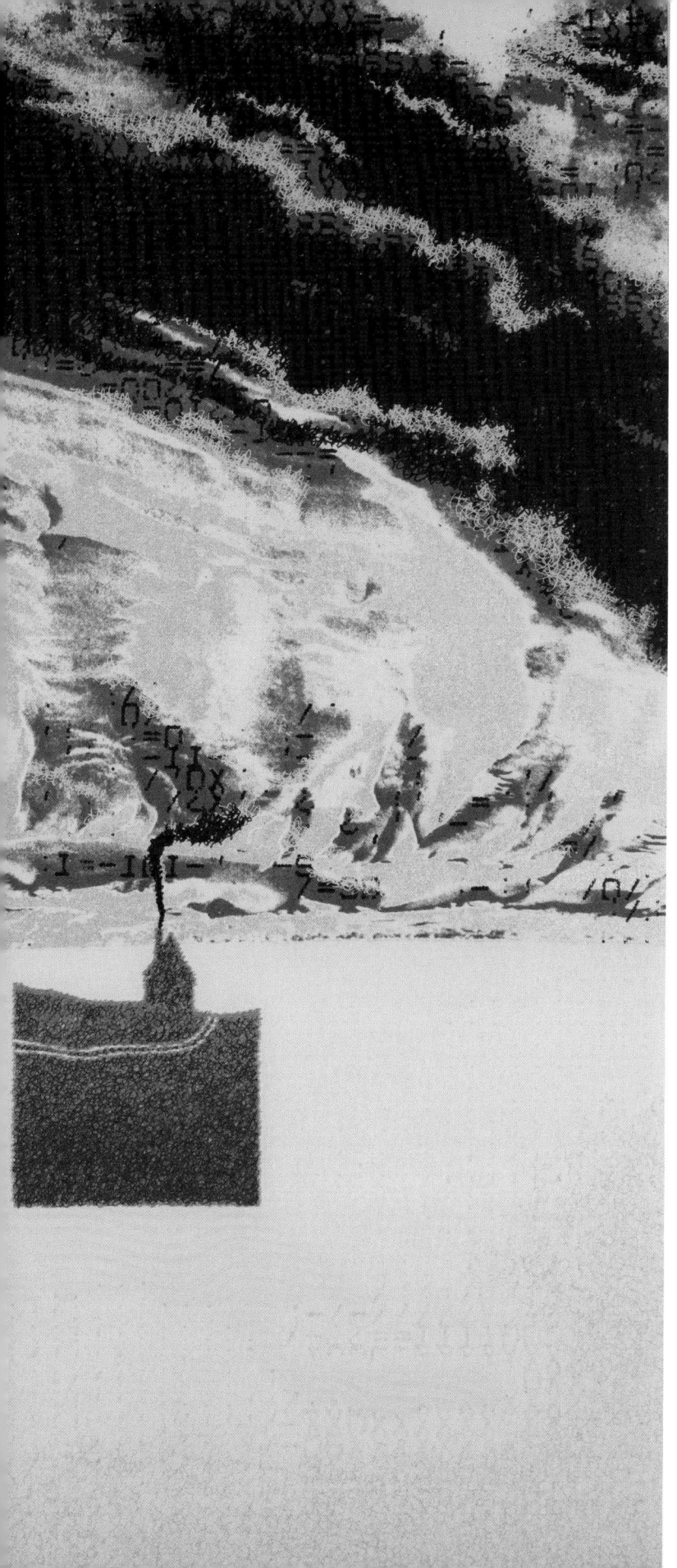

49

51. *Woodsmoke*, 1977.

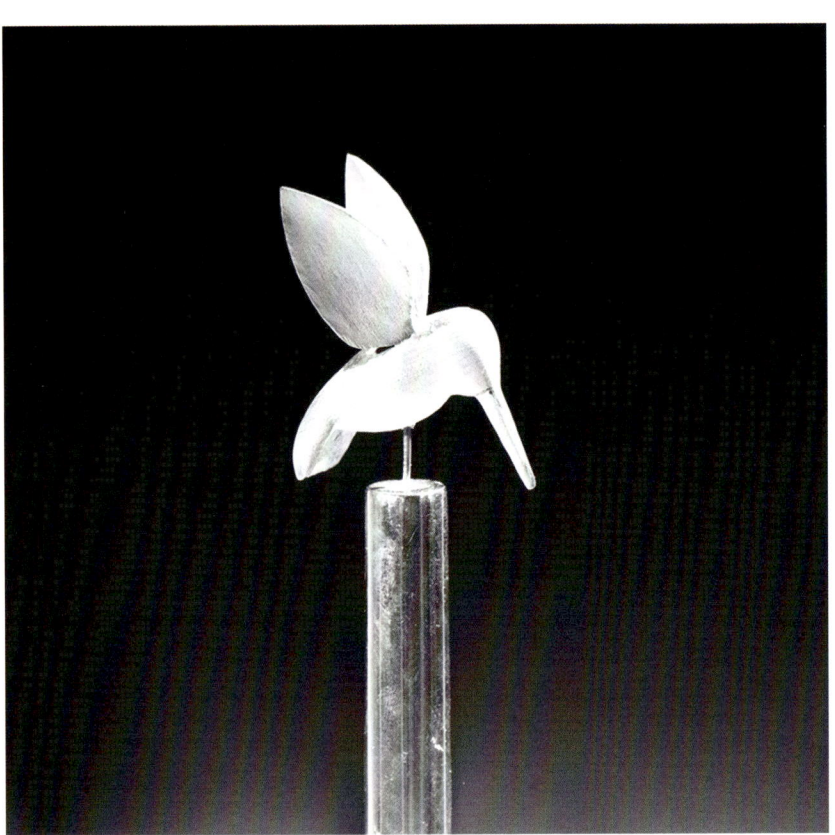

52. *Hummingbird Watching Mask* (detail), 1974. Hummingbird carved by Bertie Duncan.

Proch's inclusion of the landscape as a critical aspect of his lament and celebration of rural life is a foundational element of all his work, embracing prairie classic cultural and contemporary political traits. By the end of the 1970s, University of Manitoba professor of English and avid supporter of Manitoba artists Ken Hughes had recognized Proch's ability to analyze the interrelationship between humans and nature in his art. "What we have with Proch, in fact, is a type. As a person he embodies and gives shape to the quintessential experience of large numbers of other persons, indeed of generations. His experience of the peasant farm, the rural-urban hotel, and finally the big city make him a type of Manitoba in particular and Canada in general. . . . Through this typicality we can

see how Proch works from a base in Ukrainian-Canadian culture yet at the same time speaks clearly to others of different ethnic origins."[42]

Hughes also recognized Proch's artistic affinity with his own socialist politics:

As a creator of images dealing with the interpenetration of man (second nature) and nature (primary nature) in a specific region (Manitoba), Proch makes images that serve to define some of the makings of a national consciousness. As he both looks squarely at the land as it has been shaped by man, and at man as he has been shaped by the lands, the resulting

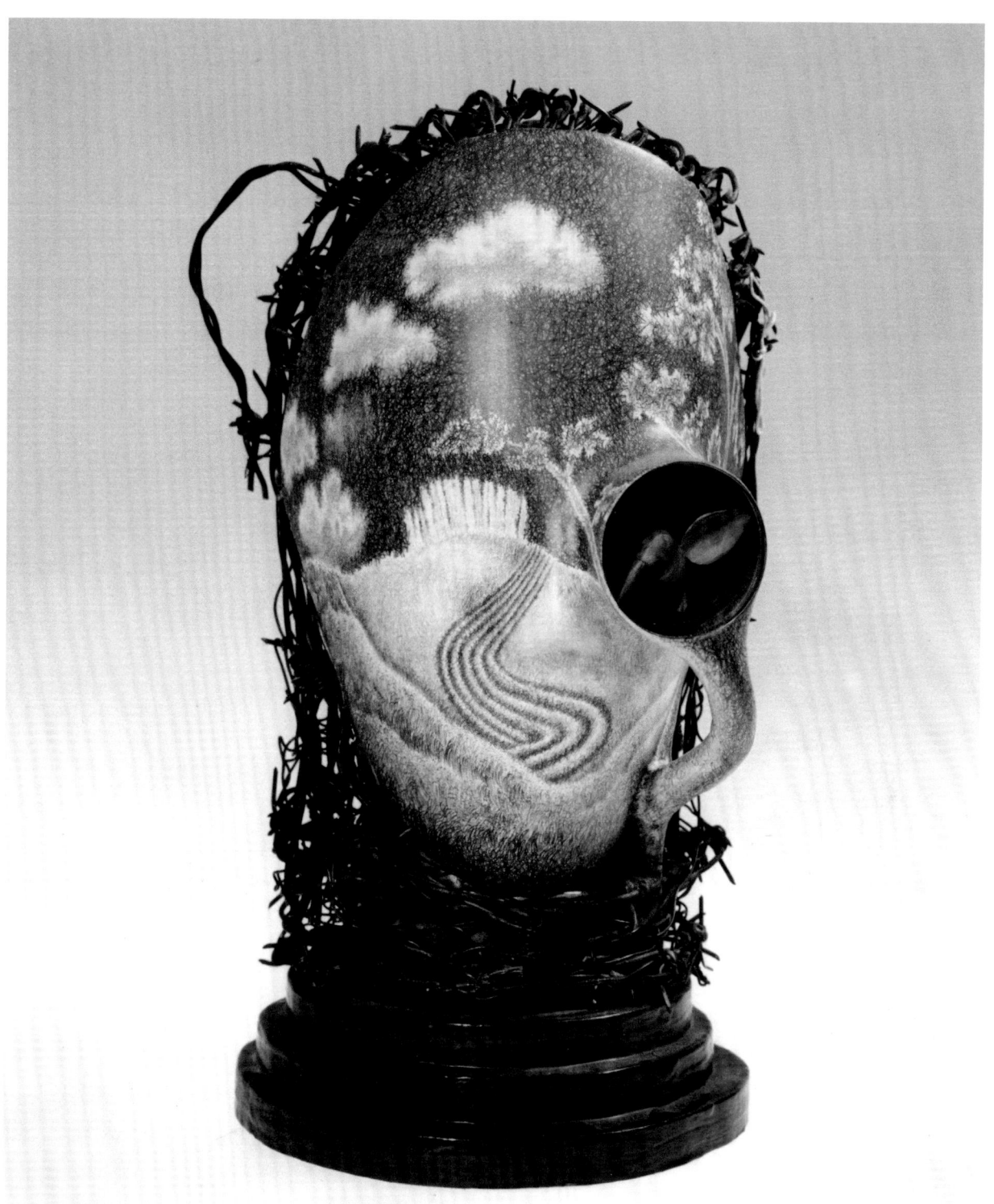

53. *Hummingbird Watching Mask*, 1974.

images he creates force others (those who wish to see at all) to see reality in his Canadian way, be they of whatever ethnic origin.

The evidence of the art indicates that Proch [is unbourgeois—or even anti-bourgeois—to the extent that he] starts with society rather than the individual. . . Moreover, he perceives things in dialectical terms so that nature is always seen in relation to man at particular stages of economic (i.e. social) development (primitive in *Walking Plow*, sophisticated advanced capitalism in *Woodsmoke*), and man in relation to nature (the masks). Both man and nature in his works are mediated through society or second nature. Nature thus ceases to be dead material or mechanical thing and becomes a living presence, a vital force in the tradition of the great Earth Mother. Because the earth lives in this sense it can be hurt and so we see in the silk-screen print *Luke's Cultivator* (1974) . . . jagged edges of a cultivator symbolically sink deep into the earth which it prepares to tear up.[43]

Jagged elements occur in both Proch's two- and three-dimensional pieces, starting with *Asessippi Tread* and *Pincushion Man*. These elements are evident again in prints such as *Walking Plow* and *Luke's Cultivator* and later in many of his *Elevator Series* sculptures. Do they denote strength, force, or fragility? His experience on the farm was simultaneously fragile and hard, and Proch presented that dichotomy and disquiet in every work, always balancing and juxtaposing fragility with harshness. As he reflected, harshness was paramount in his early work and is seen in his large silkscreen print *Walking Plow* (1972). The fragility of his surfaces, coupled with the precision of his drawing and combined with his addition of specifically chosen elements, effectively set up poignant discordant contrasts between these two sensibilities in his later masks and sculptures.

Hughes presented an evocative description of the harsh aspects of the imagery and meaning in *Walking Plow*:

From this God-sky, barbed wire . . . descends to form the equivalent of a crown of thorns in the suffering Jesus figure at the bottom, having been wrapped around a set of hands sticking out of the muskeg. This Jesus figure at once embodies the experiences of, and gives expression to, the struggles of the poor and oppressed. . . . Hands coming out of the muskeg say in the hand language of the deaf WAR and PEACE. . . . The primitive technology in the form of the single-furrow plough held by the major figure reveals him to be the archetypical peasant pioneer farmer. His twisted and contorted body speaks of his brutalization, while the solidity of his legs show him to be planted firmly on the earth.[44]

Of the aesthetics of this work, Hughes commented that the base colour is

the white of the paper, the intricately mottled graphite design [that] captures the sense of the flatness of the actual prairie. . . . The land rears up in front of the viewer as if it were a vertical cement wall rather than a horizontal landscape. . . . In effect he remakes the familiar into the distortion of prairie, a reflection of the pain of the land plowed. . . . *Walking Plow* takes as its subject the historical process of the appropriation or humanization of man of nature. The plowing of the land, the planting of the bodies, and the brutalizing dehumanization are all part of the pioneering process.[45]

This print, and a number of others of the period, were executed in black and white, a choice that effectively enhances the starkness of their subjects. The 1970s was definitely a decade in which Proch developed his evolving messages, iconography, and art making.

52

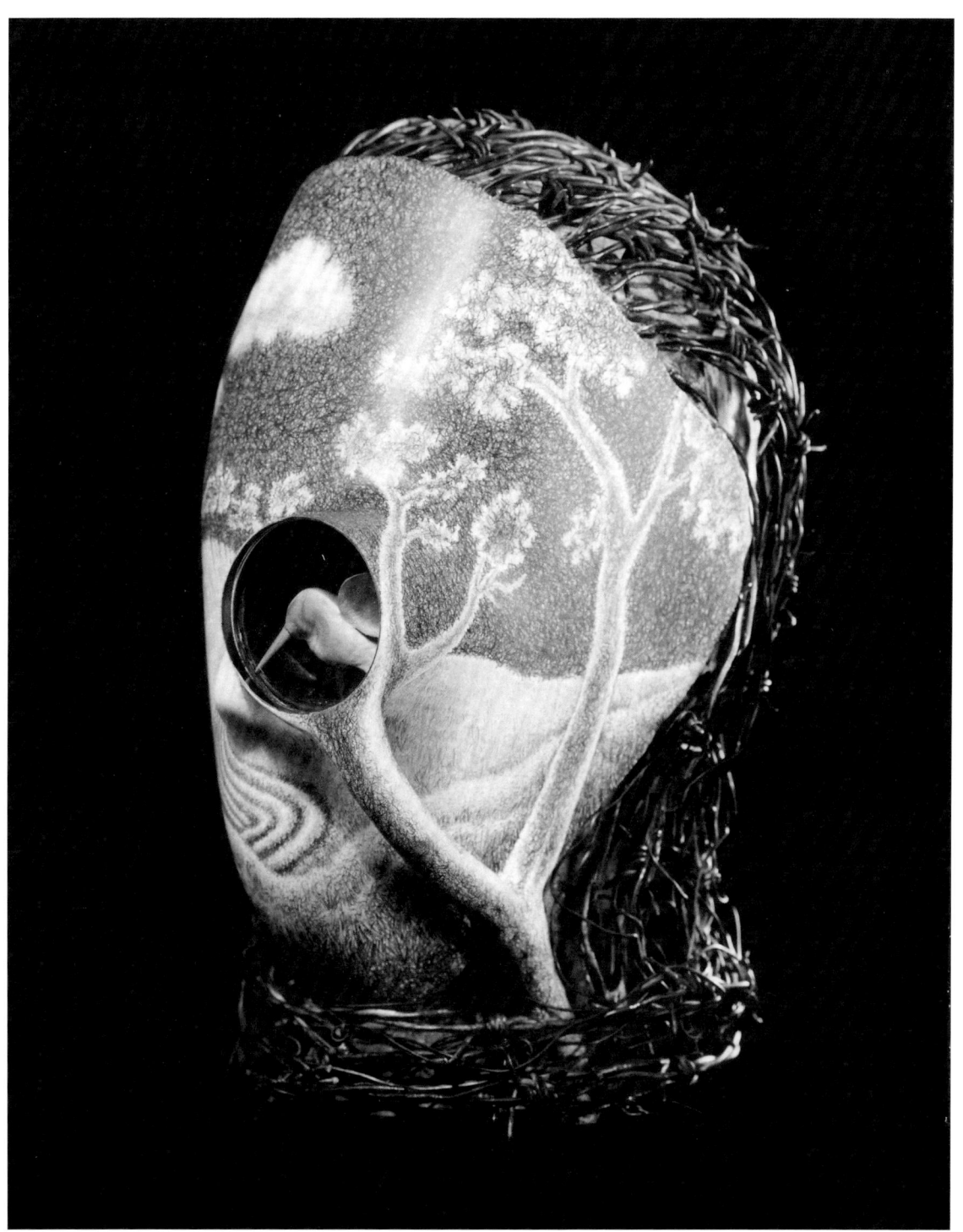

54. *Hummingbird Watching Mask* (side view), 1974.

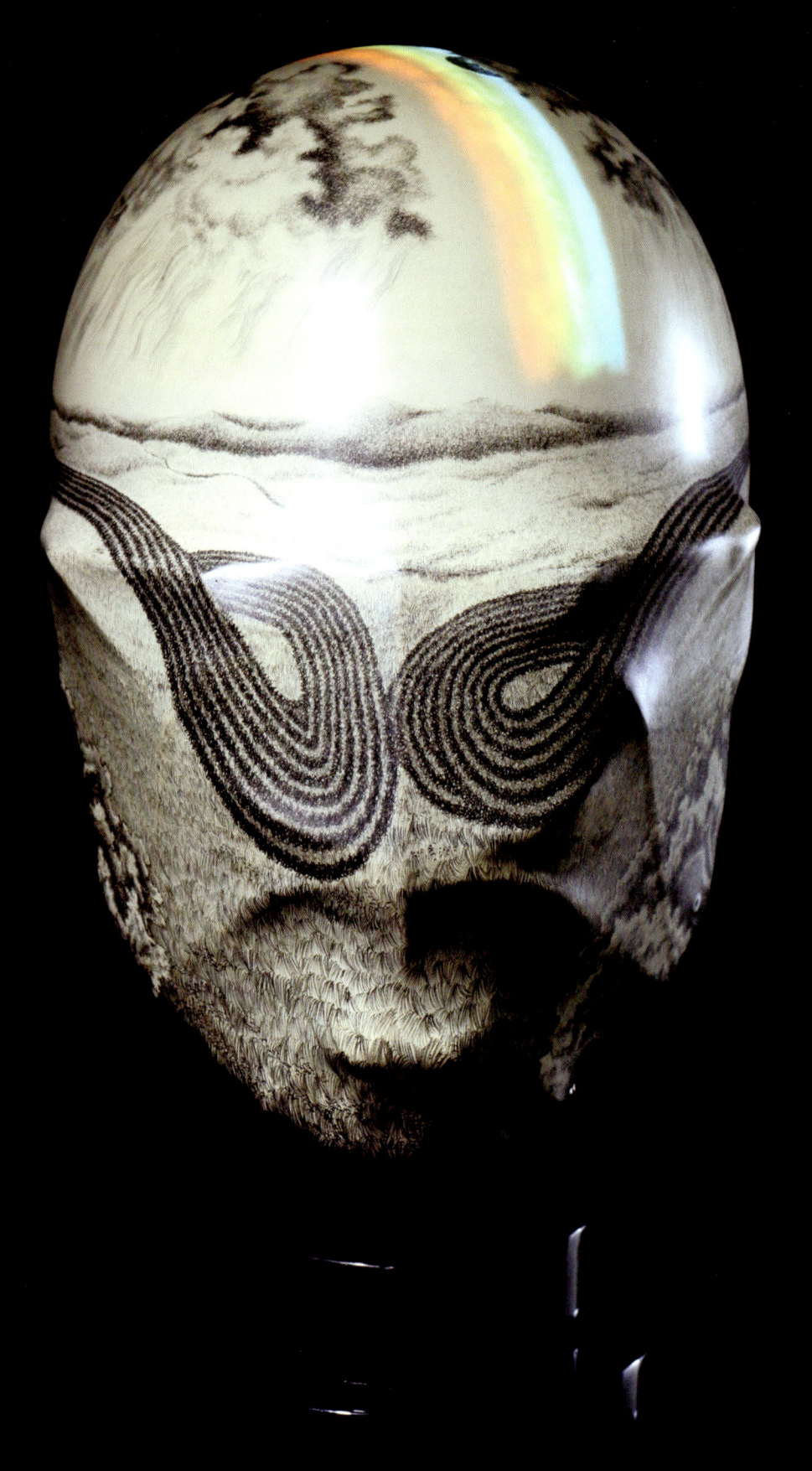

Masks: Concealing and Revealing

IN 1974, DON PROCH BEGAN creating his novel and distinct masks in addition to his major sculptures, installations, and prints. His first mask, *Hummingbird Watching Mask* (1974), was a breakthrough. A delicate wooden hummingbird, carved by his friend Bertie Duncan, is the focus. The tiny bird is placed in the mask's only eye—a round aperture in its centre. Two branches of a tree and its leaves, intricately drawn, embrace the right side of the face. Below the eye are furrows in the field. The wider landscape and skyscape cover the face and sides of the mask. The top and back of the mask's head are made from barbed wire, evoking a bird's nest. The delicacy of the bird and drawing contrast with the barbed wire. The effect is jarring, recalling the harsh imagery in his earlier prints such as *Walking Plow*. The counterpoint achieved with his deliberate juxtapositions of gentle and harsh reflects Proch's balance of nostalgia for the past with worries about the future. His 1976 *Manitoba Mining Mask*, depicting the Manitoba terrain and vegetation, develops the theme of concern about the future further. Effluent flows down the side of the work and spews from its top.

Rainbow Mask (1978), another early example, bears a number of iconographical ties to his silkscreen print *Fire Fly* of the same year, including the portrayal of lightning and the depiction of the region's geology. Peter Mellen included *Rainbow Mask* in his 1978 book *Landmarks of Canadian Art*:

> *Rainbow Mask*, one of the most startling of them all, is made of fibreglass and contains a heat sensitive neon light in rainbow colours. The entire outer surface is covered with an intricate graphite landscape drawing that has no vanishing point, suggesting a feeling of endless space. The viewer can imagine himself viewing the entire landscape with full 360-degree peripheral vision, as if he were inside the mask. *Rainbow Mask* is not only a statement about man's relationship to the land, but it has [a] deeper perception of the Prairie landscape, combining man and landscape in a unique visual experience. It is

55. *Rainbow Mask*, 1976.

not only a contemporary mask, similar to a motorcyclist's or a goalie's, but it also evokes the artist-shaman's mask of prehistoric times.[46]

This fusion of nature and human, clearly evident in the 1972 installation *The Legend of Asessippi* and in Proch's prints, continues in the masks. Some masks honour specific individuals whom Proch admired; others present various forces and elements of nature; yet others are critical commentaries on conundrums and concerns in present-day society. All his masks include traits found in his other work and build on his rural roots with his nostalgic portrayal of prairie life. The harshness of the present and his concern for the future are combined in much of his work. In creating his masks, Proch developed a unique drawing surface in the round, usually the shape of head and shoulders, emphasizing humankind's central place in and responsibility for the land and environment. External elements appended to his forms enhanced his theme.

The metaphors of masks have allowed Proch to explore physical representations, psychological insights, and global issues. Masks themselves are mysterious. Masks conceal identity, yet in Proch's work they simultaneously reveal truth, identify place, and evoke illuminating psychological inscapes. They cloak a personality while imparting the artist's penetrating insights of place, time, and person. Proch's masks see; his viewers experience. Although his masks contain the landscape, they are also objects within his landscape, describing what is there and imparting warnings about the future. As William Kirby wrote,

the masks are designed to represent what one would see with 360° peripheral vision, with what would be seen from the inside being registered on the outside. In other words, the masks are actually what they see. In addition to looking at or into the mask you are also able to see the outside world from inside the mask. Theoretically, when opened up, the landscape reads as a total view. However, there is always a frontal view—the face image—which reads as a focal point and the viewer is

inclined to stop at the front even though it reads as a continuous landscape.[47]

Much has been written about the meanings and history of masks. Patricia Vervoort provided an interesting perspective: "Traditionally, the mask suggests that something is hidden and the truth will be revealed when the mask is removed. . . . [It is] a means for human beings to temporarily transform themselves into the other beings by altering their appearance and their identity. The whole concept of the mask implies that it can be removed. Yet the odd-shaped heads, labelled masks by Proch, don't encourage removal, which [implies] . . . that there may be something more frightening underneath. Besides, the encircling landscapes are indelibly bound to the heads or masks and literally the two cannot be separated."[48]

John Graham concluded that "the mask connotes mind, the mask connotes seeing. Proch's heads are totally occupied by what they're doing; they are what they see. Proch isn't painting Canadian landscapes; he has, you might say, become the landscape. . . . There are no people in the scenes drawn on the masks: the landscape itself is human."[49]

Proch's masks have been likened to a *pysanka*, a Ukrainian Easter egg. One can recall his childhood memory of his mother creating Christmas decorations by gluing broken bits of silver glass balls onto empty eggs. The inspiration from witnessing that transformation is evident in his masks: "The mask can be perceived as the planet Earth in space. No less interesting is the interpretation of the masks as works in which the artist has transformed the art of the *pysanka*, revealing his relationship to the Ukrainian cultural tradition. One cannot react indifferently to the fantastic subjective landscapes on these masks—landscapes simultaneously earthly and heavenly, movingly delicate, and unprotected."[50]

Proch drew landscapes and placed objects in the apertures of a number of his masks, thus giving both interior and exterior views. In these works, such as *Night Landing Mask* (1982) and *Delta Night Mask—Homage à Kelly Clark* (1984), identity is revealed rather than hidden. The artist invites the viewer in, encouraging active

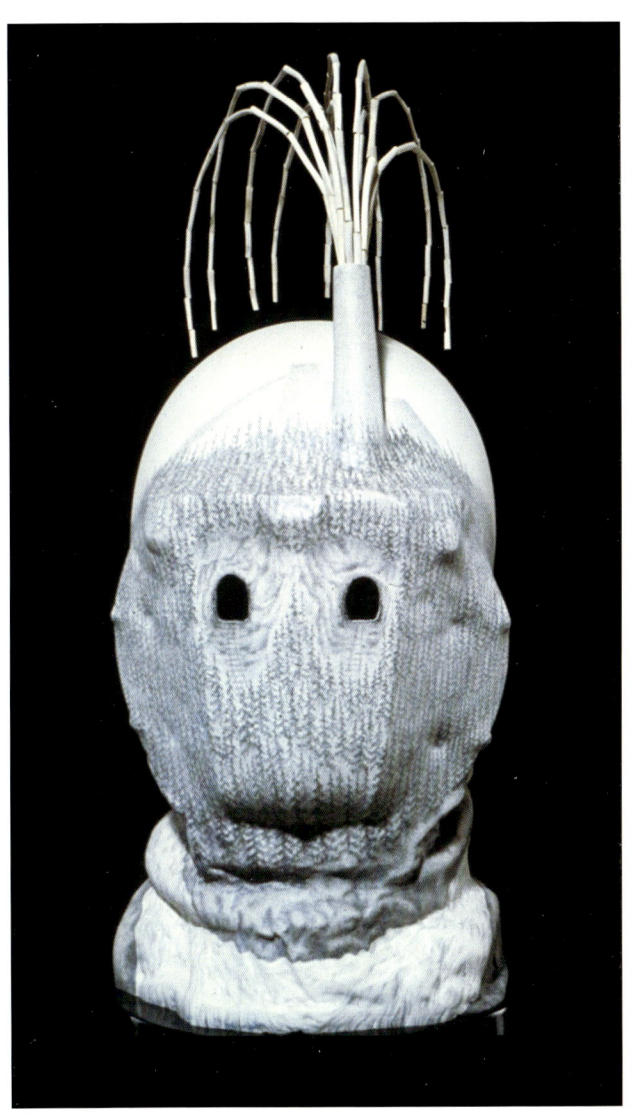
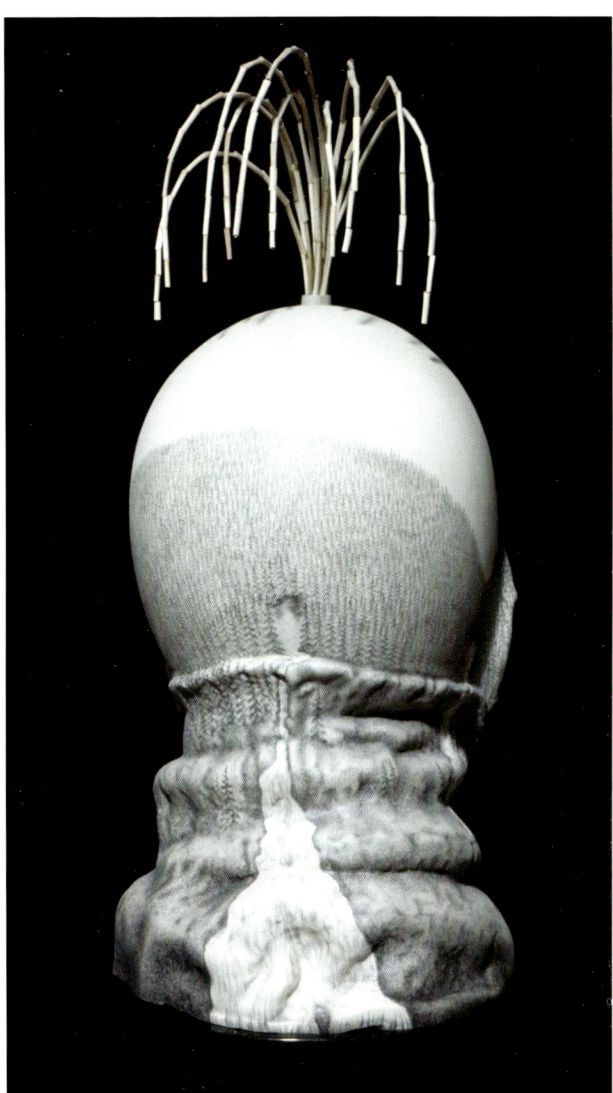

56 and 57. *Manitoba Mining Mask* (front and back view), 1976.

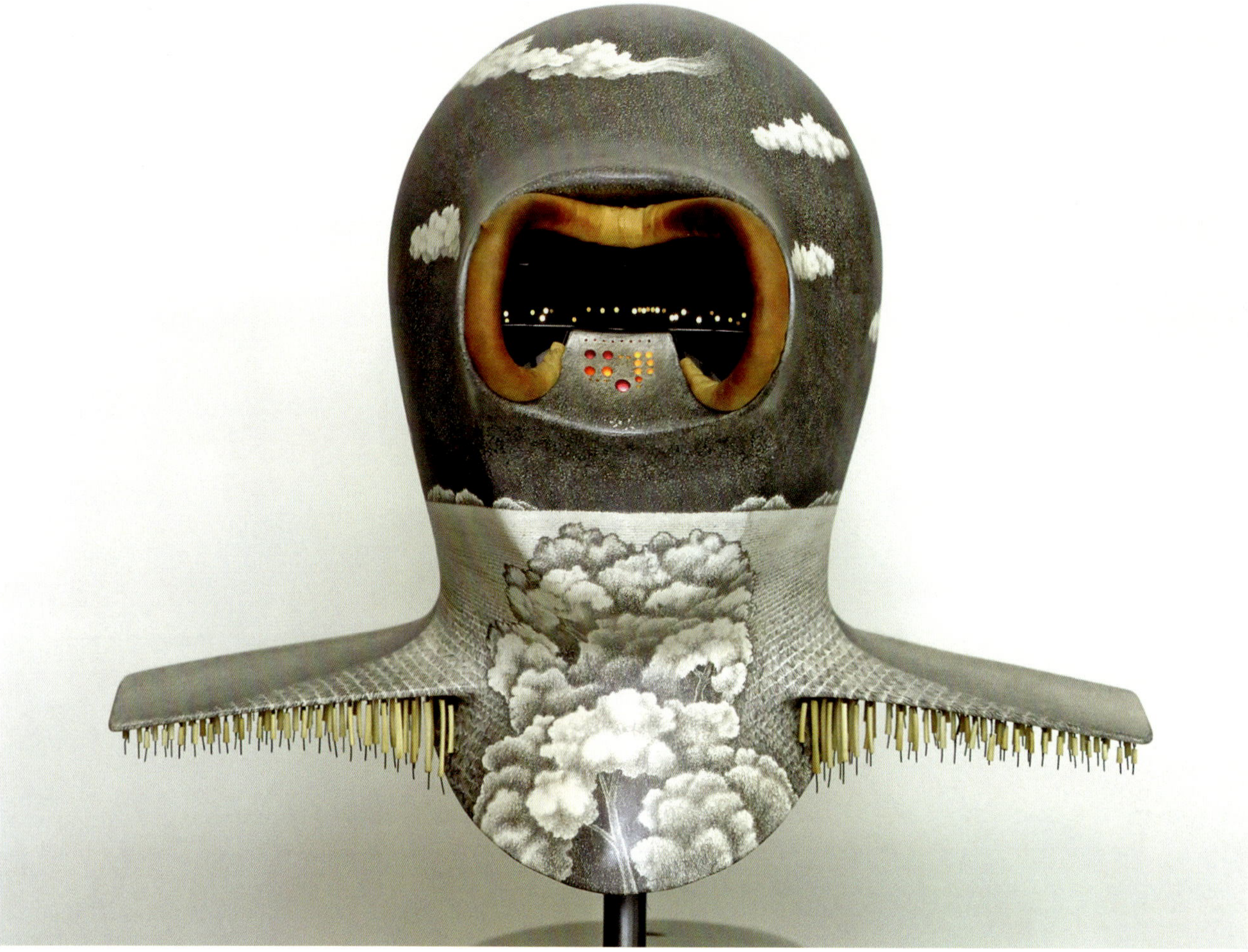

58. *Night Landing Mask*, 1982.

59. (OPPOSITE) *Delta Night Mask – Homage* à *Kelly Clark*, 1984.

engagement with and exploration of the landscape that he has conveyed in the round and his more personal thoughts and ideas expressed within. The apertures in these works are the eye portions of the masks and are rather like a viewfinder. Inside, Proch presents detailed landscapes of particular relevance to the subject of the mask itself. In *Night Landing Mask*, for instance, when one looks inside, one sees a landing strip and runway night lights. On the exterior, the artist has drawn a night skyscape with clouds, and clouds form the runway to the viewfinder's opening. Of *Night Landing Mask*, Proch wrote,

. . . it is theoretically an appliance for the face or head. The viewer may be investigative enough to visually inquire into the details of the structure to move from the exterior to the interior of the mask. With their face against the opening in the "face" of the mask, the viewer becomes the masked and is therefore "disguised" to other viewers who may be observing their interaction. This disguising marks the true definition of a mask. Once "disguised," the viewer moves from a passive to an active position, becoming a participant in the

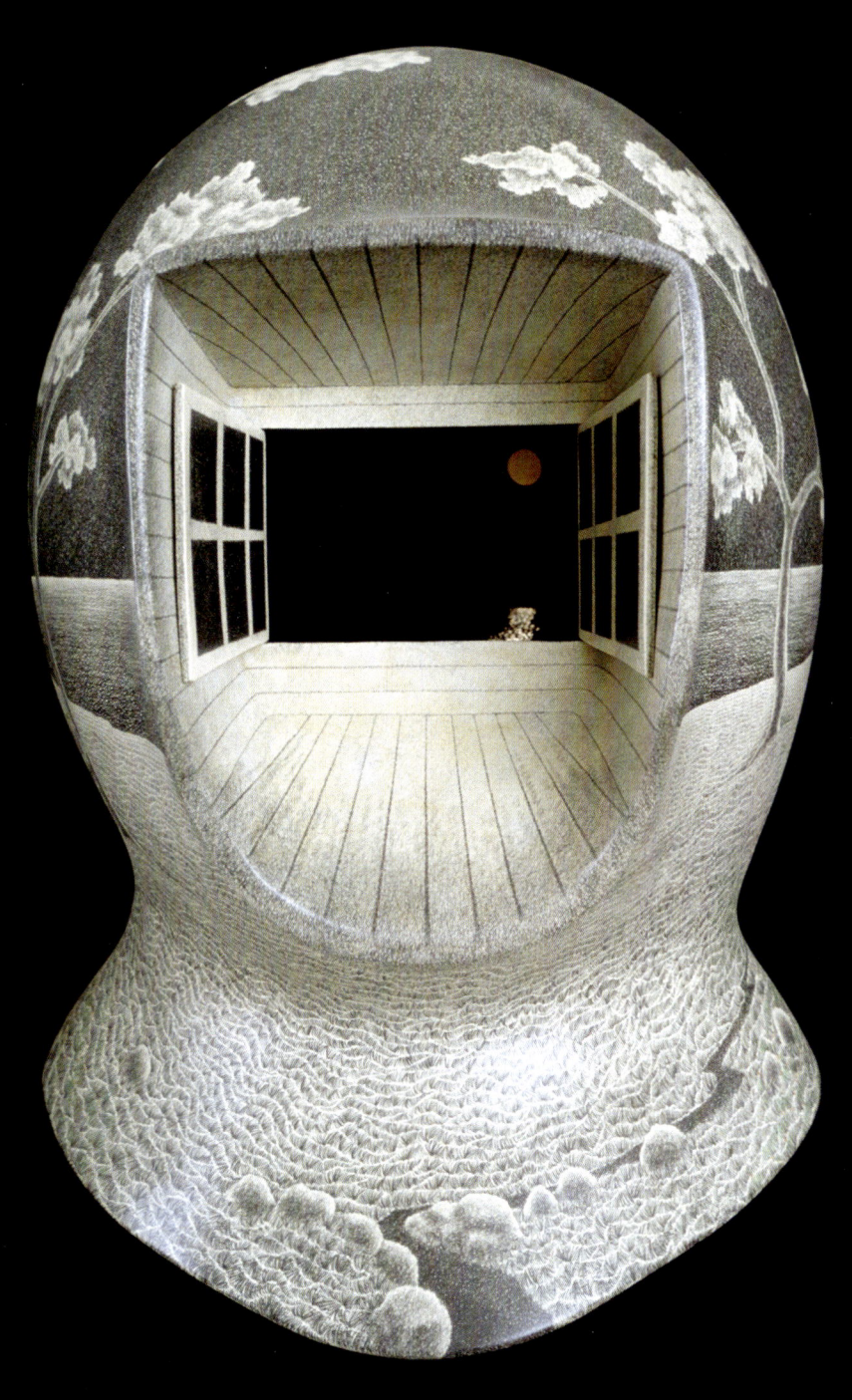

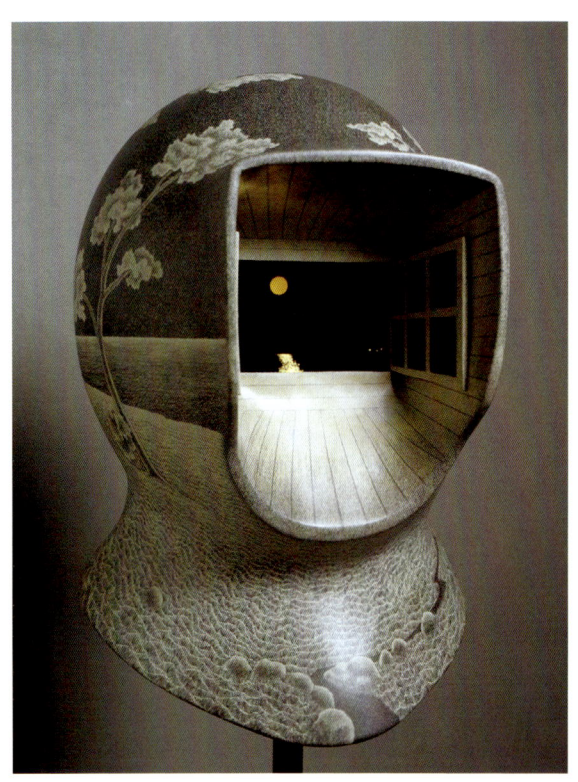

60. *Delta Night Mask – Homage à Kelly Clark* (side view), 1984.

art process. The mask's interior space is designed to become better defined, both in colour and clarity, as the viewer moves in more closely and blocks out the exterior ambient light. The viewer may then be transported in their memory to a time when they were landing at an eagerly anticipated destination. The mask is dated (the summer of 1982) by the positioning of the constellations on the horizon.[51]

Delta Night Mask—Homage à Kelly Clark is one of Proch's masks honouring friends and colleagues. Proch invites us as viewers to look inside through the viewfinder, a window. Rather than looking out the window, we look into the heart of the mask's interior, where Proch has drawn Clark's beloved Delta Marsh, Manitoba, the place where Clark did so much of his art. Clark, Proch's colleague and friend, was renowned for his drawings and watercolours. The two shared a studio from 1968 to 1973 and socialized

together over many years. Clark, with his poetic, troubled soul, explored his own psychological states of mind in his work while embodying the prairie landscape in much of it. Older than Proch, Clark was a draftsman from whom Proch learned a great deal about drawing: "He had much more experience, and I watched him draw a lot. In the 1972 show, he did some drawing on my three-dimensional forms. I spent time with him at Lake Manitoba, where Kelly had a cottage. This piece shows the view from his couch, looking out at the lake through the window, with the long beach and shallow water. We would go out at night with a drink to look at the moon."[52]

Both artists' works are steeped in deep psychological insights. Clark's are perhaps more inward and Proch's, though autobiographical in part, more societal. The works of both are approachable with their detailed and descriptive landscapes. In creating *Delta Night Mask—Homage à Kelly Clark*, Proch paid tribute to his friend with particularly poignant details of place and discernment of Clark's soul and mind. It was important to Proch to portray the Delta Marsh landscape precisely, all 360 degrees, because it was so intrinsic to Clark's life and art. Executed in silverpoint, graphite, acrylic lacquer, fibreglass, steel, and fibre optics, as curator Michelle Lavalle noted, it is a "non-conventional portrayal of landscape . . . not rigidly bound by history or tradition in the expressions of landscape. . . . [The] inspiration is from a range of sources: from the mapping of geography through science and technology to deeply personal connections with land and place."[53]

When Proch talks of these two masks in particular, he reflects on his observations about how gallery visitors approached them in the same show. He was intrigued to see that people got closer to *Night Landing Mask*. They went right up to it and put their faces on the leather-bound aperture to see inside. The detail within is reminiscent of being inside an airplane cockpit or looking out an airplane window when approaching the runway on landing. In contrast, audiences looked at, not into, *Delta Night Mask—Homage à Kelly Clark*. They engaged with that landscape in its broad sense.[54]

The apertures in all Proch's masks act as portholes into their interiors, probing the conflicting sensibilities between the inner mind and the outer world. *Waterfront Reading Mask* (2010), executed with silverpoint, pencil, coloured pencil, dyed bone, wood, and electrical elements, is a later example of his penetrating insights into the juxtapositions of inner and outer selves. The interior includes the Asessippi cabin and a minute yellow Volkswagon Beetle car.

From 2000 on, Proch's masks have become much more than renderings of a head. His departure from bikers' helmets to masks intensified his forms, subjects, and messages. John Graham insightfully articulated that first transition from helmet to mask:

> Instead of putting patterned helmets on his big back bikers, Proch began designing masks. Maybe Proch himself couldn't have foreseen how much more interesting the head is when detached from the rest of the body.
>
> Technically the masks are designed to give the viewer peripheral vision, to contain the straight line that is the prairie in some shape instead of letting it fall off the ledge of perception. But a mask has so many connotations. Alienation. Disguise. Identity. The African idea of the mask as residence of spirits. Not to mention the masks worn by contemporary man to divide him from his environments; the miner's mask, the motorcyclist's, the goalie's. The mask demands that you confront it and respond. "I have an idealistic end," Proch says. "I'd like people to appreciate a particular lifestyle that I know really well, a relationship with the land. Sometimes I think I'm asking too much."[55]

Proch also often changed the viewpoint within a single work. Many masks have several horizons—some are at chin level, some at eye level, and others above the brow. These multiple perspectives change the viewer's entry points, often confusing one's place in relationship to the scene, increasing the sense of mystery.

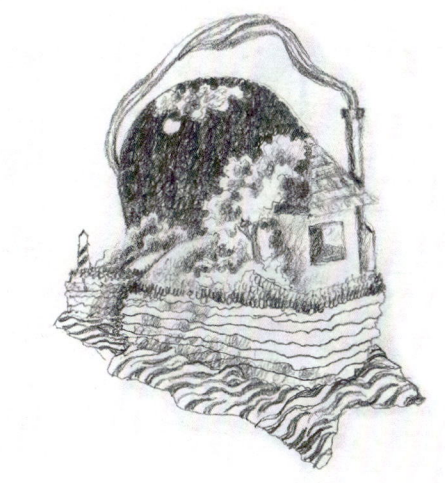

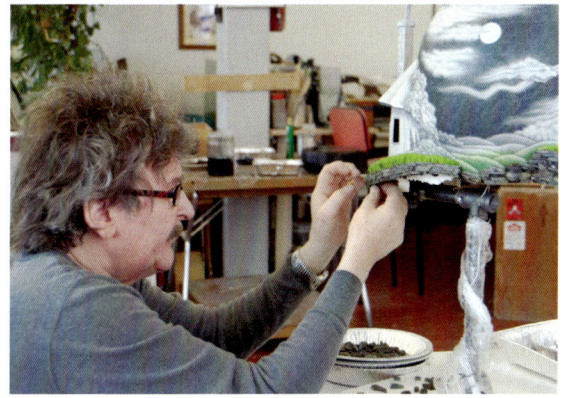

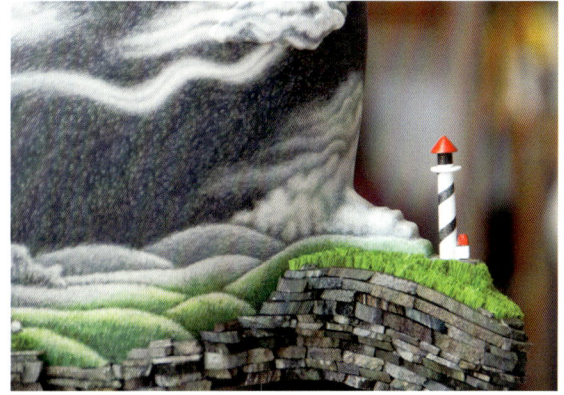

61

61. Sketch for *Waterfront Reading Mask*, 2010.

62. Don Proch working on *Waterfront Reading Mask*, 2010.

63. *Waterfront Reading Mask* (detail), 2010.

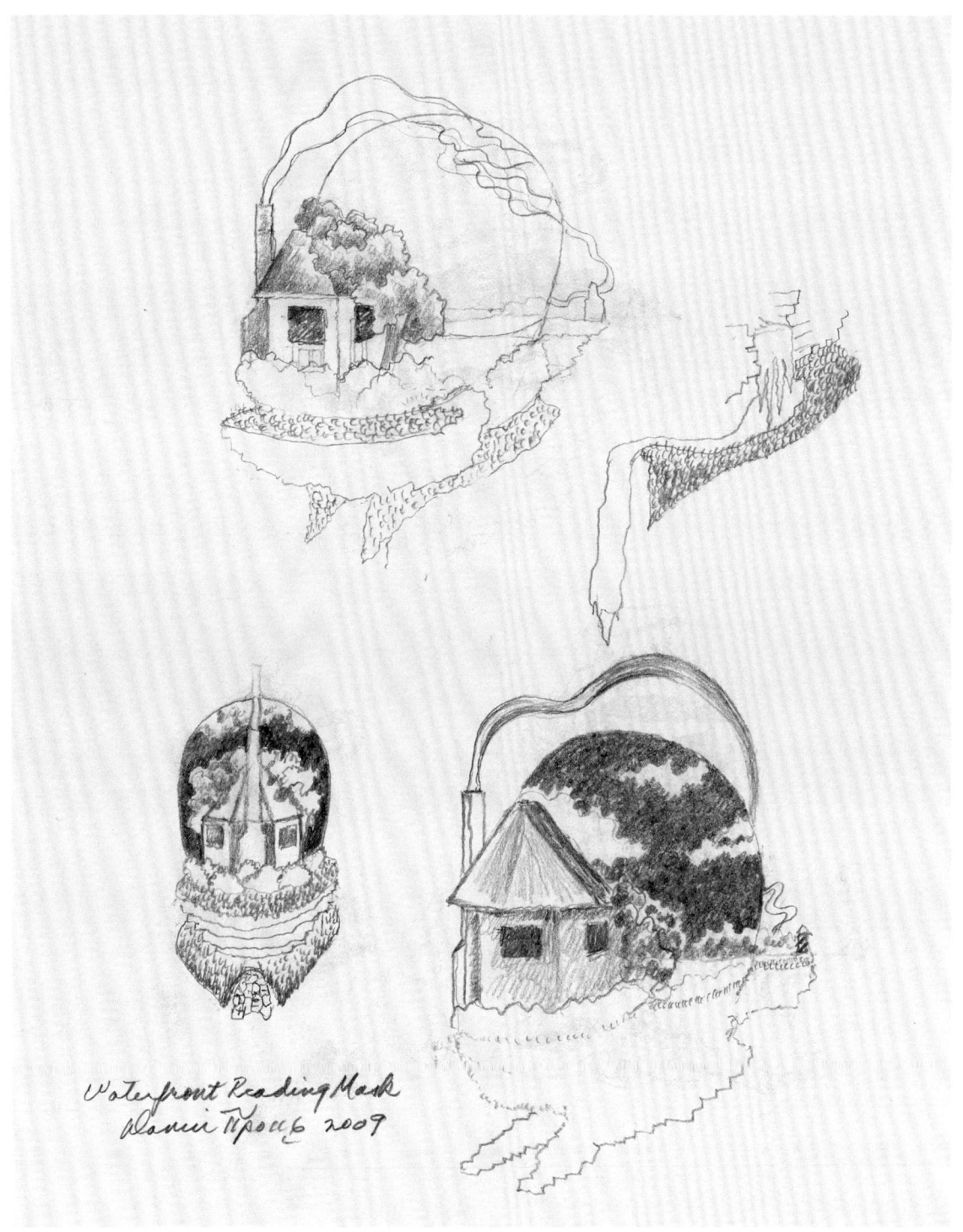

Waterfront Reading Mask
Daniel Wroth 2009

64. Sketches for *Waterfront Reading Mask*, 2009.

65. (OPPOSITE) *Waterfront Reading Mask*, 2010.

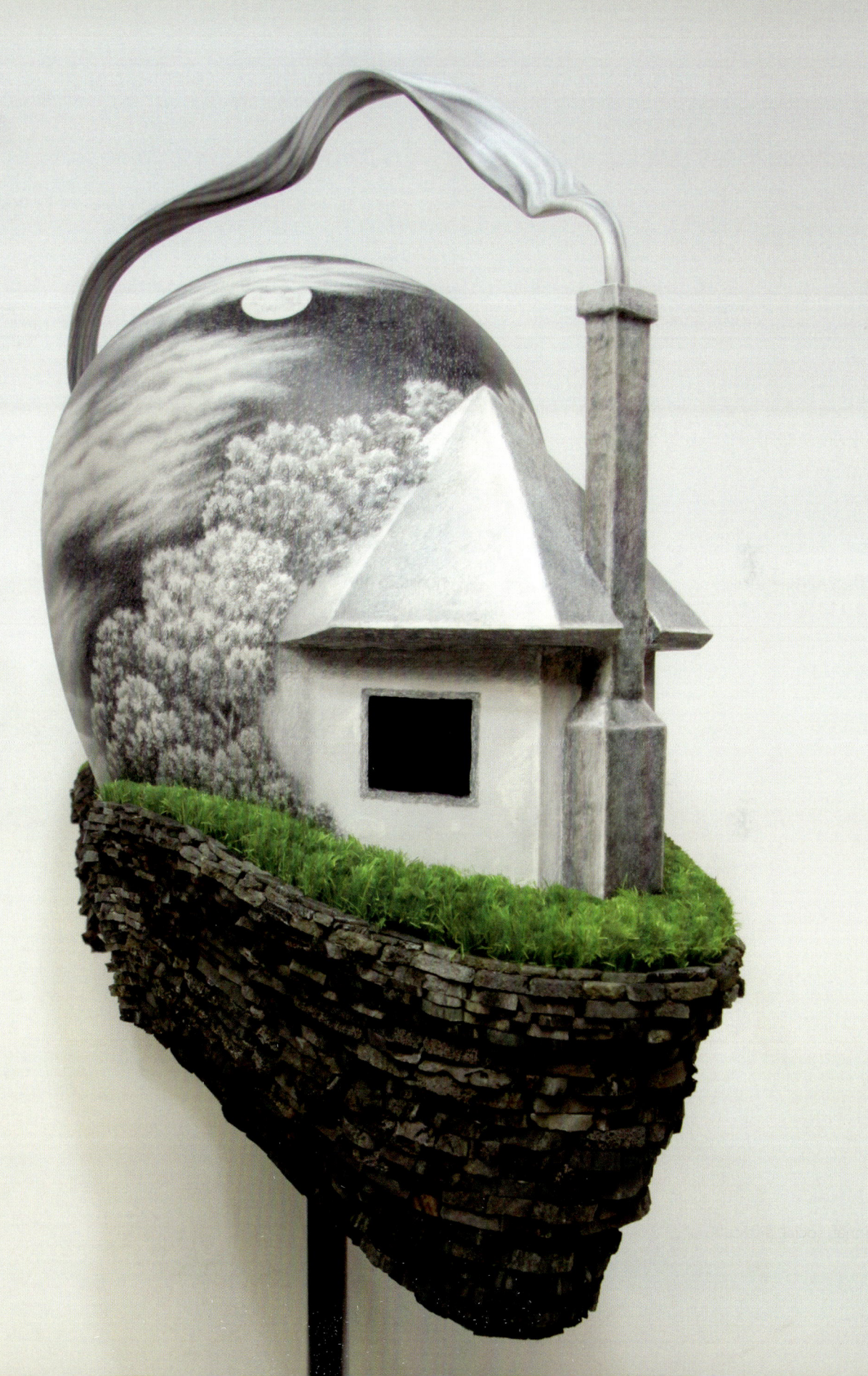

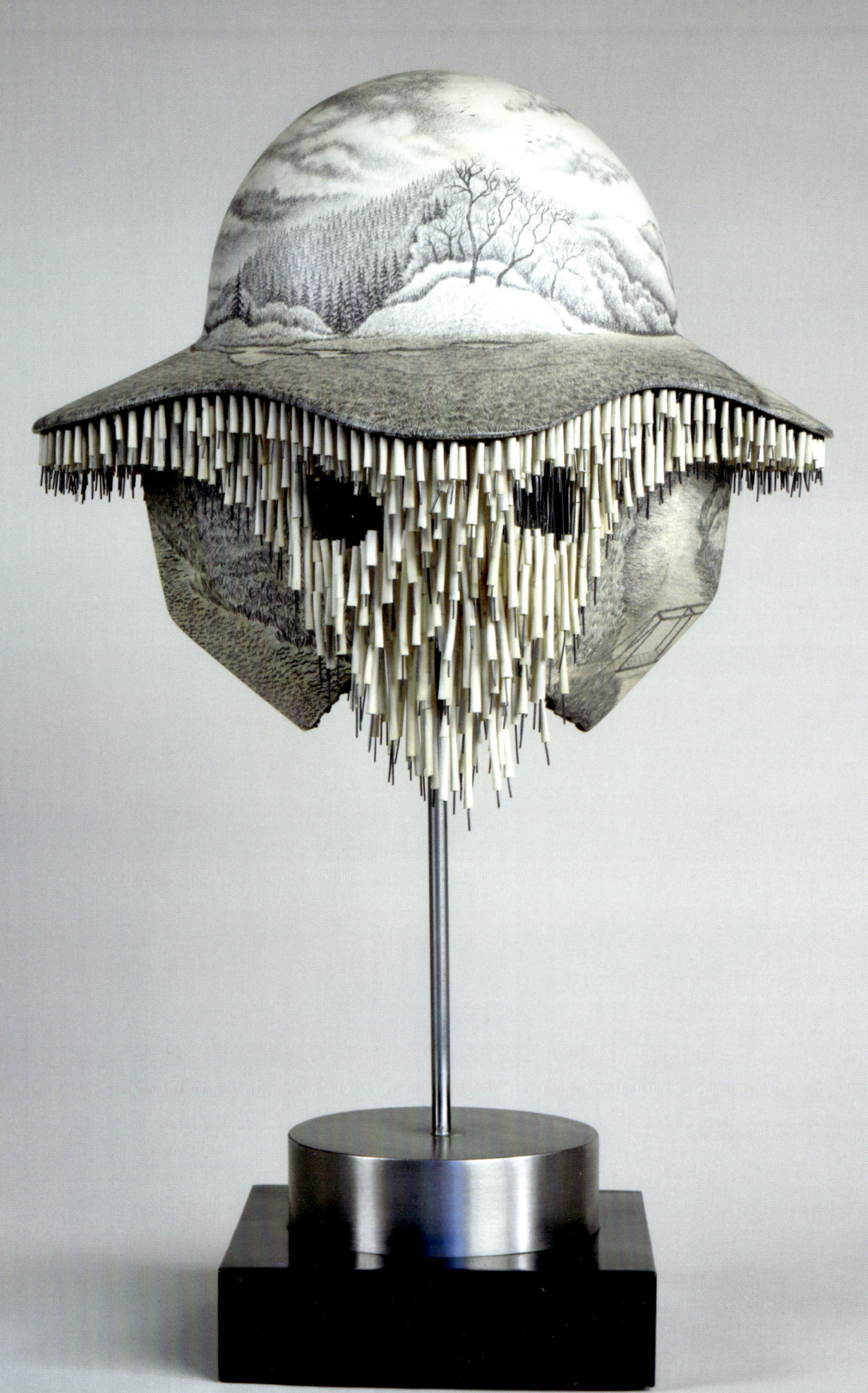

In 1980, curator Karen Allen commented on the "ritual both of process and imagery" in Proch's work. She noted his painstaking process and materials, including bones, as in his *Chicken Bone Mask* (1978), and his "constant concern for surface treatment."[56] Proch drew the landscape on the surface of *Chicken Bone Mask* with his characteristic precision and detailed furrowed fields, hills, trees, and clouded sky. Around the rim of this mask, he hung chicken bones, sewn on with catgut. Joan Sadler commented that: "Fibreglass, chicken bones, chrome, catgut and plexiglass. . . . In the hands of Don Proch such items become fascinating works of art, riveting three-dimensional pieces. . . . Proch's work is strikingly different, which he feels is the key to any artist's ultimate success or failure."[57] As Proch has said, "in this business, there's not much point in doing anything that's been done before. All the stuff I do in some way relates to the prairie landscape, or to the prairie experience in the landscape."[58]

Allen was also interested in the artist's reference to death and the spirit in his masks of this period. Proch's use of bones connotes death and nostalgia, history and geology, and links past human and animal histories:

> Though Proch's masks do not announce the incarnation of any mythic personage, they do, in a very real sense, give a manifest presence to the mythic spirit of the land. . . .
>
> Any deathly implications of the white hue are amplified in Proch's masks by the obvious suggestion of the raw bones of the skull. The masks themselves, of course, are implied reference to death. But their full connotations are much broader.
>
> The donning of the mask as a means of summoning an absent spirit is a central practice of shamanistic rites. . . . In several of Proch's own masks there is an implied interchange, or fusion, between the human and imagistic elements. In others of his masks, the shamanistic notion of the mask as protection from evil spirits might be inferred.[59]

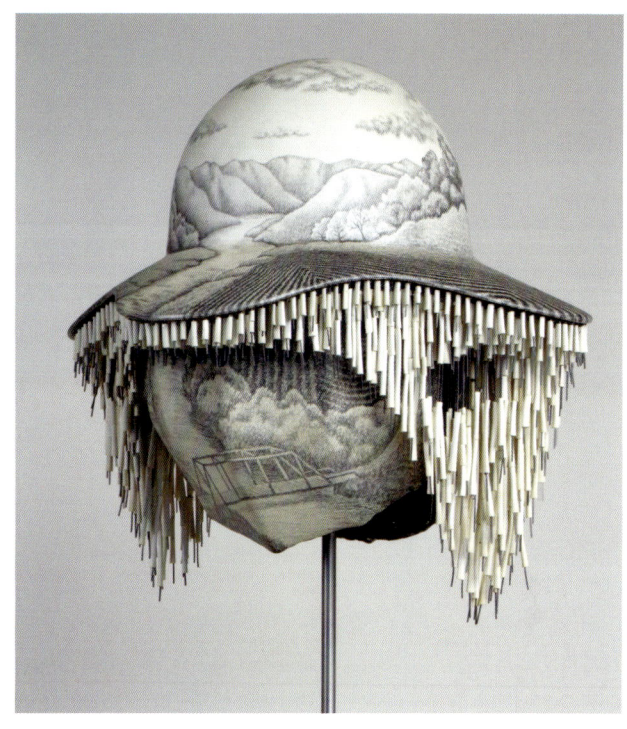

66. (OPPOSITE) *Chicken Bone Mask*, 1978.

67. *Chicken Bone Mask* (side view), 1978.

Proch incorporated chicken bones into a number of his masks, including *Night Landing Mask*, in which bones hang from the shoulders at the bottom of the mask. Evoking the past and both wild and domesticated fauna of the Asessippi region, the bones as symbols of life and death mark another connection to his roots on the family farm in this rural part of the province.

In an exhibition in 1987, California writer Clyde McConnell discussed the interpretation of the landscape in the works of a number of contemporary western Canadian artists, including Proch, and their establishment of "eloquent geographies of the imagination in which each of us can seek our bearings in space, time, and personal collective history." McConnell defined the "geographic imagination" as an "affair of places" in which the artist "strongly depends on our intuitive sense of place, our imaginative mobility, and our capacity to read the iconography of locale."[60] The understanding of place defines our community, while our personal experiences define the depth of our emotional, social, and cultural outlooks. Both perspectives are the essence of Proch's masks. His experiences and understanding of the intensity of place enhance his personal engagement with his viewers as they enter Proch's psychological space, in which he looks backward and forward simultaneously.

Graham surmised about Proch's inner and outer perceptions that "the masks' seamless fusion of the human and the natural makes them into magic. Their affinity with space masks suggests their identity of inner space and outer space, the log cabin and the space cabin, the prairies and the galaxies."[61]

Proch's depictions of human impacts on the land are deliberately devoid of representations of the human figure, though many are drawn on his crafted fibreglass human forms of the human head. As Vervoort writes, "Proch's surface for drawing and the drawing itself present human and landscape fragments in combination, [but] neither is self-explanatory."[62] His frequent inclusion of furrows in the fields and buildings essential to the farming business are only some of the marks of human intervention.

Graham described Proch's technique in building his early masks: "Proch constructs his life-size masks from fibreglass. He uses helmets to start with, to give the initial shape. For the front parts, he uses a frame covered with silk, which he then covers with fibreglass. The bottoms, corresponding to the necks, are made by putting fibreglass over a neck from a turtle-neck sweater, folded the way he wants it: the sweater neck remains inside. . . . The whole piece is sanded down with files, rasps, electric sanders. On these one-white surfaces, Proch draws his scenes, giving a face to the prairies."[63]

Proch draws with silverpoint, graphite, and coloured pencil. Thin layers of archival varnish secure the actual drawing and prevent smudging. Proch started using silverpoint early, inspired by a visit to New York: "In the mid-60s, I went to New York and saw a Picasso show at the Museum of Modern Art. Included in the exhibitions was a bunch of drawings for *Guernica*, studies done with sterling silver wire on plaster-of-Paris panels. They were beautiful pieces. Because the silver oxidizes with age, it turns a sort of sepia colour. So when I came back to Winnipeg I got some sterling silver wire. . . . I just loved the quality and

tone of it. It seemed that the oxidation made it much more sensitive."[64]

Proch initially used gesso to build his forms. He then tried fibreglass and gesso together. He soon found, however, that gesso was harder to work with and did not adhere as well as fibreglass. Preferring to draw directly onto fibreglass, he stopped using gesso.

Proch commented on his early masks that, "in retrospect, they seem to be a grouping, rather like my 1972 exhibition, each being a significant work in itself, yet together they create a larger whole."[65] They collectively defined the issues that have absorbed him throughout his ensuing career.

Homages and Tributes: Admired Colleagues

Proch has created pieces specifically to honour those whose friendship and art have had special meaning for him. In addition to his *Wild Bill Lobchuk Back Forties Mask* (1976) and his *Delta Night Mask—Homage à Kelly Clark* (1984), Proch has paid tribute to Jackson Beardy, Vic Cicansky, Joe Fafard, and most recently Gord Downie. Each of these works take different forms, as masks, as sculptures, and, for Fafard, as a two-dimensional work. As Proch has said, these were people whose "art I followed closely as it was happening, and they are all people whose art I respect." He met Cicansky, for instance, at the Grand Western Canadian Screen Shop, where "there was lots of experimentation. We didn't discuss what we were doing, we just did it."[66] Proch got to know Cicansky well through their cross-Canada exhibitions and openings. They also had a common dealer in Regina, Susan Whitney, who represented them for many years along with Fafard and Thauberger.

Wild Bill Lobchuk Back Forties Mask was one of Proch's few wearable masks. Lobchuk's rural roots are clear in this piece. Grass hangs down from the rim and the furrows and cut grain are depicted over the entire surface.

68. (OPPOSITE) *Wild Bill Lobchuk Back Forties Mask*, 1976.

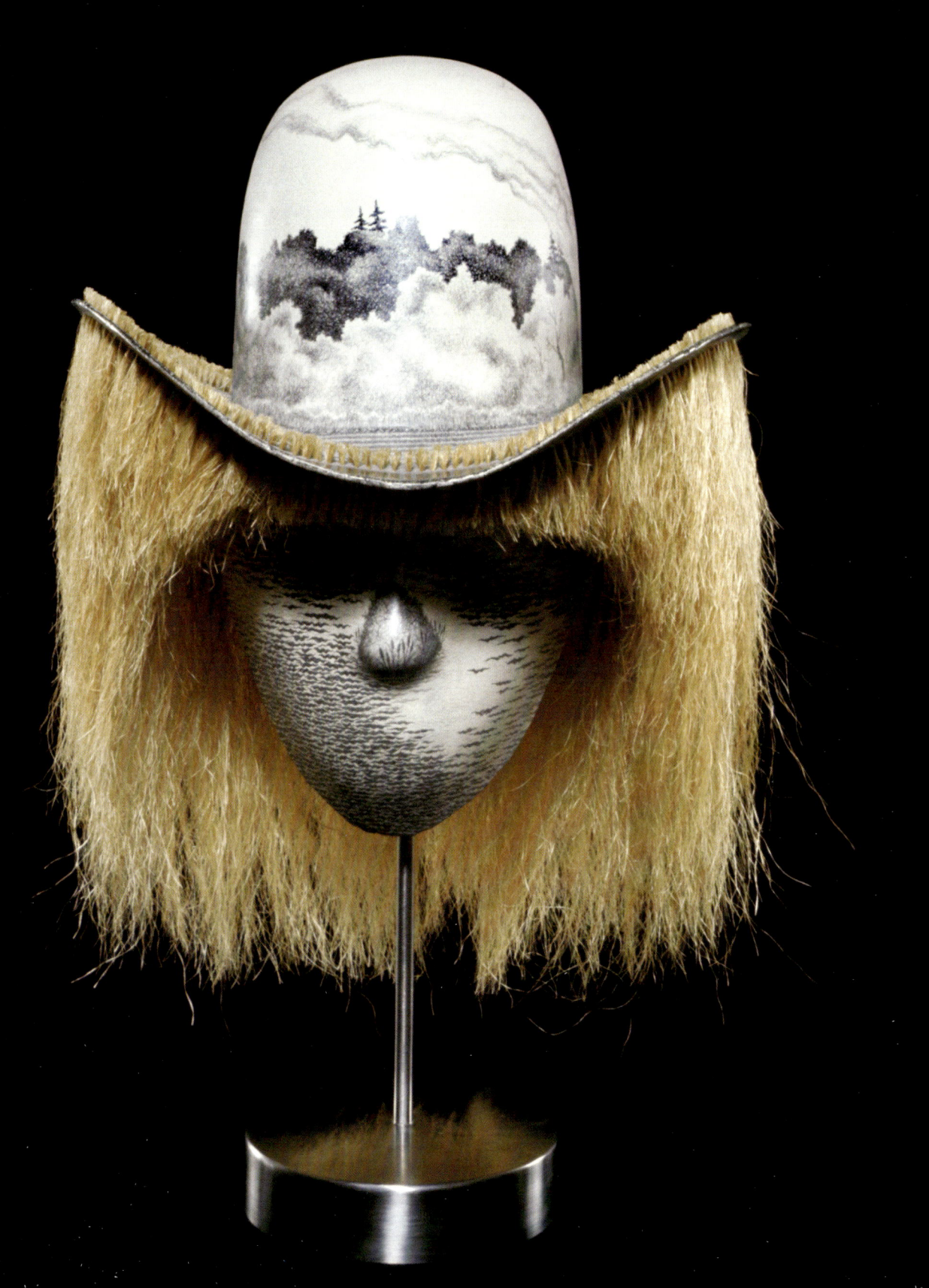

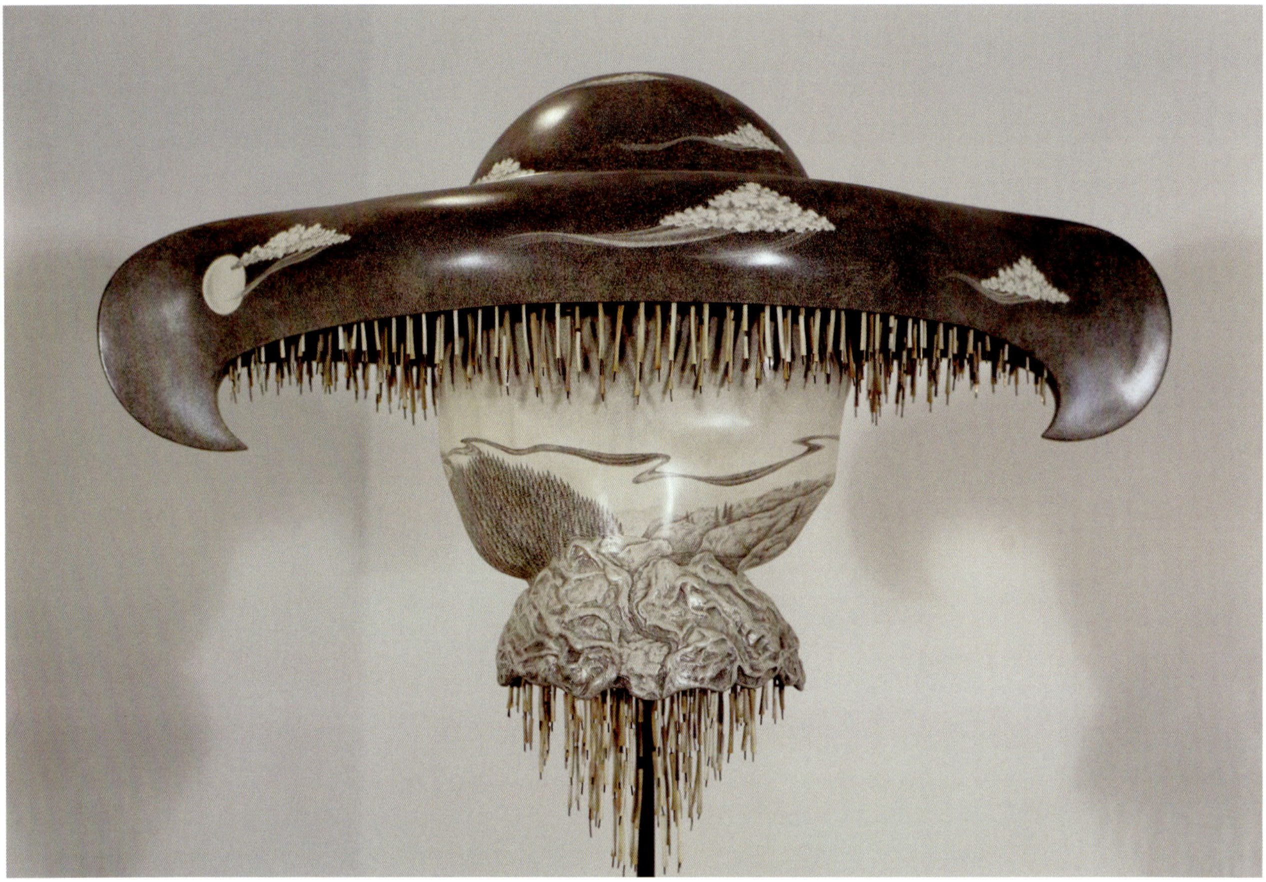

69. *Blue Canoe Mask*, 1985.

This mask captures Lobchuk's personality and the intensity of his quest for change in the art world. The 360-degree landscape has a flock of geese in their characteristic "V" formation pointing to new futures and directions, thus underlining Lobchuk's strong, vocal advocacy for new directions in the arts scene in Winnipeg and beyond. Just as the geese fly in numbers, so did Lobchuk and his colleague young artists band together collectively in protest in the late 1960s and early 1970s to garner fairer remuneration and credit for their art.

As we have seen, First Nations themes and interests have been an important part of Proch's art. One Manitoba Indigenous artist who made an impact on Proch was Jackson Beardy, one of the founders of the Indigenous Group of Seven and a colleague printmaker at the Screen Shop. A leader in the Indigenous and Manitoban communities, Beardy contributed significantly as an artist

and as an early Indigenous voice on federal and provincial commissions. He was one of the Screen Shop artists who travelled to Paris for their 1978 exhibition in the Canadian Cultural Centre. His early death at forty, in 1984, was a passing that affected many in the Indigenous and arts communities of Manitoba. Proch created *Blue Canoe Mask* (1984) in tribute to Beardy:

> *Blue Canoe Mask* is one of my favourite masks It deals with Jackson Beardy. After the Beardy tribute at the Legislative Building we all went to the Aberdeen Hotel for drinks. Then I went home and did the drawing for the piece and the next day I came to the studio and started working on it. I finished the piece on Friday, crated it on Saturday and put it on a plane on Sunday. I haven't seen it since. Now it lives in New York. . . . It's in the shape of about a three-foot-long, upside-down canoe.

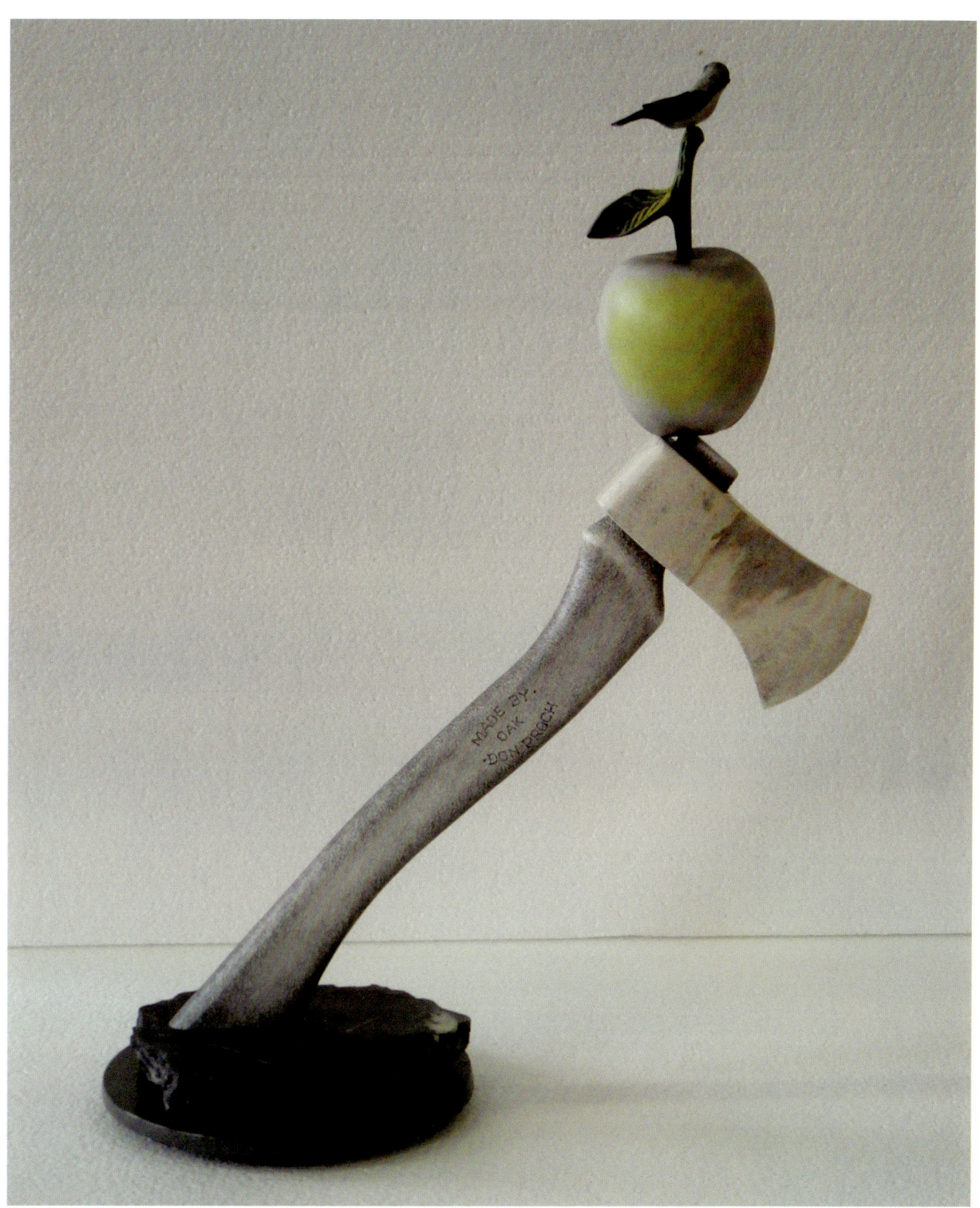

70. *Balance – Homage à Cicansky*, 2010.

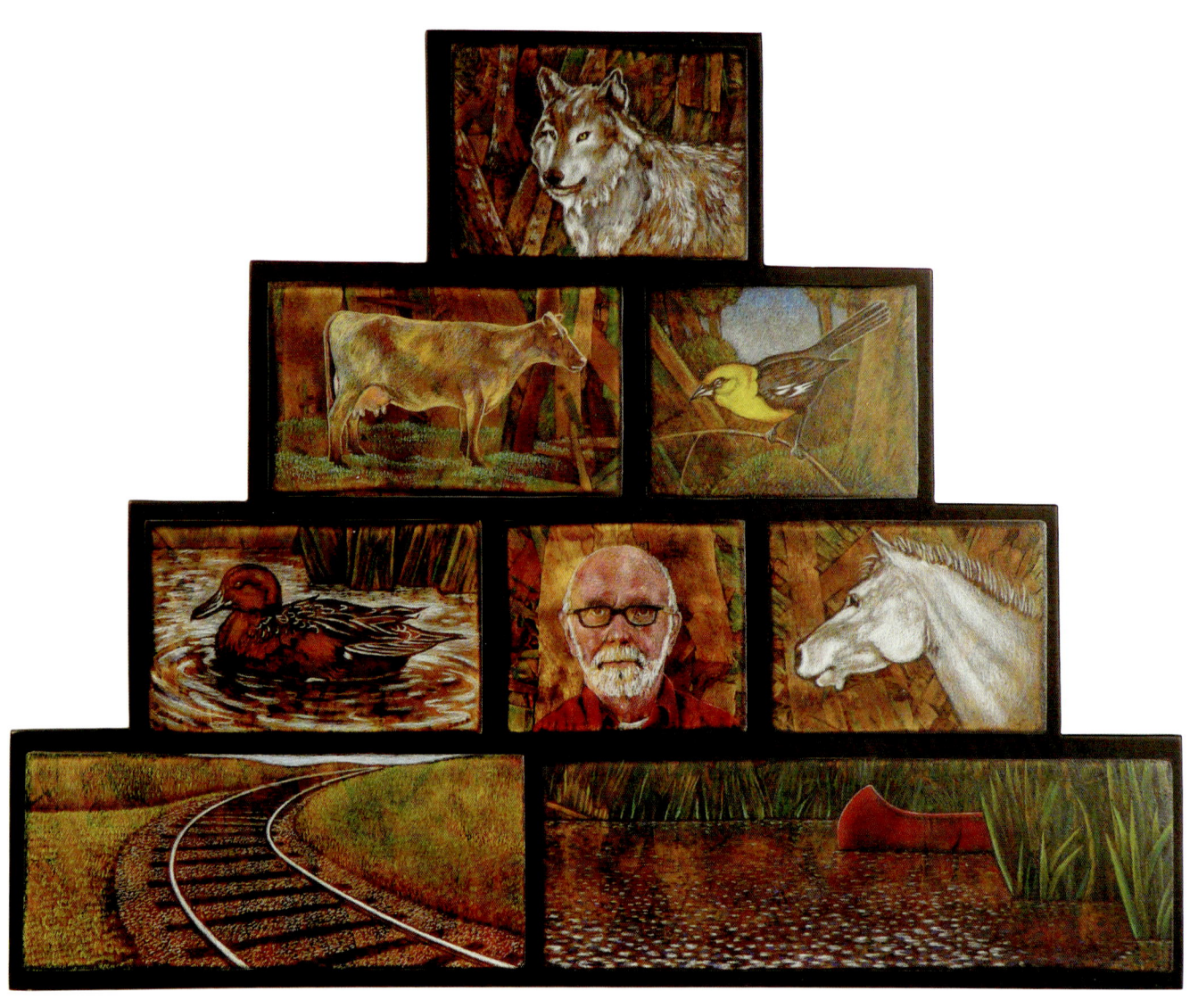

71 Joe – A Portrait, 2016.

The crown of the head rises about the bottom and around it there is a northern Manitoba spruce tree landscape. Smoke comes from the spruce forest which goes around the head and round the face and back of the head. Then it goes back up into the canoe. The canoe has chicken bones falling down all around like rain. It's quite a daring piece. On each side there's a moon and a cloud on the prow of the canoe and there's a blue halo around the moon. The rest is all greys.[67]

Balance—Homage à Cicansky (2010), shows Proch's sense of humour and ingenuity. An apple, red on one side and green on the other, is balanced on the end of an axe. This cast bronze, wood, steel, and carved bone maquette is 51 x 51 x 7.5 centimetres, and its imagery evokes Cicansky's tables and ceramic sculptures of foods and cupboards. Here the bone axe head combines the natural grain of the bone and Proch's characteristic drawing, in pencil and coloured pencil, which depicts the prairie sky on one side and the landscape on the other. The overbearing human hand on nature is unmistakable; Proch's wit in the juxtaposition of the apple and the axe emphasizes his message of reality. Unfortunately, the anticipated large public installation of this work has never been realized.

In 2016, Proch paid tribute to his close and long-time friend, Joe Fafard, in *Joe—A Portrait*. This eight-sectioned, two-dimensional landscape, shaped as a pyramid, is done in pencil and coloured pencil on sanded and stained fibreglassed wood. A face-on portrait of Fafard is its centre. Other sections show aspects of the land around Fafard's farm and animals, the focus of many of Fafard's ceramics and bronzes. A wolf, cow, horse, yellow-headed blackbird, and duck are all included, as are the ever-present train tracks and Fafard's pond and red canoe. This tribute is a visual biography of Fafard.

The Gord Landscape with Passing Comet (2017) includes all of Proch's characteristic elements yet with a unique poignant twist. It honours Gord Downie, lead singer and lyricist of The Tragically Hip, diagnosed with a brain tumour in 2016. He died a few months after Proch completed this work. The sculpture is constructed on a pole, as *Red River Flood Mask* was twenty years earlier. Downie's hat is on top of the pole, his collar and tie lower down. There is no face, no eyes, no facial features. Instead, three tiny chrome-plated waterfalls, tears, fall from the front of the hat into the empty space that would have been the forehead. Proch commented that the work "is based on two lines from Gord Downie lyrics—the two lines being, 1. 'At the hundredth meridian where the great plains begin' (the top ½ of the piece); 2. 'Settled in, Into the pocket—of a lighthouse on some rocky socket' (jean jacket collar [real] with lighthouse tie/neckpiece)."[68]

Where Proch's earlier masks had rolled turtlenecks for their collars, this piece has a jean jacket as its collar. The lighthouse, representing the beacon that Downie has been in Canadian culture, becomes the tie and connects to the base of the sculpture. Proch's dyed and stacked tiny bones are the neckpiece, and they extend onto the front of the base. The Asessippi Valley landscape is drawn on the hat in subdued black-and-white tones, showing the valley's rolling hills, furrows, a sweeping rail line, grain elevators, and clouds. A chrome stream flows out from the one green field. A field in gold is beside a bright red elevator. The strength of the red and gold, and their contrast with the rest of the subdued landscape, enhance the poignancy of the work. Proch's signature clouds are drawn around the collar with his unique chrome cloud forms judiciously affixed to both the hat and the collar. Downie's hats were often adorned with a feather. Proch includes the feather in the shape of a comet, meticulously depicted in its three parts: the nucleus; the coma, a fuzzy cloud around the nucleus; and the tail, extending outward and pointing upward. This tribute, rich in meaning, its various elements all evident in Proch's prior work, takes on additional connotations. This was not the first mask in which Proch did not depict the face. His wearable *Sunflower Shade Mask* (1975) was a precursor of this form of expression. Here Proch drew a row of sunflowers at eye level, and the stems were joined with catgut strings connecting the jaw section which was suspended from the eyes. The catgut was the only colour on the work.

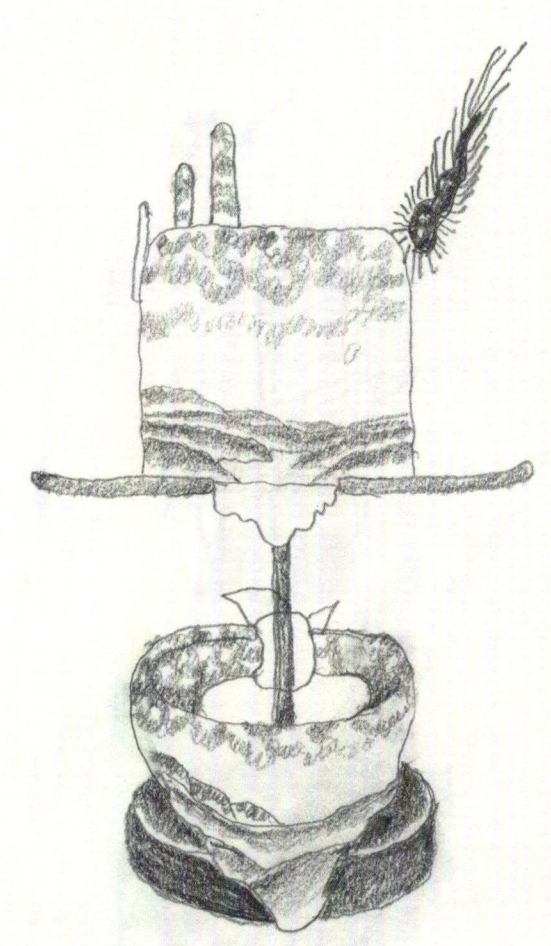

- vertical fiberglass clouds - chrome clouds
on opposite side of meteor. chrome pond
on hat flowing over brim. Some chrome
on brim toward back of hat. Bandana
partially slumped over base.

"The Gord Landscape with Meteor" - 2017
Donie Kpouc

72. Sketch for *The Gord Landscape with Passing Comet*, 2017.

73. (OPPOSITE) *The Gord Landscape with Passing Comet*, 2017.

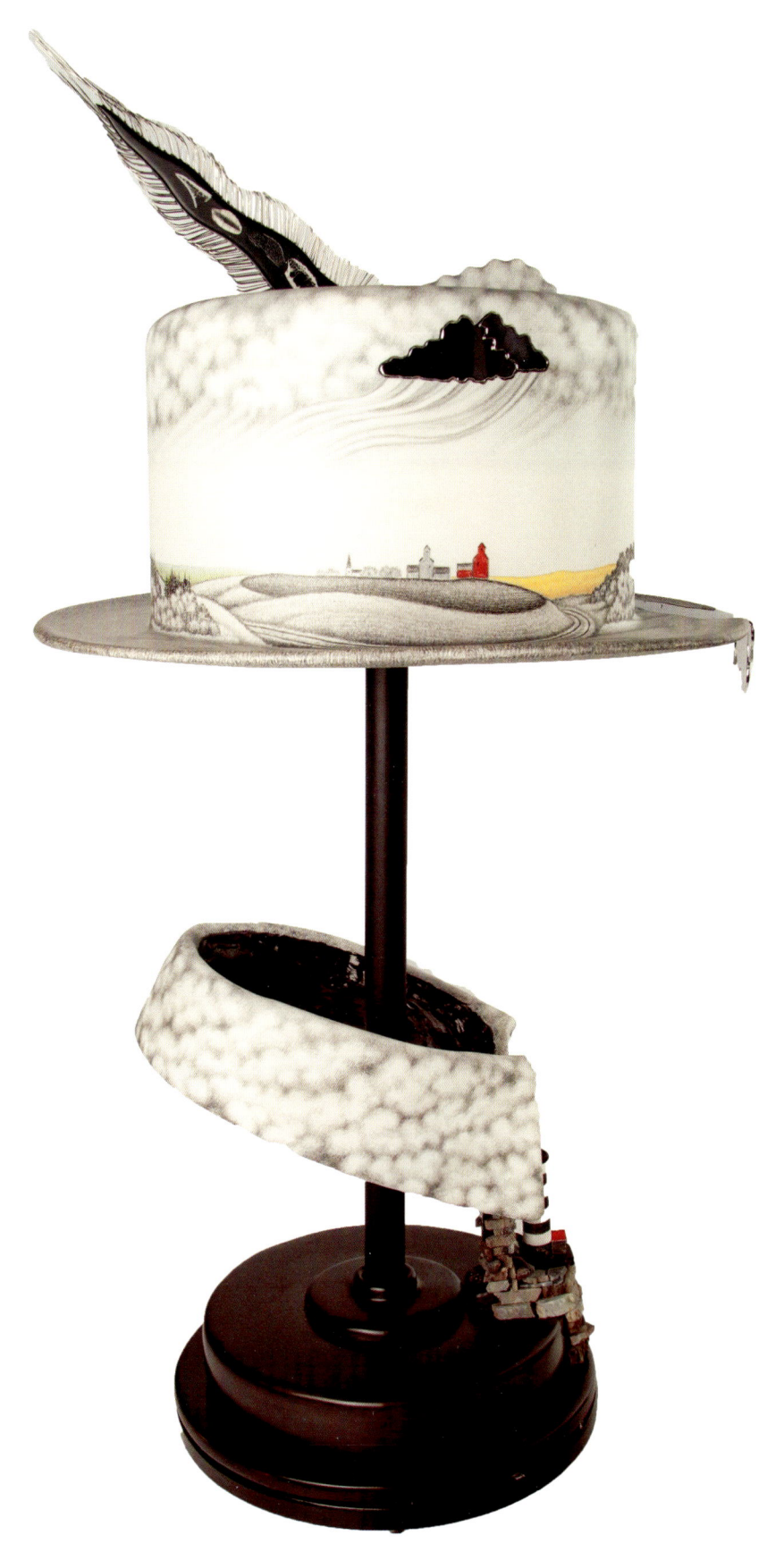

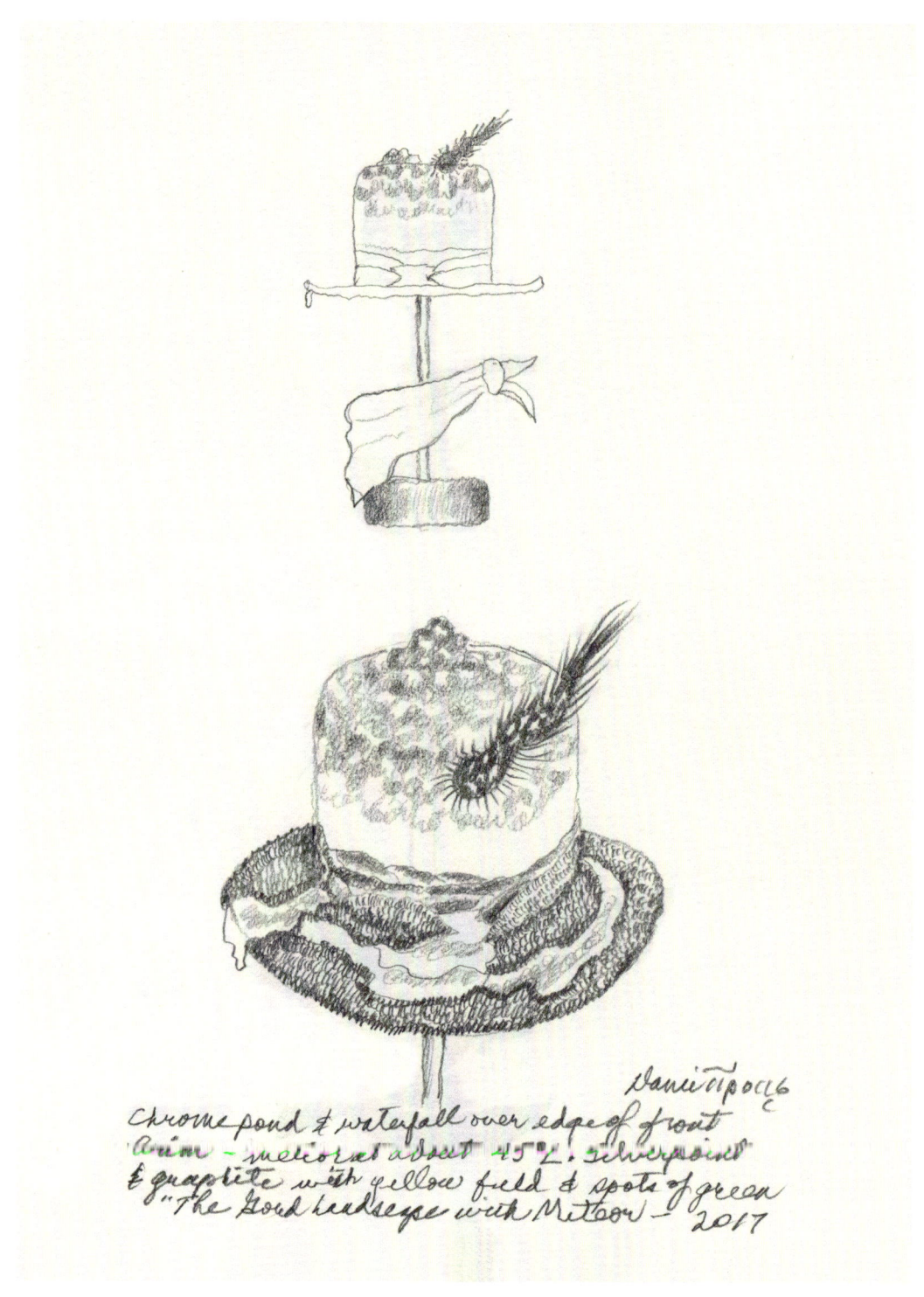

74. Sketch for *The Gord Landscape with Passing Comet*, 2017.

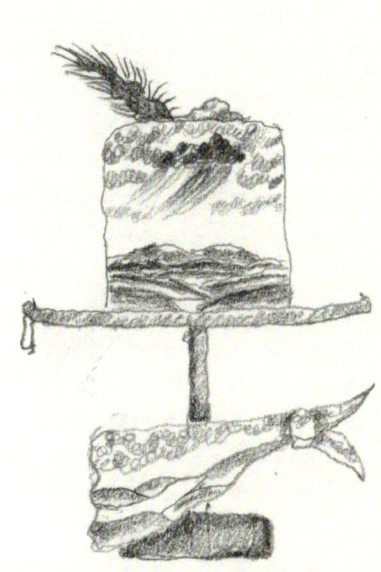

"The Gord Landscape with Meteor" – 2017
waterfall in front – meteor slanted
toward back – chrome around brim
no chrome on bandana – mountains on
one side – prairie on other. Wear Typ. 6

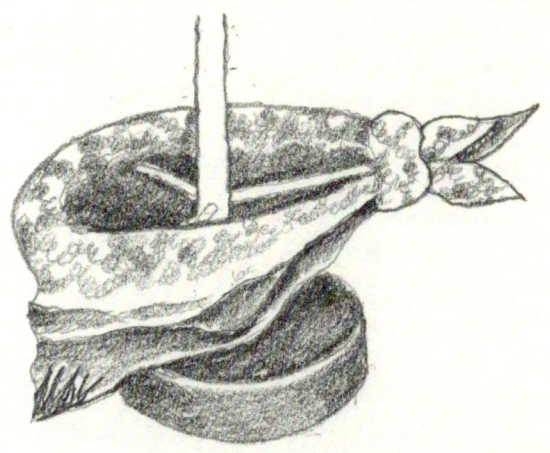

75. Sketch for *The Gord Landscape with Passing Comet*, 2017.

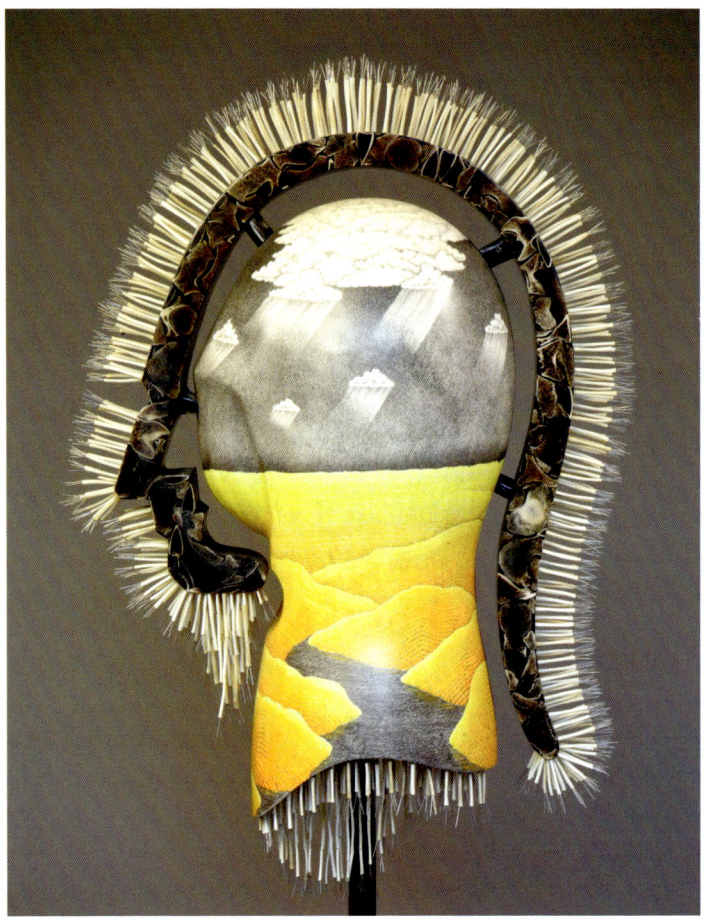

76. *Great Plains Mask* (left side), 1986.

Continuing Indigenous Preoccupations: *Great Plains Mask* (1986)

Proch's continuing respect for and knowledge of Indigenous cultures of the plains are evident in many of his pieces. Seen in *Pincushion Man* and *Blue Canoe Mask*, the important histories and contributions of Canada's Indigenous Peoples are frequent themes in his art. *Great Plains Mask* (1986) is a prime example. In this work, Proch added the profile of a face on top of the fibreglass form of the head and neck, on which he drew a landscape of farmland. The horizon line is at the mid-point. Fields of grain cover the neck and chin with Proch's characteristic elegant sweep of linear patterning. A roadway flows over the hills on one side of the surface drawing. A cap of clouds in the grey sky covers the top of the head with parallel lines of rain falling from some of them. Chicken bones with chrome pins, reminiscent of porcupine quills, form a fringe around the whole. Tracing its outer shape, they are inserted into the linear dark form, and appended to the mask. The sharp points of the pins hang below the neck facing outward. Proch said that he "wanted the piece to have a silvery halo [reflecting the northern lights] surrounding the drawing and saw them as a halo of electricity."[69] The chicken bones and steel pins together evoke that halo, emanating electric energy into the atmosphere.

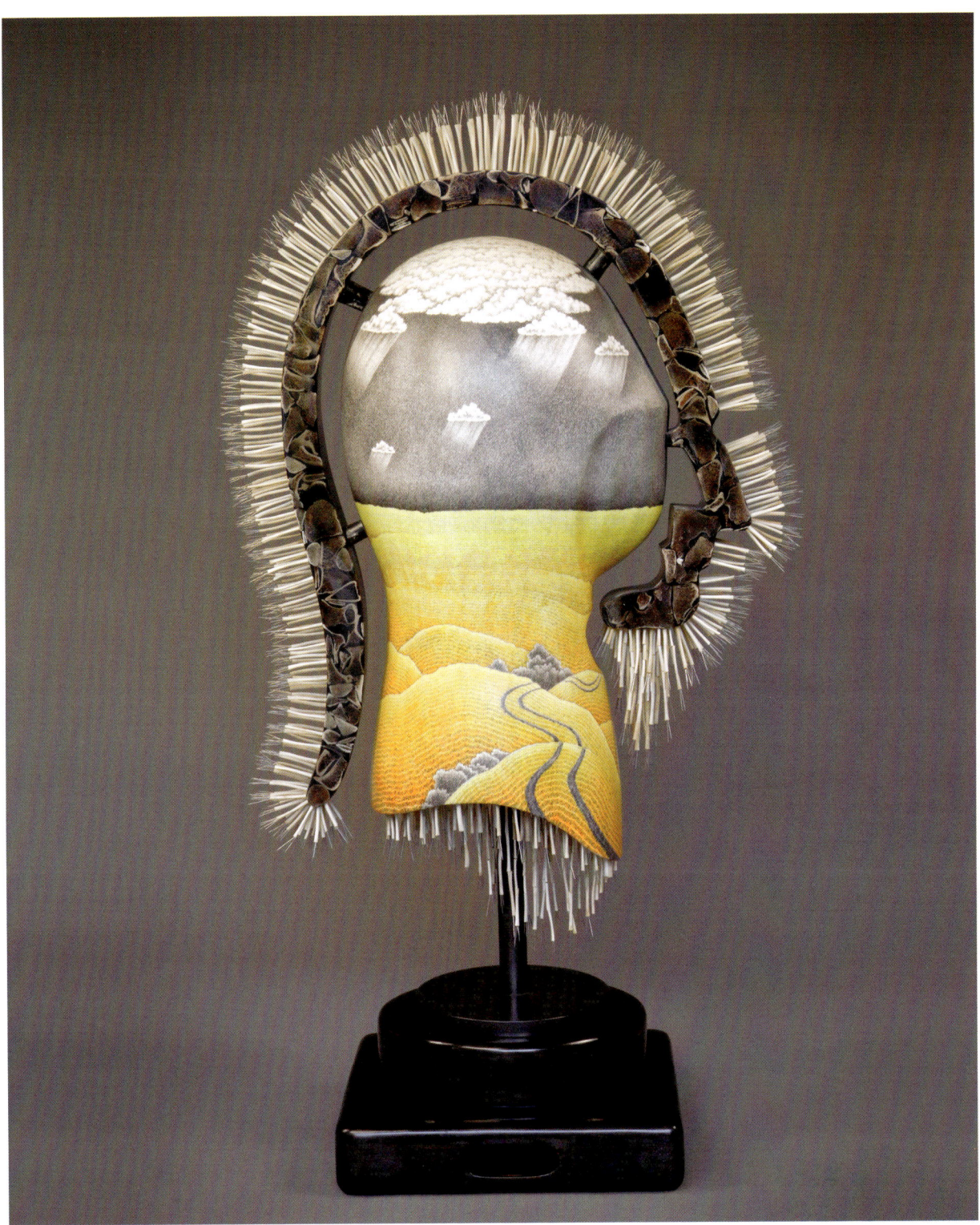

77. *Great Plains Mask* (right side), 1986.

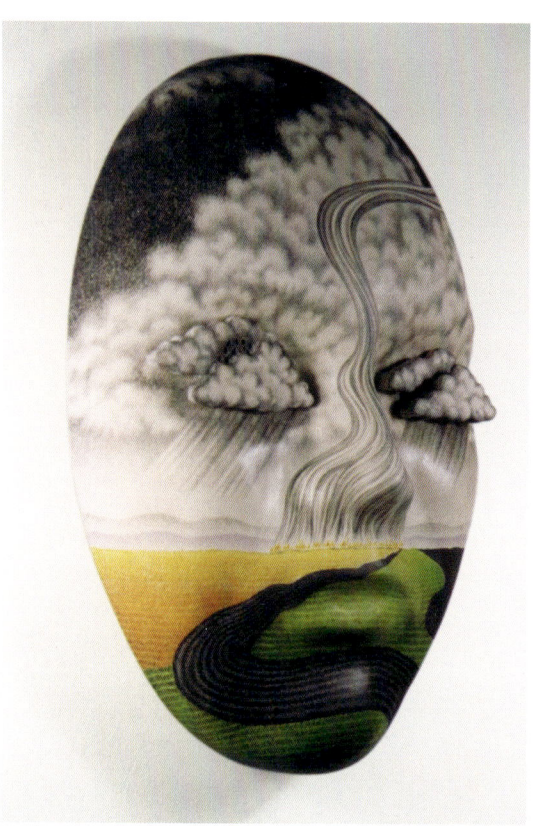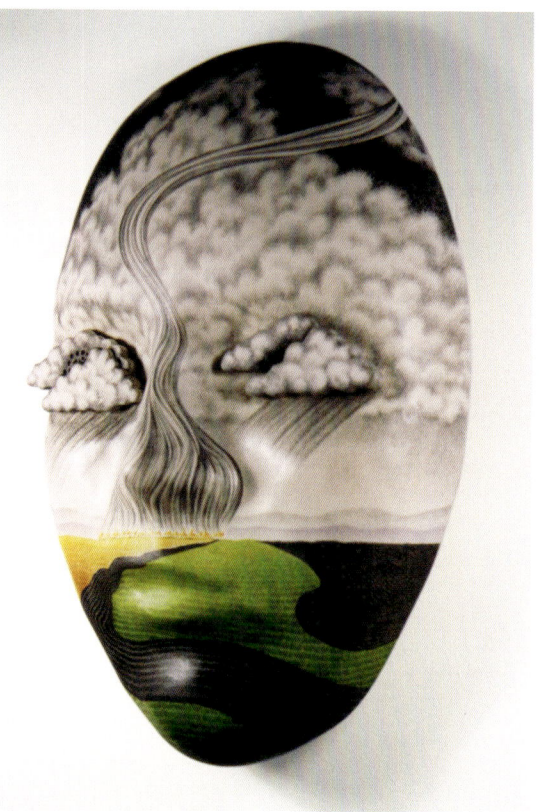

78 and 79. *The Farm As A Memory Mask* (78. left angle, 79. right angle), 2000.

80. (OPPOSITE) Sketch for *The Farm As A Memory Mask*, 2000.

Memory and Nostalgia:
The Farm As A Memory Mask (2000)

Proch fuses memory of the past with the present and the future, providing layers of reading and meaning echoed by his layering of drawing and materials. Where do memory, nostalgia, and the preservation of history intersect in his visual vocabulary with his dire warnings about unsustainable societal and environmental changes?

As its title suggests, *The Farm As A Memory Mask* (2000) holds one answer, based on Proch's memory of the farm. The drawing on this mask shows his familiar prairie landscape, its horizon line low, with the sky filling two-thirds of the form. Fields in the lower third proffer yellow and green grains. Cultivation lines run from the lower right across the field and up to the centre point of the horizon. The sky is filled with clouds. There any nostalgia ends. The closed eyelids reveal rain streaming from the eyes. A tornado spins down the forehead along the nose. Executed on cast Laguna white clay, this silverpoint, graphite, and coloured pencil drawing is deceptive. On first view, it portrays a gentle and perhaps rather idealized view of a farm. The artist's poignant message is jarring, highlighting climate change as it increasingly causes dramatic and devastating weather systems. It shows a deep sadness and sense of loss, as expressed in many of his works and conversations. Proch's preliminary drawing for this mask clearly depicts the counterbalance of the lyrical landscape with interlocking circles of furrows contrasted by the lightning and tornado.

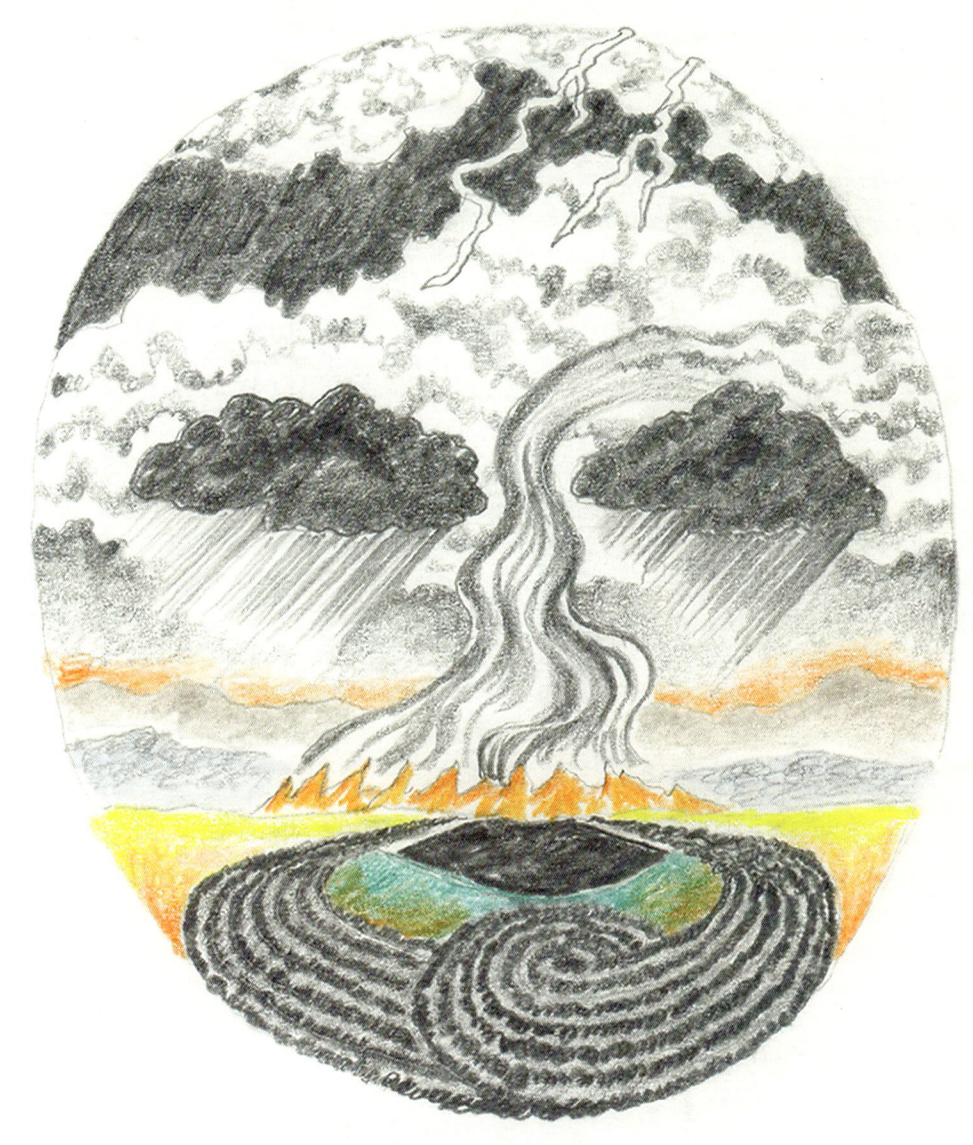

"The Farm Ash Memory Mask" - Marie APoule

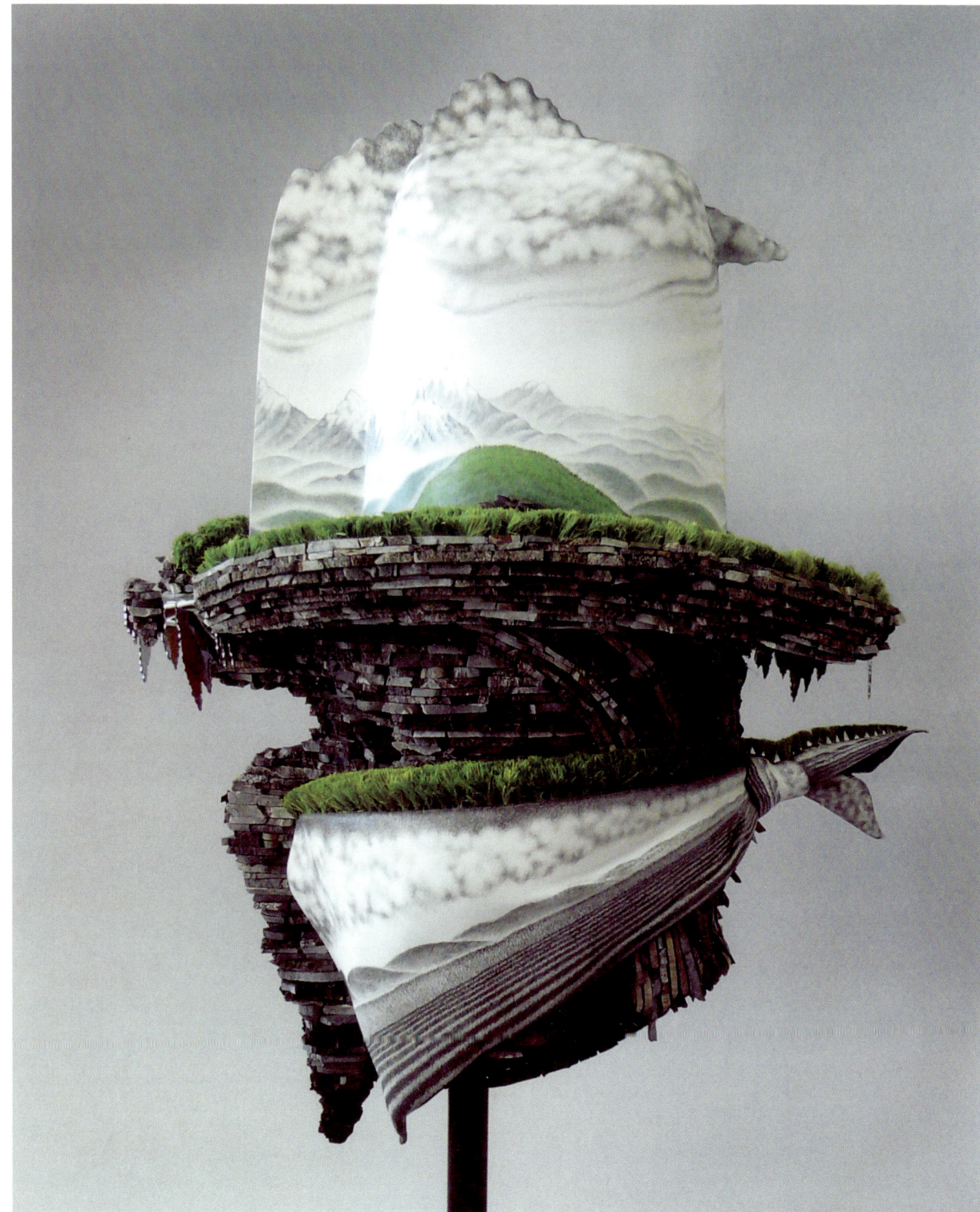

81. *Bandana Mask*, 2013.

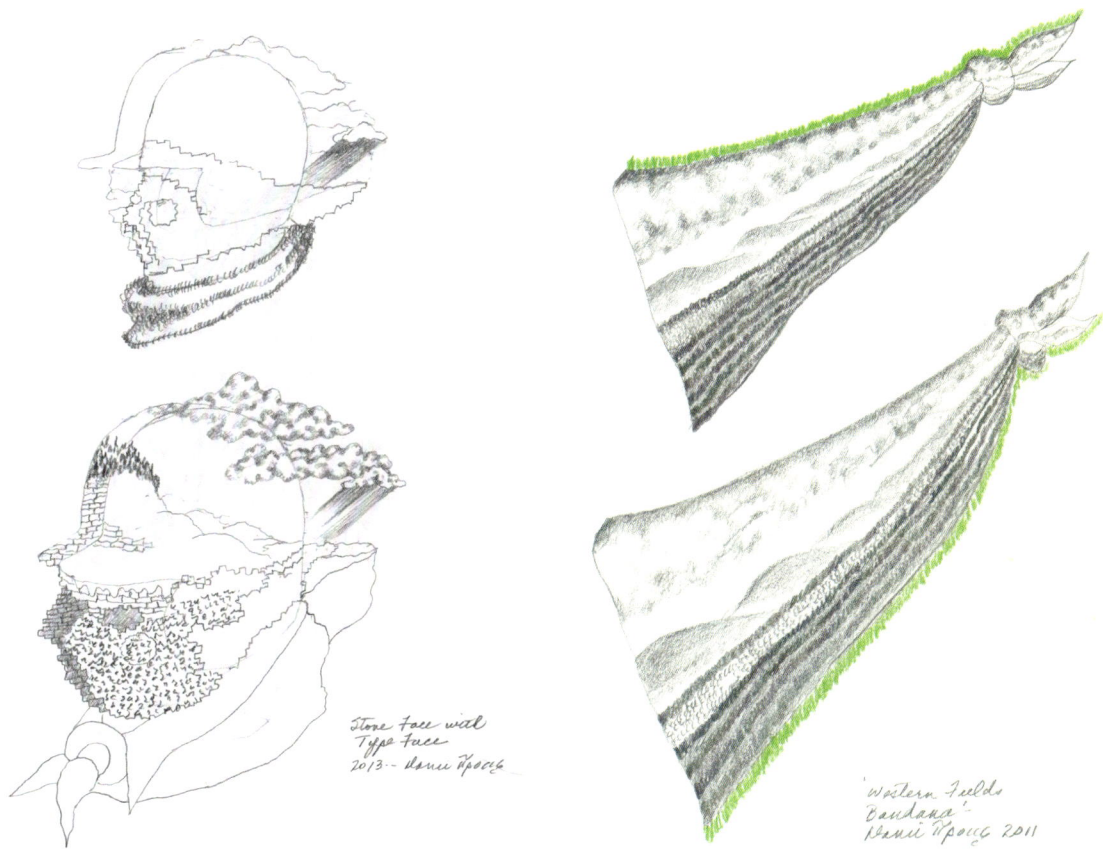

82 and 83. Sketches for *Bandana Mask*, 2013 and 2011.

The Mask Extended, 2000 Forward

The forms for Proch's later work, though titled "masks," have become more complicated sculptures. Their only reference to a mask is that they are faces or spaces for faces, heads, and necks. These increasingly complex forms symbolically imply the intellect, thoughts, and history of the "person" as well as the artist. *Bandana Mask* (2013) is a case in point. The bandana, built with stacked bits of bones on one side, evoking the geology and history of the prairies, has an exquisitely drawn black-and-white prairie landscape on the other. Sisal, representing grass, runs around the neck. Like *Wild Bill Lobchuk Back Forties Mask*, the upper half of this much later work is a hat. The brim of *Bandana Mask* is made of bone pieces to which Proch has added chrome waterfalls at various points, and the drawing of a mountainous landscape surrounds it. Three-dimensional cloud formations project beyond the hat, parallel to the tie of the bandana below. The face, built with tiny stacked bones, is indented in the eye area, increasing the sense of introspection about the past. Proch's sense of place is redolent. In addition to the wide view of the landscape and sky, Proch has delineated the subterranean geological formations of the Asessippi Valley—the very base upon which the landscape is built. He probes its geology as he layers both the past and the present with the future. The work has a penetrating, all-seeing look.

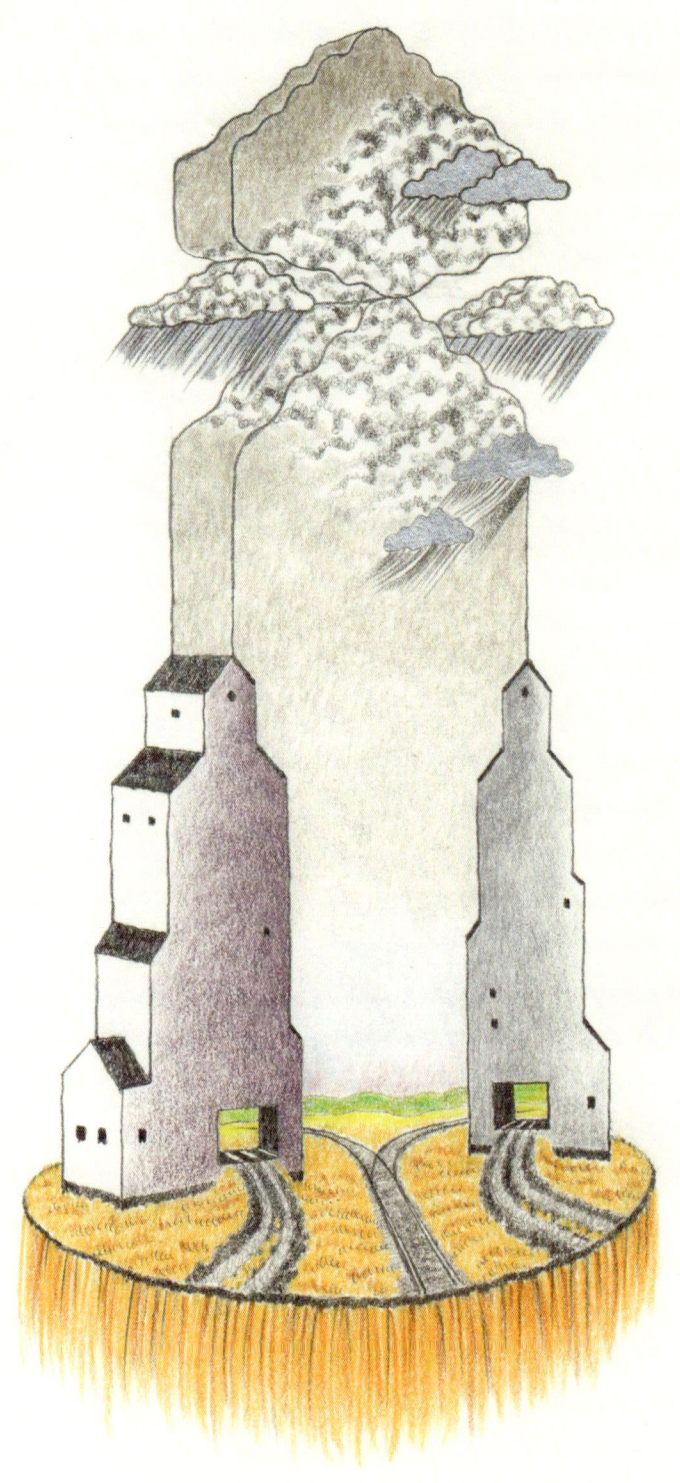

Dark French Grey at peak. Horizon a more muted green. Slightly
longer "root system" in proportion to piece. Linear plywood will
enrich color. A more irregular circumference with small
channels & mirrored "puddle areas.   Blanci Thpouch / 99

Layered Sources and Mixed Materials: Reflections and Futures

ALL PROCH'S THEMES address human impacts on the land. Core to his unique and creative five decades, these themes are expressed as icons of farming, grain elevators, or furrows cut into the land. Iconographical elements consistently recur throughout Proch's work in his portrayals of the horizon, skies, and landscape, his aesthetic approaches and psychological insights emphasizing these endangered prairie icons. Proch's sources and representations are inextricably woven together throughout his work, some identifiable, others more private. Many are traceable to his early years, consciously and unconsciously. All project contemporary concerns about the universal scarring intrusions on the land.

Proch, the constant experimenter, continues to mix new and old materials, farm implements and natural elements, always achieving a deliberate, sensitive surface. He contrasts textures and surfaces with his delicate and fastidious colouring. Values emanating from all of his works through his truly peripheral view of the prairie simultaneously define its history, human and geological, its beauty, and its peril. Exploring the interior and exterior, and the physical and psychological, Proch portrays the prairie reality, the consciousness of prairie people, and pressing prairie issues.

Railways, Pathways, and Grain Elevators, 1970s

Railways and pathways permeate Proch's art in all media—prints, drawings, sculptures, and masks. Railway tracks are the focus of *Night Rail* (1976), a silkscreen print in which one track leads to the cloud at the vanishing point and another runs horizontally along its lower edge. This directional juxtaposition points to the ambiguities of life today counterbalancing opposing ideas regarding their resolution.

Tracks also provide a focal point in *Rocky Mountain Mask* (1978). The black-and-white drawing on this mask has a rail line running in a continuous

84. Drawing, 1999.

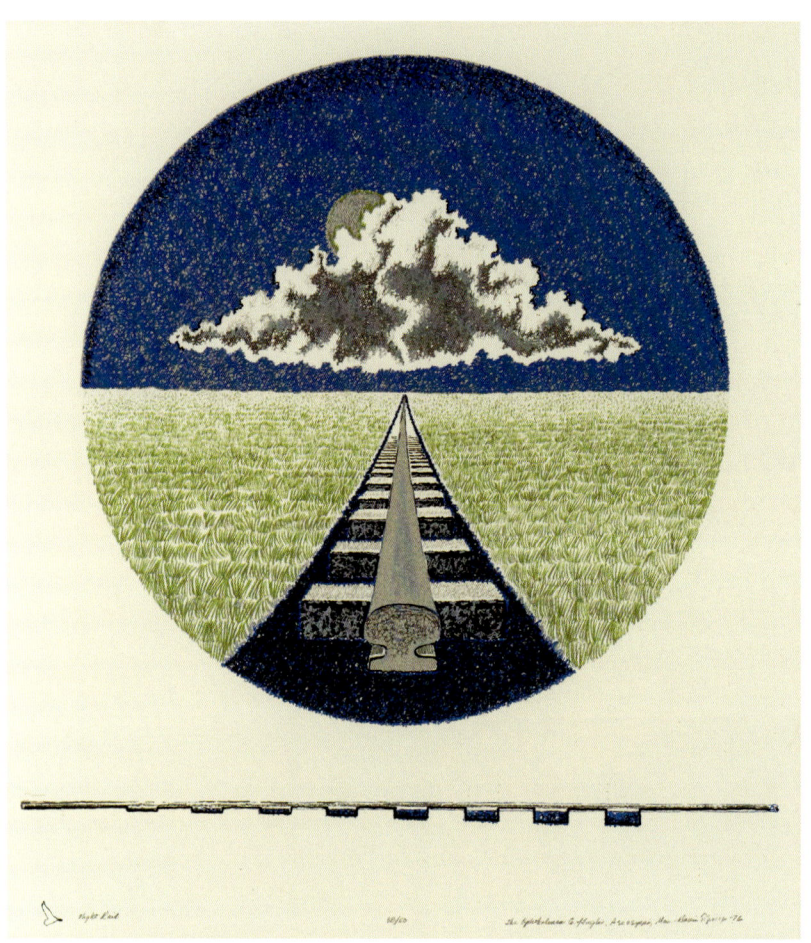

85. *Night Rail*, 1976.

circle through the eyes as tunnels and around the chin and back. This seemingly directionless continuum imparts an ominous sensibility to the work as a whole, foreshadowing the perils of shipping hazardous materials by rail and the rapidly changing technologies of transport. The sides and back of the head of this work proffer views of the forests in the mountains executed in minute detail. The cheekbones on either side of the rail lines are raised, creating a three-dimensional profile. This combination of a frontal view and a side profile in the one work gives a heightened human dimension to the sites of train accidents and derailments, such as that in Hell's Gate, British Columbia, in November 2017, and its resulting fuel spill in the Fraser Valley. A waterfall cascades down one side of the head and flows down the nose. Proch's use of his unique iconographical symbol, his stylized nickel waterfalls, denotes increasing environmental perils.

Why, one might ask, is this inclusion of pathways and rail tracks so important? Do they point back to history, or do they denote present realities? Or, given the ambiguity as to where they lead, do they depict a contemporary psychological conundrum, setting the known past against the unknown future, raising poignant questions as to where the present is taking humanity? Paths, trails, roads, and railways are indelible and continuing parts of human history, the means over the centuries for people to move from one place to another. In Proch's work, it is often unclear where the roads and rails go. Nowhere? Somewhere? Proch's *Incline* of 1976, an unsettling drawing of a figure tied under the railway track, draws into question the troubling links between rails and people. He never made the final work of this drawing. The rail ends; the figure is clamped into place. Dark in meaning, one can only query if it refers to the now, or the longer-term future.

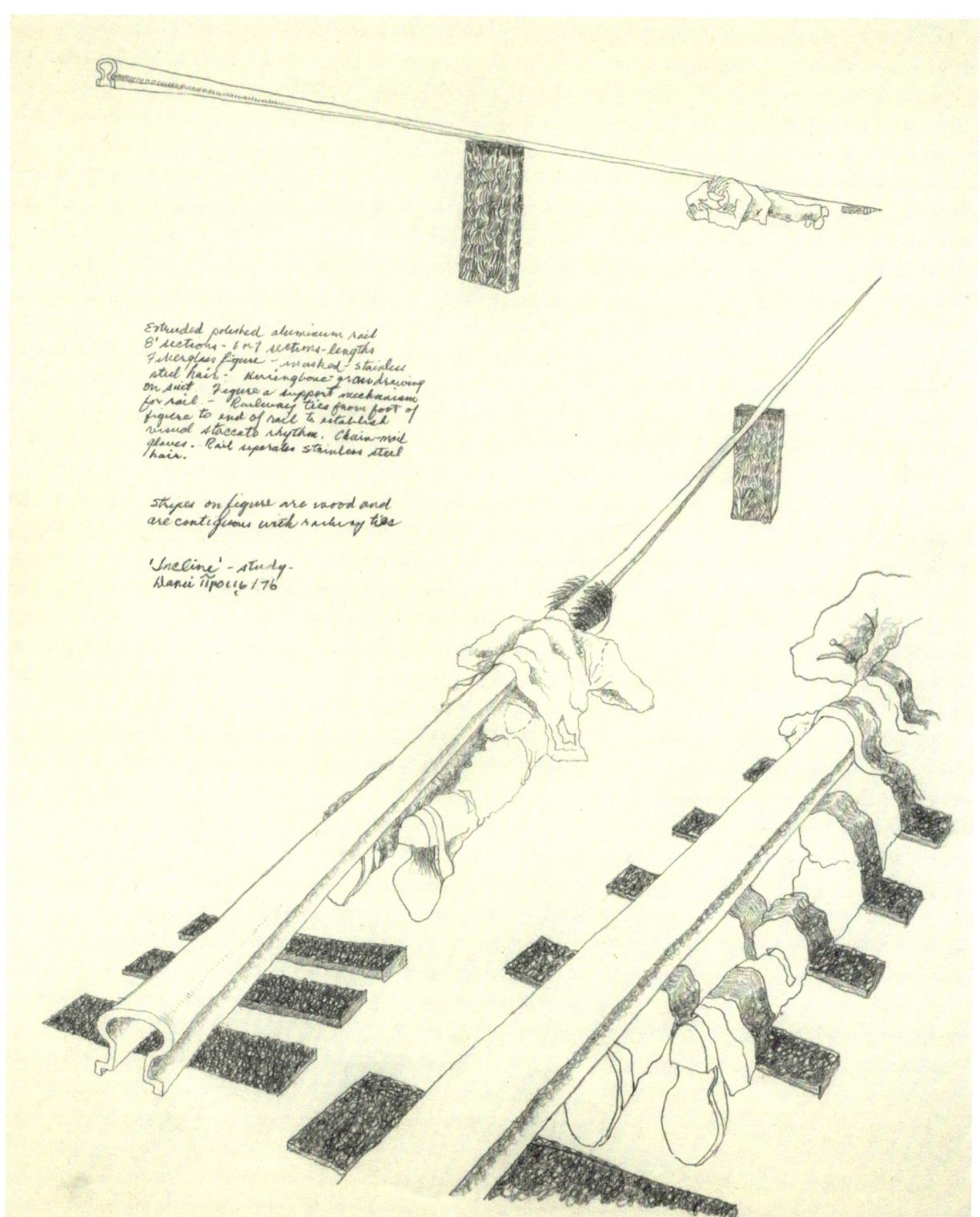

Extruded polished aluminium rail
8' sections - 6 or 7 sections- lengths
Fiberglass figure - masked - stainless
steel hair. Herringbone grain drawing
on suit. Figure a support mechanism
for rail. - Railway ties from foot of
figure to end of rail to establish
visual staccato rhythm. Chain-mail
gloves. Rail separates stainless steel
hair.

stripes on figure are wood and
are contiguous with railway ties

'Incline' - study -
David Upole 6 / 76

86. Sketch for *Incline*, 1976.

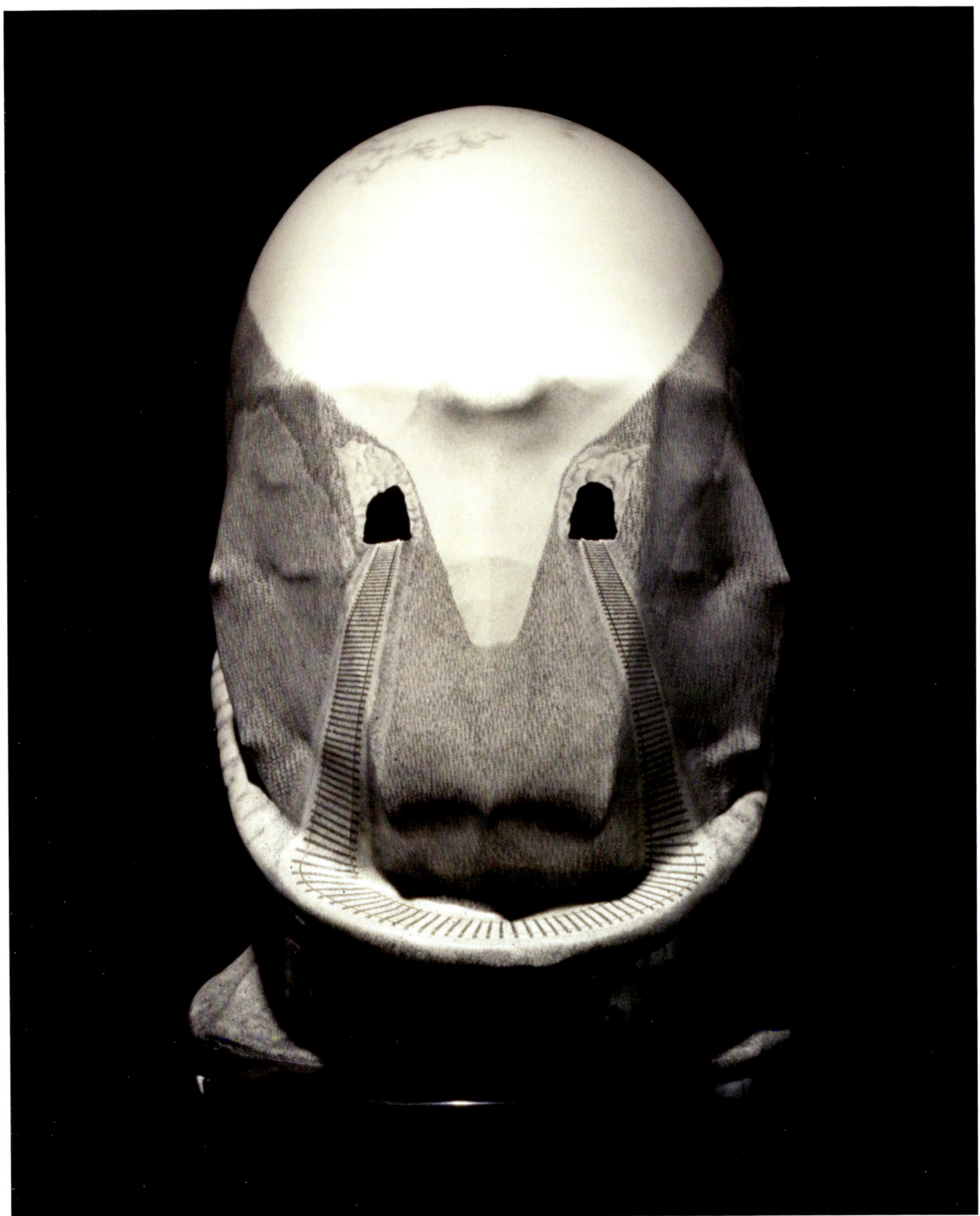

87. *Rocky Mountain Mask, 1976.*

Grain Elevators, 1980–2000

It is not surprising that grain elevators, part of Proch's life since his childhood, are such an essential element of his work as forms for drawing and as subjects. For Proch, elevators represent societal and farming transformations. Many rail lines on the prairies are now unused, and the iconic wooden elevators are all but gone, replaced by huge cement silos built farther and farther apart. As he immortalizes the historical and personal significance of elevators, Proch is keenly aware of their importance to the economic development of the West.

His *Elevator Series* of the 1980s and 1990s is compelling both as an entire series and as individual works. For each, Proch constructed the three-dimensional sculptural form of an elevator, often with the sky with appended clouds around it. As with all of his constructions, the form became his drawing surface. In this series, he again used combinations of multiple materials—grass, binder twine, and nickel-plated chrome—each with specific and personal significance. His drawings, like those on the masks, are done in coloured pencil, silverpoint, and graphite, and all depict aspects of the Asessippi Valley landscape and rural life. A foreboding and uncertain future is highlighted by dark, ominous skies, sharp points of acid rain, jagged edges, and lightning streaks.

The exhibition *Grainscapes: Sculpture by Don Proch* (1997) at Winnipeg's Oseredok Ukrainian Cultural and Educational Centre included a number of his multifaceted and intuitive elevator works. Curator Steve Prystupa wrote that they "express his own being and his human and environmental values . . . probing the physical reality and consciousness of real prairie people, prairie landscapes and real prairie issues. . . . [Proch] captures a live-in, close-up view of his subject and reveals its mystery and beauty as well as its starkness."[70]

In *Prairie Junction* (1989), for instance, two elevators are on either side of a stylized elevator form. Its various pieces are fitted together like a jigsaw puzzle, a compositional technique that enhances the vital farm and industry collaborations to get grain to

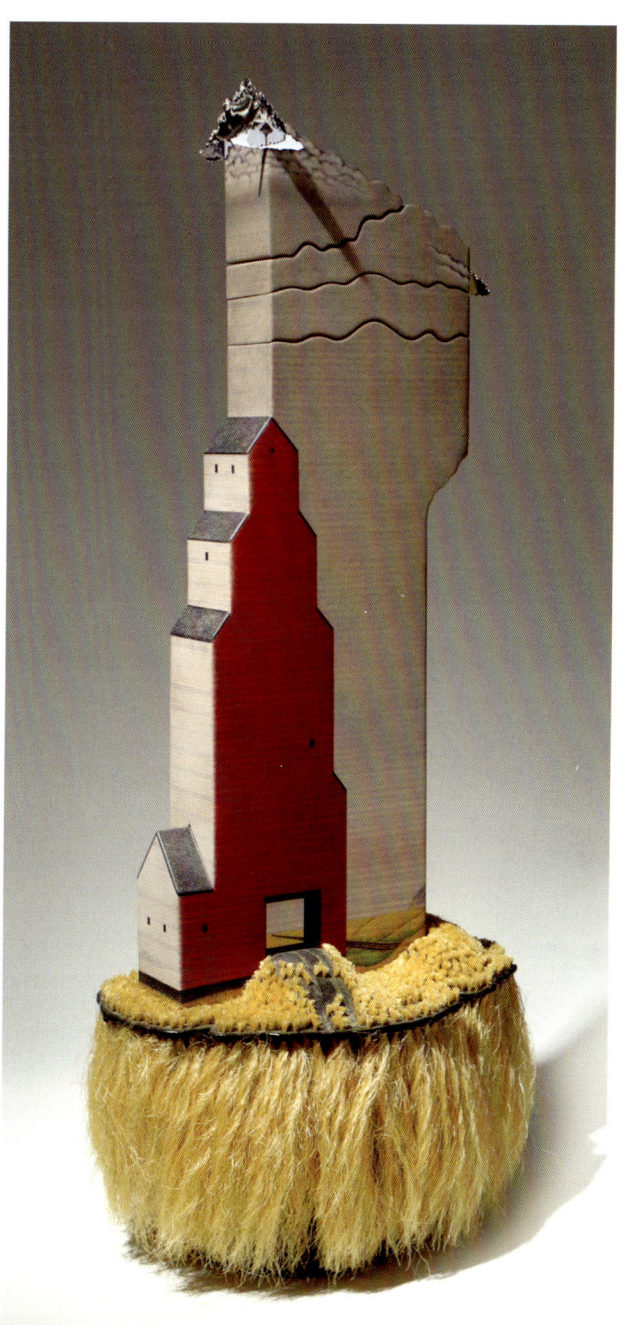

88. *Prairie Monolith*, 1996.

87

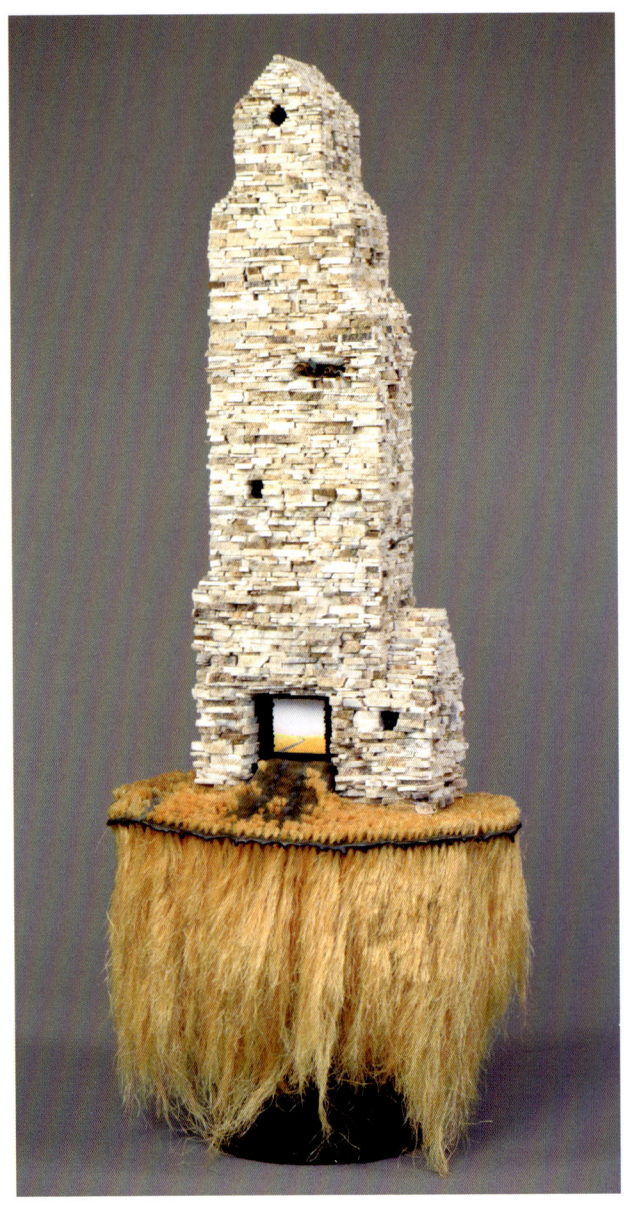

89. *Root Systems*, 1995.

market. In this work, as in others, the roads go through the elevator drive-throughs. The railway track branches in two directions and runs between the elevators. The preparatory drawing is precise, and the notations are clear. As Proch noted in his sketchbook, "Dark French Grey at peak. Horizon a more muted green. Slightly longer 'root system' in proportion to piece. Linear plywood will enrich color. A more irregular circumference with small channels & mirrored puddle areas."[71]

Prairie Monolith (1990) is another expression of Proch's personal perspectives and experiences and his explorations of the relationship between farmer and land. As Garth von Buchholz wrote,

> *Prairie Monolith* has the same kind of black base, with the flaxen strings woven into the surface and clustering below, but in this one, the elevator, the sky and the clouds are all joined in an organic whole, as if they were something one could excise from the landscape but never separate entirely.
>
> The silver clouds at the top crown the three of four layers of sky (like layers of soil), while the sky below shows a blue horizon with the field of grain that almost overlaps with the red elevator beside it. Even through the open door of the elevator, you can see the field continue, as if the farm and the farming are one, organic process.
>
> The other elevators are variations of this technique, with different themes. *Vanishing Landscape* features clouds above the elevator suspended by thin silver rods to represent rain. The shape of the elevator itself becomes the sky, with an image of clouds near its roof, a winding country road down its centre and wash of red at the base.[72]

Proch's sketchbook notes for *Prairie Monolith* contain many specific details of the imagery he planned to portray, and his materials and approaches to colour. One page includes a precise drawing of one view of the full elevator, the attached sky and landscape, details of its sky and

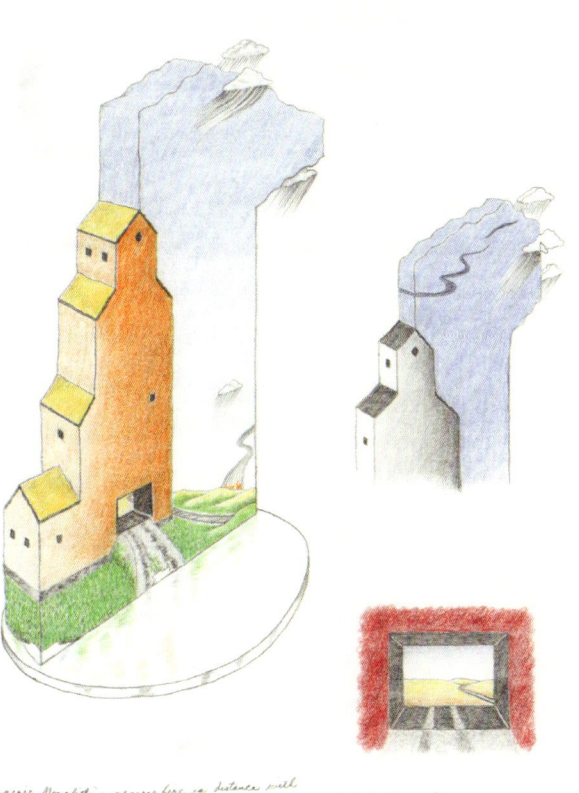

"Prairie Monolith" - prairie fire in distance with smoke snaking through sky. Chrome 'water puddles' in roadway & corners. Graphite over orange for richer color. For Sisal base have green at base of elevator blend into a burnt orange to meld with natural color of sisal. Madw Prystupa/96

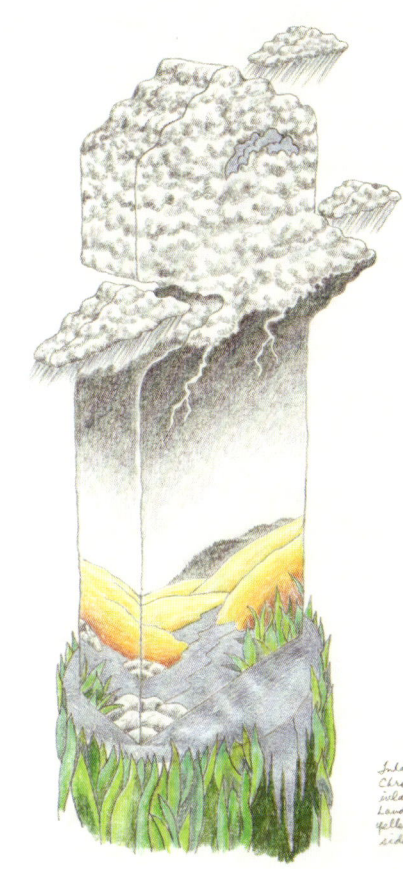

Inlaid copper lightning, Chrome & nickel clouds inlaid in drawn clouds. Landscape changing from yellow to green on opposite side. Dawie Prystupa 98

90. Sketch for *Prairie Monolith*, 1996.

91. *Home Grain*, study, 1998.

clouds, and a specific idea for the view through the drive-through. Proch's notes articulate "prairie fire in distance with smoke snaking through sky. Chrome 'water puddles' in roadway & corners. Graphite over orange for richer color. For Sisal base have green at base of elevator blend into a burnt orange to meld with natural colour of sisal."[73]

Other notations and sketches for works in this series specify the inlay materials that Proch would incorporate: "Inlaid copper lightning, chrome & nickel clouds inlaid in drawn clouds. Landscape changing from yellow to green on opposite side."[74] In some cases, he used silver pencil in the drawing to denote where he intended to use silverpoint in the final work and where he planned to inlay the chrome. In still others, he talked of his proposed "root system," specifying the length of the grasses to be used on the base. *Root Systems* (1995), for instance, is made with layers of stacked, tiny, brick-like animal bones, and Prystupa noted that its "dark base has 'crops' of wheat woven into it, while below the surface, the long golden strings (made of corn flax?) reach to absurdly disproportionate depths below the surface, clustered beneath the sculpture."[75]

Proch's notations often document his colour sensitivities and desired grey tone gradations. *Home*

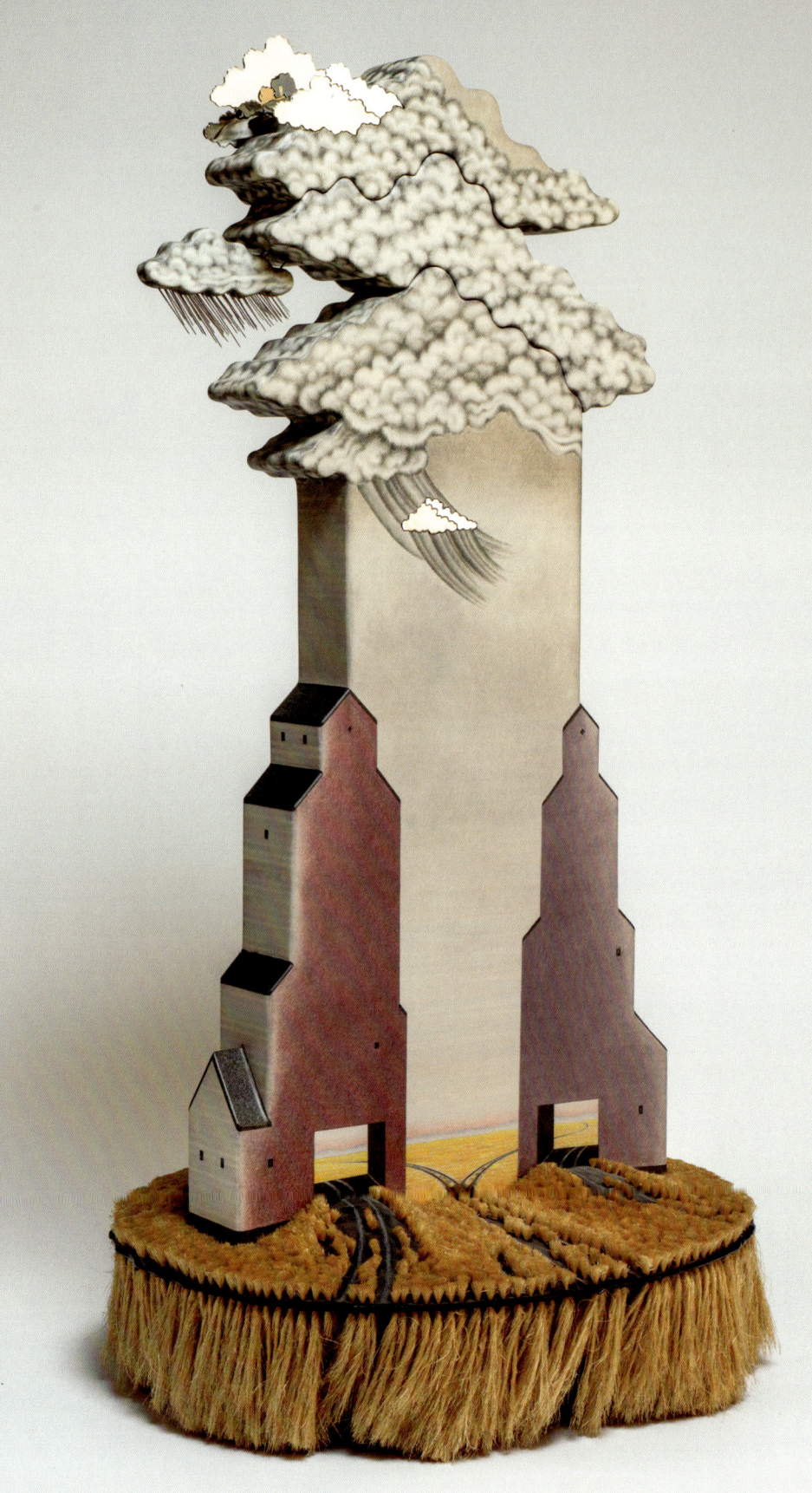

Grain (1997), for instance, is a blending from the blue in the upper portion of the elevator to white and greys, which then morph into the red in the lower section and the drive-through. The drawing shows the base in detail, with sisal and grasses. In this sketch Proch noted "Home Grain. Bring blue down below 3rd roof. Grain Scape—clouds drawn at elevator peak. Maroon on one side, graphite on other. Sisal bottom."[76] In other preparatory drawings, he stipulated his intended connections between the various portions of a work—the elevator with its attached landscape or skyscape, the clouds, and in some instances inverted shapes.

The sky forms the major focus of *No. 1 Gold* (1995), the red elevator on one side representing only half of the height of the work. The landscape is a tiny portion at the bottom and is reflected in the nickel-plated chrome base. Proch's decision to render the landscape so small, coupled with his judicious use of reflection, effectively adds distance to the road running toward the elevator and gives a greater sense of space to the work as a whole. The sky is formed in three parts, including two appended at the top. Three stylized clouds are attached to the side of the work by rain formed from sharp-pointed steel rods, which emanate from each cloud. As always, Proch's drawing is precise, and his application of colour is smooth, imbuing a gentleness despite the ominous pointed projections of steel from the clouds.

Prairie Junction (1989) shows the elevator with its drive-through in the middle.[77] As in so many of Proch's works, the landscape covers the work itself. The drive-through was to become an element in other works in his *Elevator Series* of the 1980s and 1990s, and after the turn of the century it was to become a full subject of its own, with works such as *Colville's Horse Races through the Prairie Drive-Thru Gallery, Brushing Past John Nugent's "No. 1 Hard," Heading West to Haida Gwaii* (2016). An early articulation of the theme is seen in *Prairie Sentinel* (1994), in which the horizon is seen through the open tunnel in which farmers unloaded their grain. This vista through the drive-through is a continuation of the landscape depicted in front of the elevator. Cloud formations follow the contours of the field; its colour is

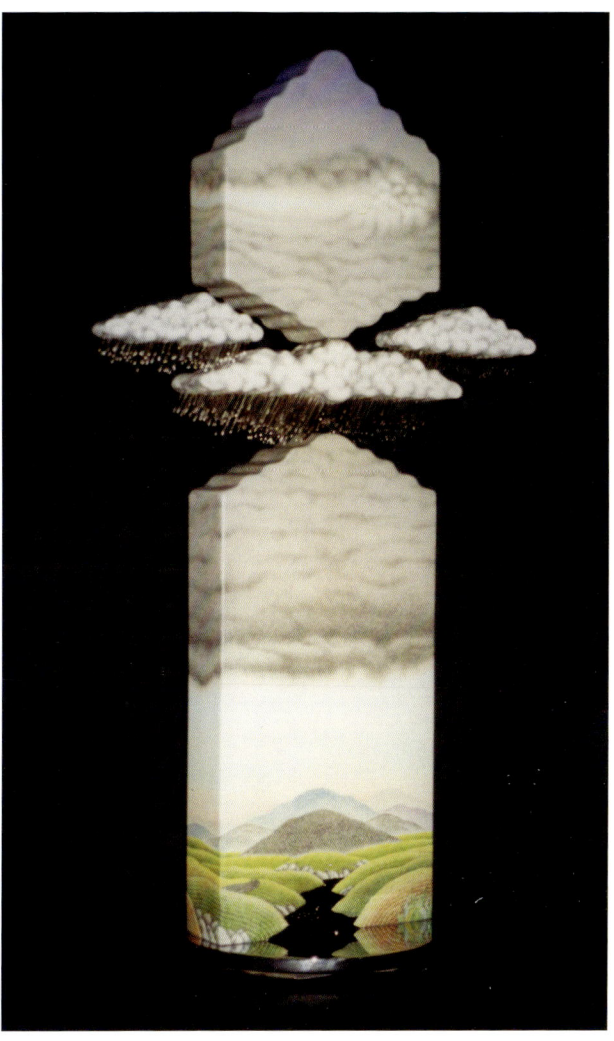

92. (OPPOSITE) *Prairie Drive-Thru*, 1988.

93. *Prairie Trail*, 2002.

natural—the gold prairie grains, green grasses, and soft blues characteristic of late-summer skies. As before, the entire surface is covered with Proch's intricate and smooth pencil workings. The rhythm of his markings, parallel to the ground, flows across the sky and the elevator. The artist's engineering knowledge is evident as three external clouds are attached off centre by pointed diagonal protrusions of rain. These sharp outthrusts splice the calm of the overall aura, thus magnifying the perturbing overtones of the work. While this vertical sculpture is balanced, it seems to be off balance, further enhancing present-day environmental unease.

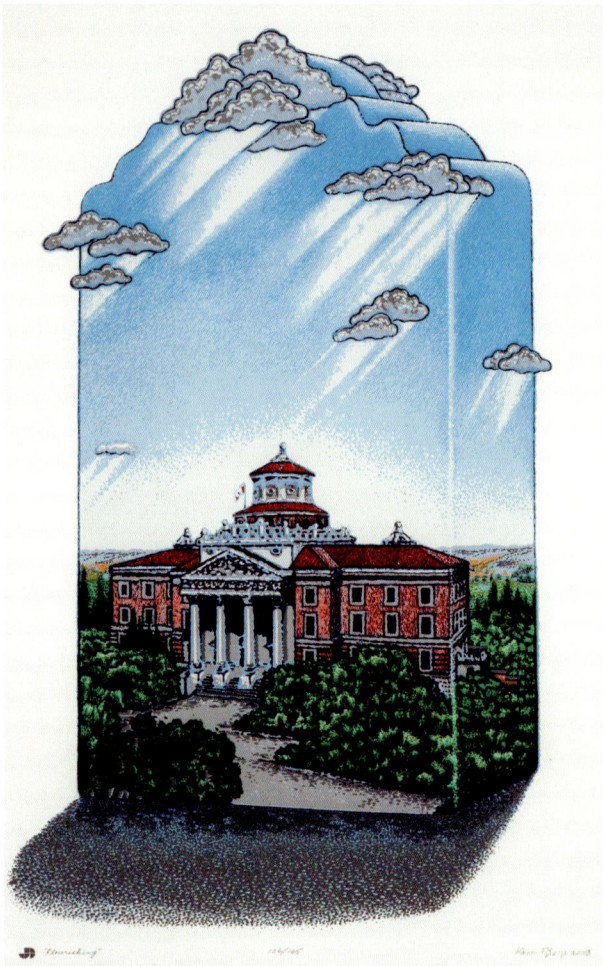

94. *Flourishing*, 2008.

95. (OPPOSITE) *Through the Artist's Eye Moon and Pine Bough* (side view), 1990.

Prairie Trail (2002) takes Proch's affixing of elements to the top of a work yet a step further. Although its shape is that of a stylized elevator, there is no reference to an elevator in this drawing of the prairie landscape with a trail running through it. Four sections are added to the basic form and comprise approximately half the work. Three are cloud formations, each with detailed drawings of cumulus clouds. The largest and uppermost, a blue skyscape above the clouds, has two nickel-plated inlaid clouds. Rain falls

from both inlays. From one, the rain is shown with Proch's typical parallel straight lines; from the other, the rain flows horizontally across the skyscape. Characteristically, the pointed steel, evoking acid rain, adds a harshness to the otherwise serene image. A master of setting up dichotomies and contradictions within a single work, Proch again builds up conflicting and opposing sensibilities in the mind of the viewer.

His silkscreen prints carry the elevator theme into his two-dimensional works, such as *Flourishing*, the 2008 commission from the University of Manitoba. Here the shape of an elevator encases the university's administration building, as if the elevator itself contains the university's history, a university originally founded in 1877 as an agricultural college. Proch effectively underlines the all-encompassing importance of agriculture to the province as a whole and to the livelihoods of its citizens. He does so both as a graduate of the university and as a child of the province's agricultural business. In addition, this work highlights the importance of education as the gateway to a secure future.

Although beautiful in every detail, his art nonetheless meddles with our psyches as Proch poses vexing and increasingly pervasive questions. What *is* in those clouds? Acid or worse? Do we care? What is our responsibility in addressing these dire threats to the balance of nature? In his *Elevator Series*, Proch seems to predict changes in weather patterns that will irrevocably alter farming practices. He certainly suggests that contemporary lifestyles have destroyed past lifestyles and even, perhaps, the meaning and practicality of elevators in getting grain to market. Do we know the essential role of these vanished prairie icons? The irony in his work is palpable.

In 2018, Proch returned to the elevator theme again. These later pieces incorporate more chromed elements than his earlier ones. His precision is evident as he creates these new pieces—each copper cloud shape, before being chromed, is numbered and carefully fitted to ensure the proper fit and that the relationships of the parts in the work's final assembly are correct.

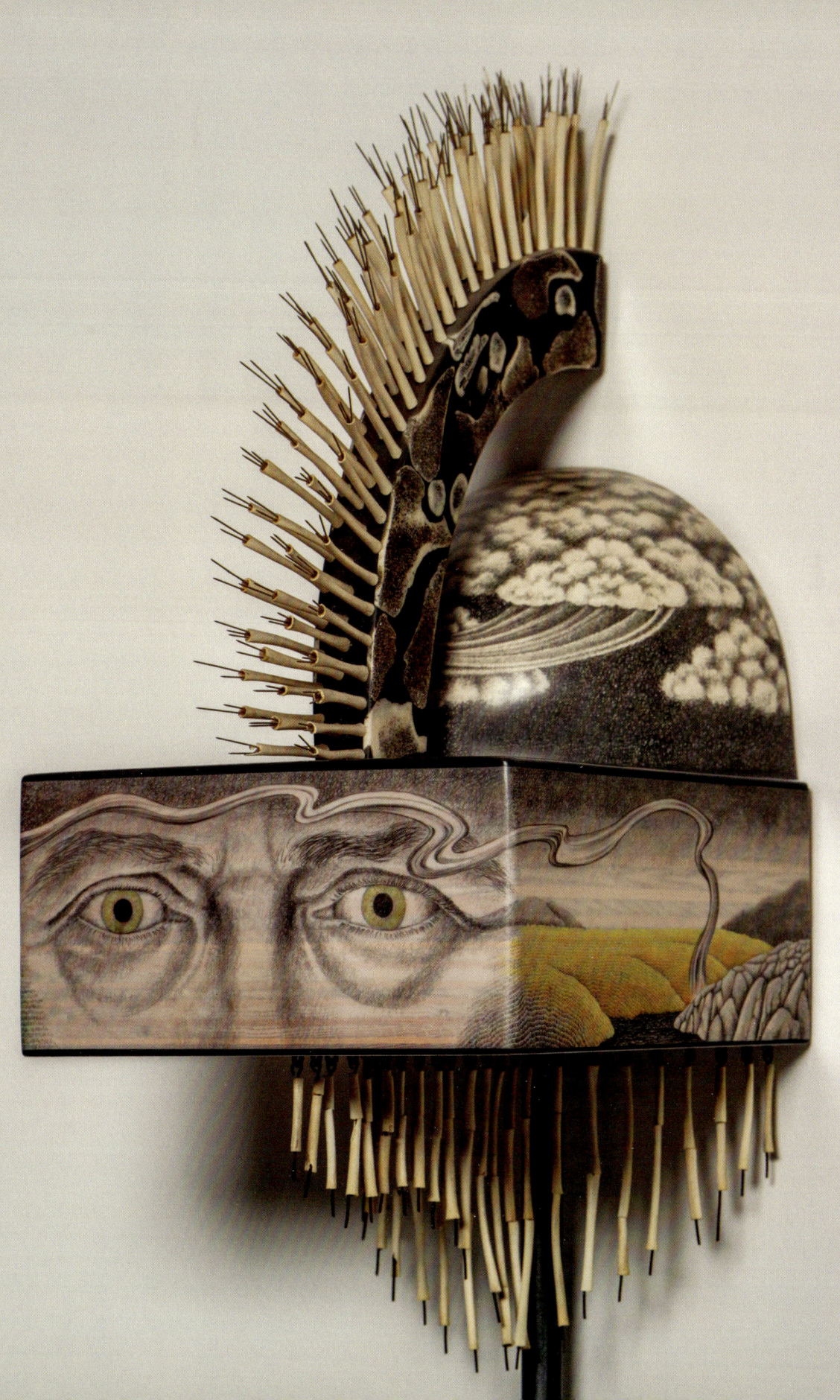

Visual Progressions:
Aesthetic and Psychological

Proch has been a true environmentalist since childhood, and his knowledge and experience of rural life continue to inform his significant body of two- and three-dimensional works. Fed by indelible intuitive, intellectual, and emotional impressions from his youth, his deep respect for the land evolved into a well-articulated and increasingly deep concern about the long-term impacts of human treatment on nature. From the 1980s on, the intrinsic relationship between people and nature, and the natural cycles of birth, growth, death, and regeneration, are elegantly and jarringly embedded in all of his work.

Through the Artist's Eye (1989), a summary of Proch's thoughts to that point, unites the power of the landscape and the impact of human interaction with it. This work proffers a two-way gaze—the work to the viewer and the viewer to the work. A self-portrait, his two piercing eyes fill one side of this sculpture. Engaging with this work, the viewer, on close observation, sees "that the left pupil (when facing the piece) is hollow. Upon closer observations one can see lights inside the piece and when you put your eye up to the opening (the pupil) you see a night landscape with moon The moon, stars and several constellations reflect on the water. Hence the title. Who is studying whose vision? Or is this the artist's pupil identity?"[78]

The details of the forehead drift into a smoky haze. The brow becomes a vapour trail as the face morphs into the landscape with golden grain at the adjacent edge. The vapour trail terminates in some rocks on the lower right of the second side of the work, tying the two sides together Hanging below and set above are chicken bones, with sharp-edged metal points aimed outward, characteristic of Proch's masks of the period. On top, a half-moon-shaped sky is covered with clouds from which more vapour trails emanate. Not a mask, though akin to his masks, this work stands on a black pole and penetrates the viewer's psyche at eye level.

Memories Juxtaposed:
Recurring Connections

Precision, detail, and delicacy are the trademarks of Proch's drawing, his consistent primary artistic endeavour. Strong stylistic, iconographic, and psychological links recur among his drawings, prints, and three-dimensional works. Ideas and images also reappear and are recycled through his various series. Proch's visual progression can be seen clearly through each decade as witnessed in his masks and elevators. His non-linear, cyclical development as an artist, with images based upon specific preoccupations of the moment, always reconnects to his core concerns.

Proch's unique layering of past, present, and future, simultaneously superimposing nostalgia, reality, and anxiety, imbues all his drawings, prints, sculptures, masks, elevators, drive-throughs, and installations with a sense of unease. The consistency of his core focus, balancing memory, communal and personal, and his intertwining of land and humanity, results in his robust advocacy for urgent action to restore respect and care for the environment. Mixing vanishing nostalgic icons and the beauty of the prairie with poignant and jarring truths, Proch articulates a clarion call to turn away from the perilous precipice of devastation.

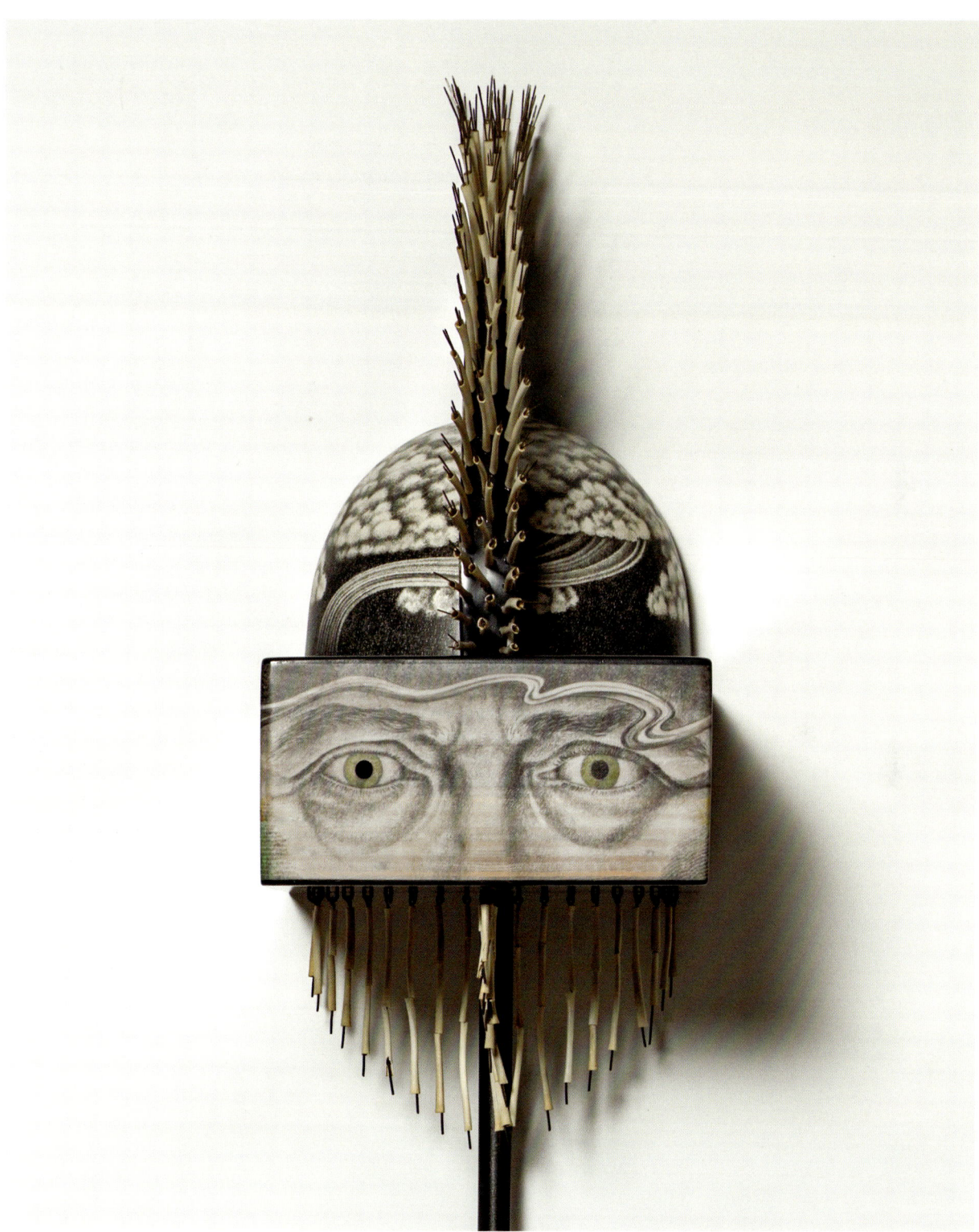

96. *Through the Artist's Eye Moon and Pine Bough* (front view), 1990.

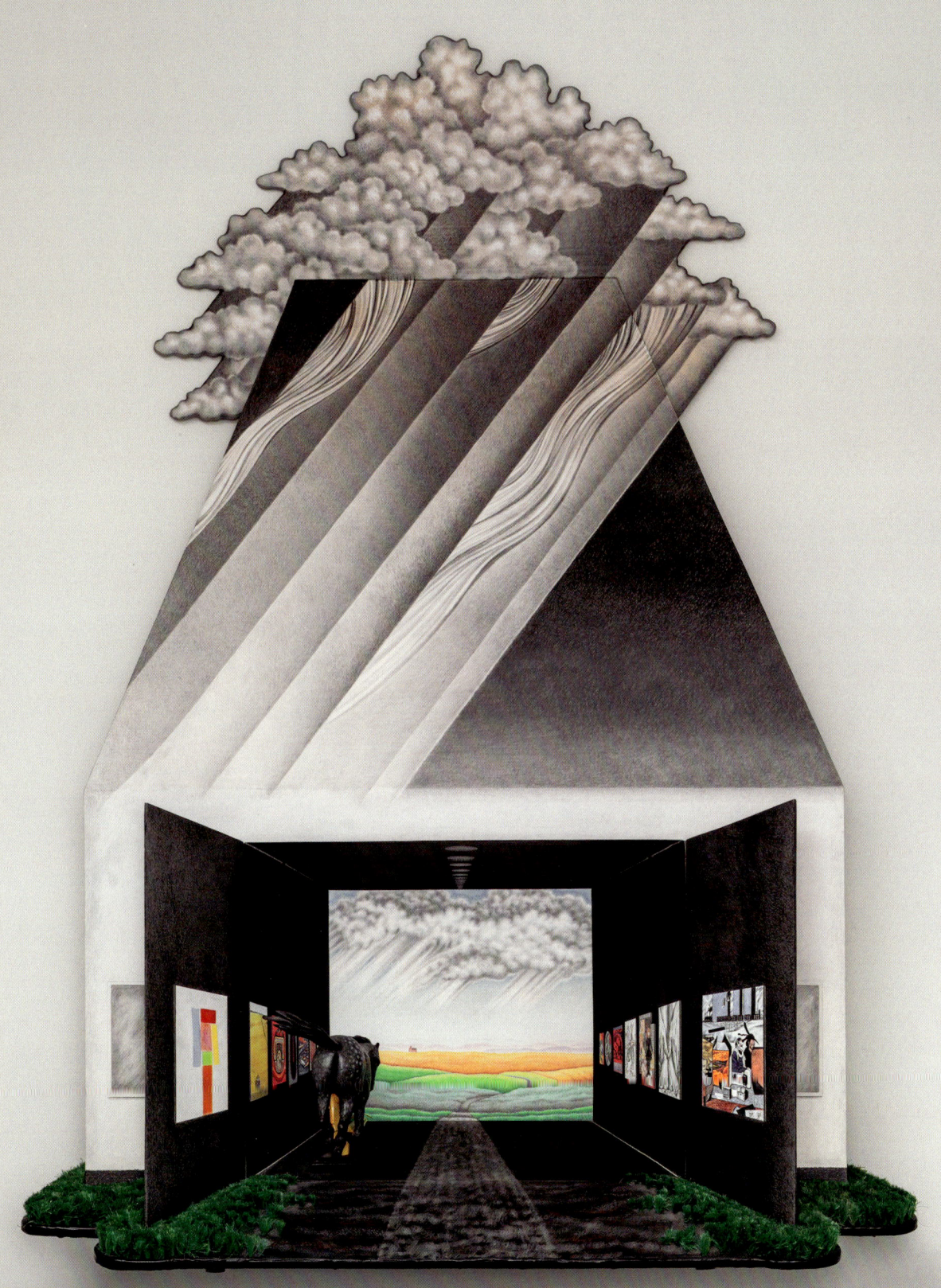

A Prescient Societal Voice: Masking and Mapping

COLVILLE'S HORSE RACES through the Prairie Drive-Thru Gallery, Brushing Past John Nugent's "No. 1 Hard," Heading West to Haida Gwaii (2016) shows a horse galloping through the drive-through, past the works of art that Don Proch depicted in his gallery on the interior walls of the sculpture. The horse's tail flies behind, evoking speed, just as the crouched position of the figure on the bicycle had more than forty years earlier in Asessippi Tread.

Proch expanded his depiction of the grain elevator in his Drive-Thru series. Initially inspired by the drive-through of the elevator itself, the point where grain is unloaded, the site shifted as the concept of the work progressed. It became the machine shed: "The image I had in mind was a large farm machine shed often set away by itself in a field."[79] The drive-through becomes a gallery in which Proch, as artist and curator, includes the best-known art of his colleagues, some of Canada's leading artists, "whom I knew and whose work I admired."[80] By bringing the art of others—Kenneth Lochhead, Jack Bush, William Kurelek, and Ivan Eyre—into his own meaningful central place in this work, Proch effectively unites his two lives—a farm boy turned environmentalist and acclaimed Canadian artist. The horse galloping through Proch's gallery is reminiscent of the horse galloping along the railway track toward an approaching train in the famous painting by Nova Scotia artist Alex Colville, Horse and Train (1954). "I was hoping that the horse had run free of the train and continued on a cross country journey where his curiosity led him through the drive-thru gallery," said Proch.[81] The horse had appeared in one of Proch's earlier works, The Journey (1988).

The developmental sketches and drawings for this seminal work fill a number of pages in his sketchbooks and were done over several years as Proch developed the concept and details of the work. Listing critical structural details, aesthetic decisions, materials, colours, and measurements, they specify the supports and construction required. For example, the note on one page reads: "Attach steel plate to top and bottom of box. Horse bolted through steel pipe set in corner of recessed door opening. Steel plate where horse touches

97. Colville's Horse Races through the Prairie Drive-Thru Gallery, Brushing Past John Nugent's "No. 1 Hard," Heading West to Haida Gwaii, 2016.

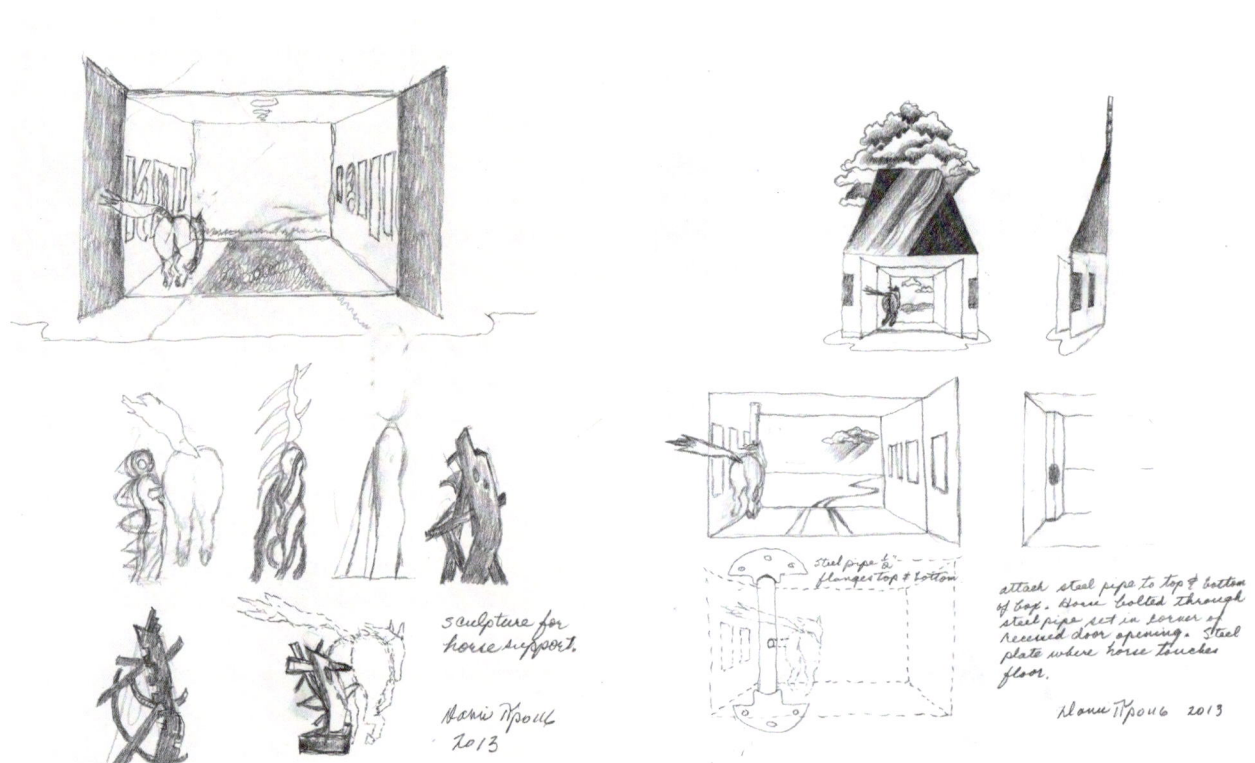

98 and 99. Sketches for *Colville's Horse Races through the Prairie Drive-Thru Gallery, Brushing Past John Nugent's "No. 1 Hard," Heading West to Haida Gwaii*, 2013.

floor."[82] His year of engineering studies obviously had a beneficial effect on his art.

The roof is superimposed by the sky and clouds. Wind-swept rain pours down in slices of geometrical diagonals parallel with the shafts of light in the landscape through the drive-through. Proch added sisal, as grass, on either side of the open doors of the drive-through, adding texture to counterbalance the fluffy clouds.

In *Colville's Horse Races through the Prairie Drive-Thru Gallery, Brushing Past John Nugent's "No. 1 Hard," Heading West to Haida Gwaii* (2016), the drive-through is a real and physical opening and serves as a pathway for Proch into personal and communal psyches. Are we driving? Moving from the past? To what future? A greenish acidic quality in the greys imparts a luminous eeriness, presenting a foreboding look at the future. One can also conjecture about Proch's reflections on the past, when horse-drawn carts, not motorized vehicles, were used to deliver grain. Constructed like a theatre stage, this drive-through heightens the dramatization of the passage of time from the 1930s and 1940s, through the heady 1960s and 1970s represented by his choice of specific contemporary works of art, to present-day environmental crises.

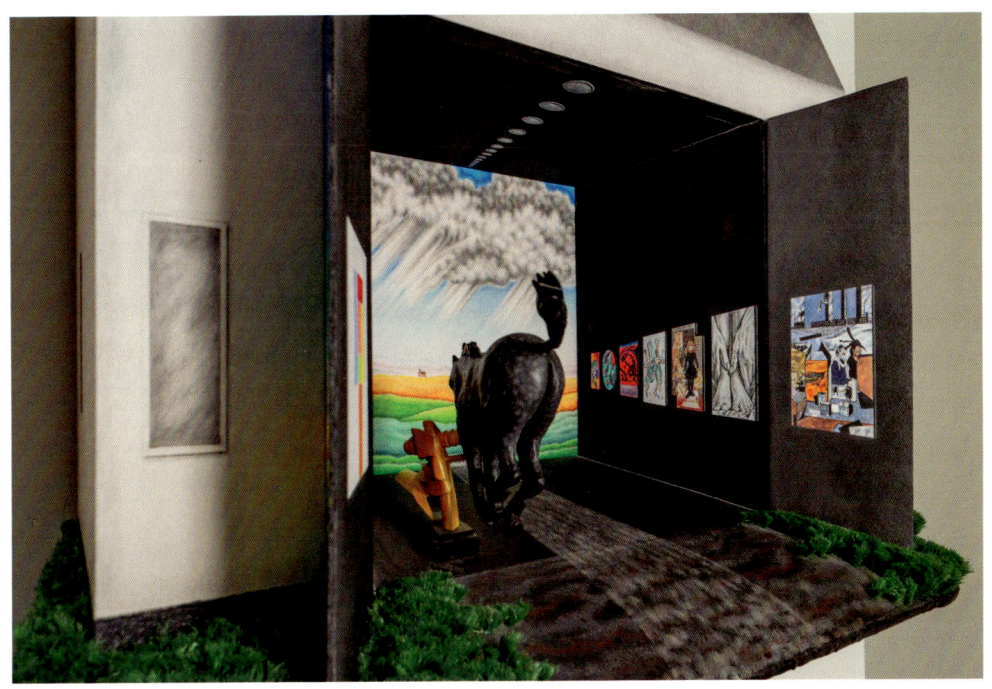

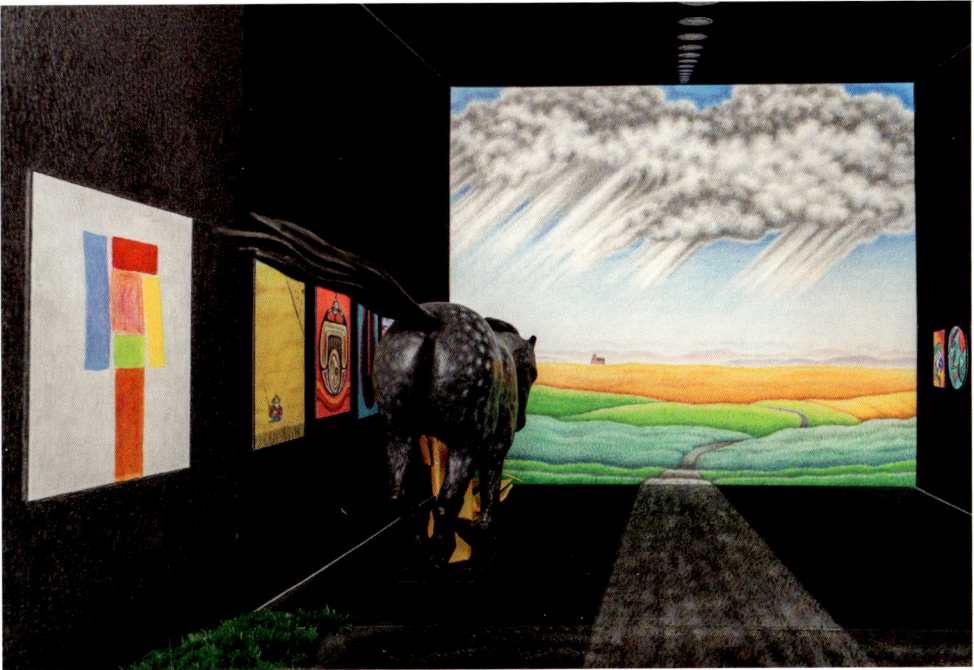

100 and 101 (details). *Colville's Horse Races through the Prairie Drive-Thru Gallery, Brushing Past John Nugent's "No. 1 Hard," Heading West to Haida Gwaii,* 2016.

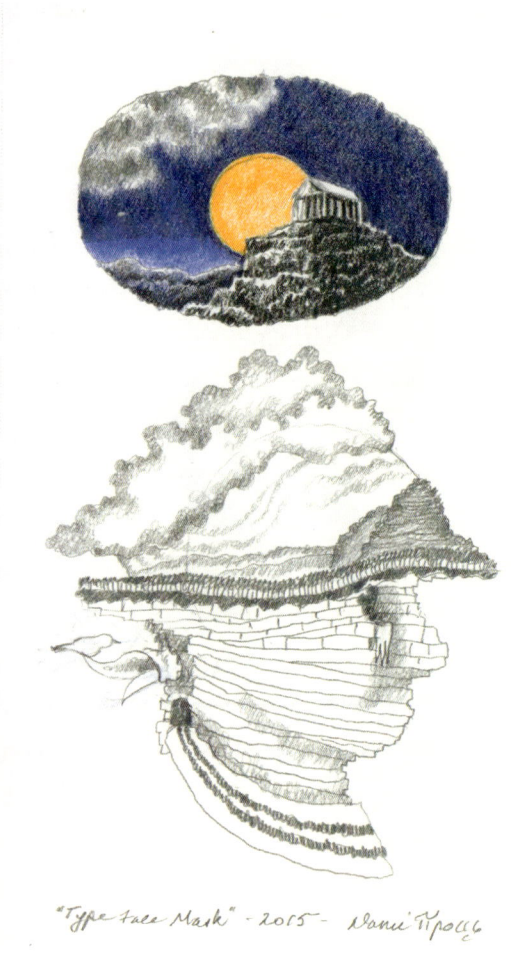

"Type face Mask" - 2015 - Danu Proch

102. Sketch for *Typeface Mask*, 2015.

103–106. (OPPOSITE) Sketches for *Typeface Mask*, 2012–2015.

Typeface Mask (2017)

Juxtapositions of materials, ideas, and images, those important links in Proch's roots and messages, continue in his sculpture *Typeface Mask* (2017). The past is elevated, even enhanced, with his incorporation of stacked tiny bones and the typeface once used by a rural newspaper. The present is shown in the lyrical landscape of prairie hills drawn on the bandana. The future is foreshadowed by a tear, the waterfall in one eye. A tiny white grain elevator, made of wood, is placed in one eye in front of the full moon in a midnight blue sky. Proch's iconography again underlines the negative effects of contemporary lifestyles and acid rain on how we live and the crops that farmers grow.

The various items on his work table while creating *Typeface Mask* were carefully ordered, and those that Proch appended or embedded give specific effects, adding multiple visual and psychological meanings and contrasts. His use of old metal type on one half of the face in *Typeface Mask* adds a unique three-dimensional textural element. Each letter is affixed at different lengths to create the work's outer form and its contours and shadows. An old Selectric typewriter ball forms the cheek. The letters mark direct associations with the two-dimensional press of rural newspapers, such as the *Western Producer* and the *Farmers' Almanac*, the purveyors of weather, community and rural news, and commodity and financial markets. Proch recalls going to the printing shop of the local newspaper, the *Russell Banner*, owned by the father of a childhood friend. Many years later, when metal type became obsolete, Proch was given the trays of discarded type. Using the type as he did in *Typeface Mask* simultaneously gave him a direct connection to his past and enabled him to reinvent the future.

Tiny bits of dyed bones build the other half of *Typeface Mask*, thus deepening the multiple layers of meaning, juxtaposing his Winnipeg studio with his prairie life, the bones denoting the rural and the typeface the urban. The dyed bone fragments render a detailed, soft-hued palette, not unlike the subtlety and intricacy of his coloured pencil drawings. Proch stacked the bone

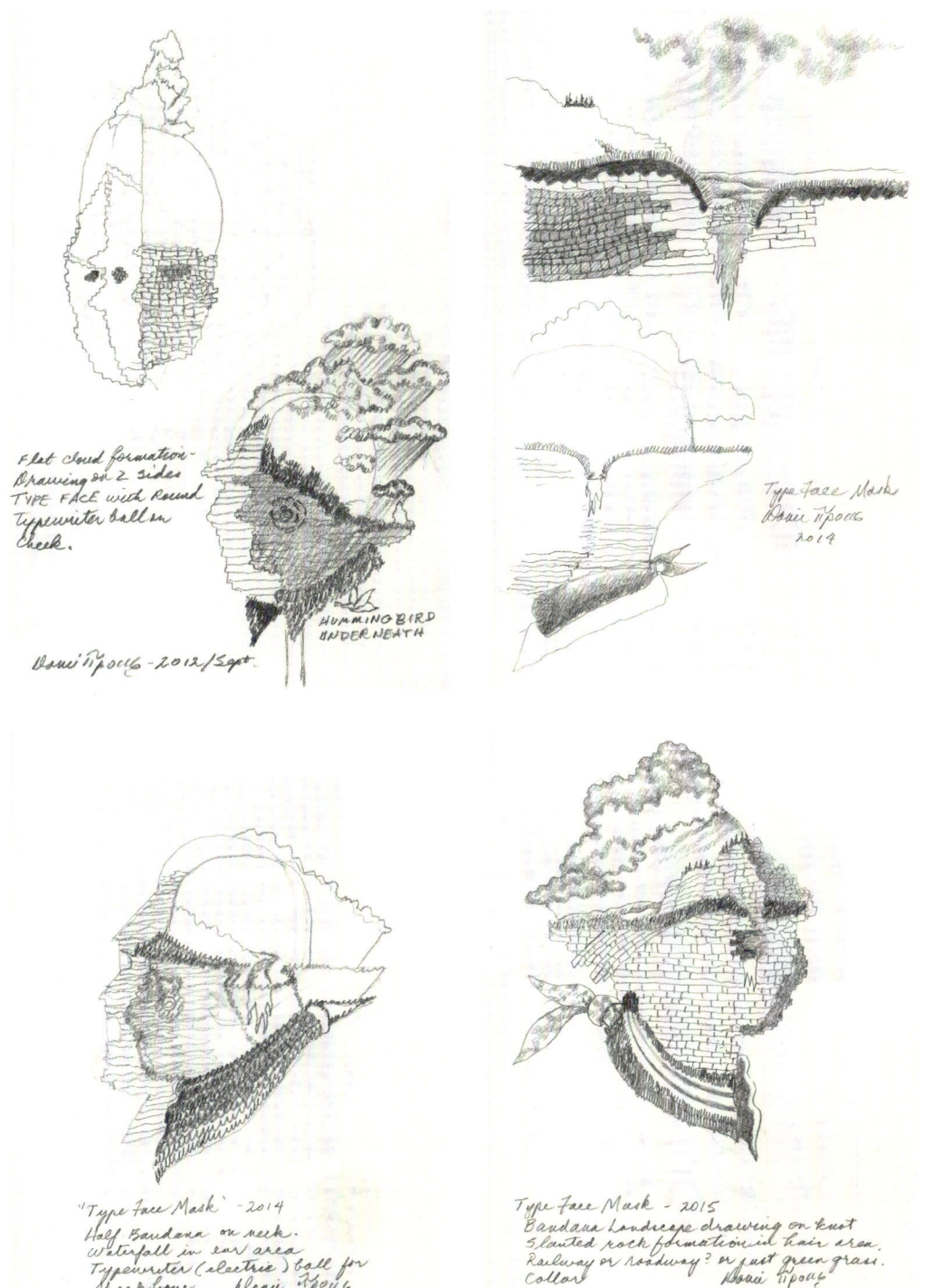

Flat Cloud formation.
Drawing on 2 sides
TYPE FACE with Round
Typewriter ball on
cheek.

HUMMING BIRD
UNDER NEATH

Daui Тромс - 2012/Sept.

Type Face Mask
Daui Тромс
2014

"Type Face Mask" - 2014
Half Bandana on neck.
Waterfall in ear area
Typewriter (electric) ball for
cheekbone.   Daui Тромс

Type Face Mask - 2015
Bandana Landscape drawing on knot
Slanted rock formation in hair area.
Railway or roadway? or just green grass.
Collar   Daui Тромс

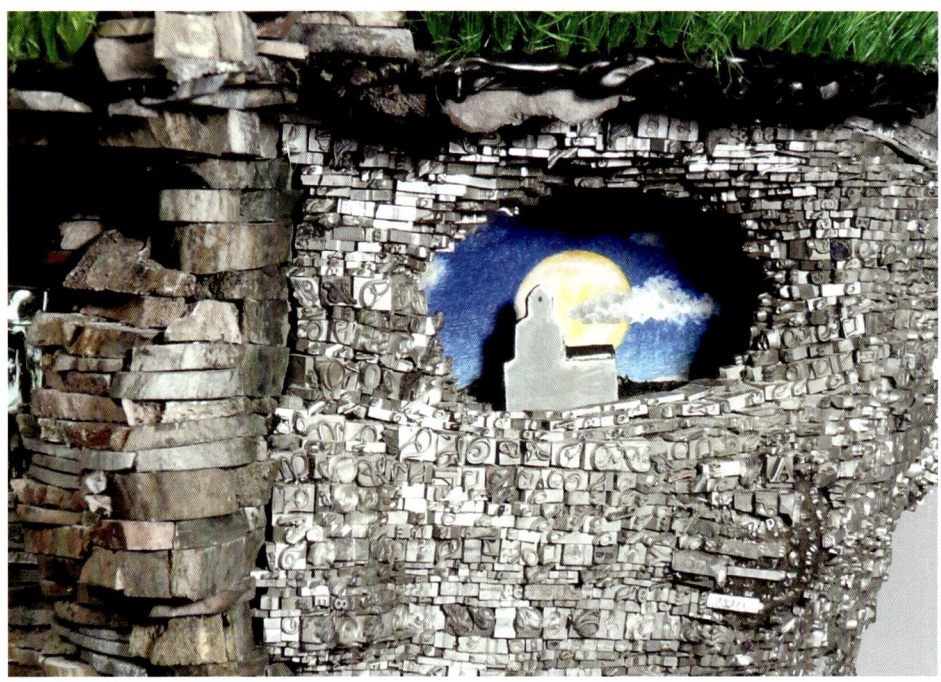

107. *Typeface Mask* (detail), 2017.

108. (OPPOSITE) *Typeface Mask*, 2017.

fragments on top of each other, much as one builds a brick wall. Some are placed with the porous side showing, others with the smooth edges facing outward. This deliberate ordering reflects the dichotomies of one's inner self and outer self and the inner and outer sensibilities of a community. Like the metal type, the bones introduce another texture, emphasizing physical realities and contemporary psychological quandaries.

Process is core to Proch's work. His sketchbooks reveal the essence of his ideas and his intense and detailed thought processes for each work, both his two-dimensional and his three-dimensional works. The sketches dating back to 2012 for *Typeface Mask*, completed in 2017, for example, show the progression of his ideas over the years of its development. The sketches include notations for the collar, "cast aluminum tie—sisal green on the collar." Below other sketches articulate ideas for other details included in the final work: "Half-Bandana on neck; Waterfall in ear area; Typewriter (electric) ball for cheekbone."[83]

Many pages in that particular sketchbook are devoted to the concepts in *Typeface Mask* and particularly the interior of the right eye (as one faces the mask). Proch's first sketched idea for the eye was to have the Parthenon in the interior of the eye. Proch drew that version both in pencil and in coloured pencil, and in each rendering he had the full moon behind the Parthenon. He drew another version with Stonehenge in the eye. In the final work, however, a grain elevator, his local icon, is set in front of a dark blue sky and a full harvest moon. His reason for the change? As recognizable as his first two ideas were internationally, he thought that they lacked local currency and impact. Symbolic of his past, the elevator carried his personal and poignant warning about environmental sustainability.[84] In his notations, Proch also worked out the piece's many details, such as the chrome waterfalls, shaped like tears, one falling out of the left eye and the other out of an ear over the face made of natural bone and metal type. The cumulative effect is visceral and disturbing. The contemporary transitions in farming and the consequential negative human impacts, which Proch witnessed, alarmed him, and he was determined to bring his concerns to worldwide attention.

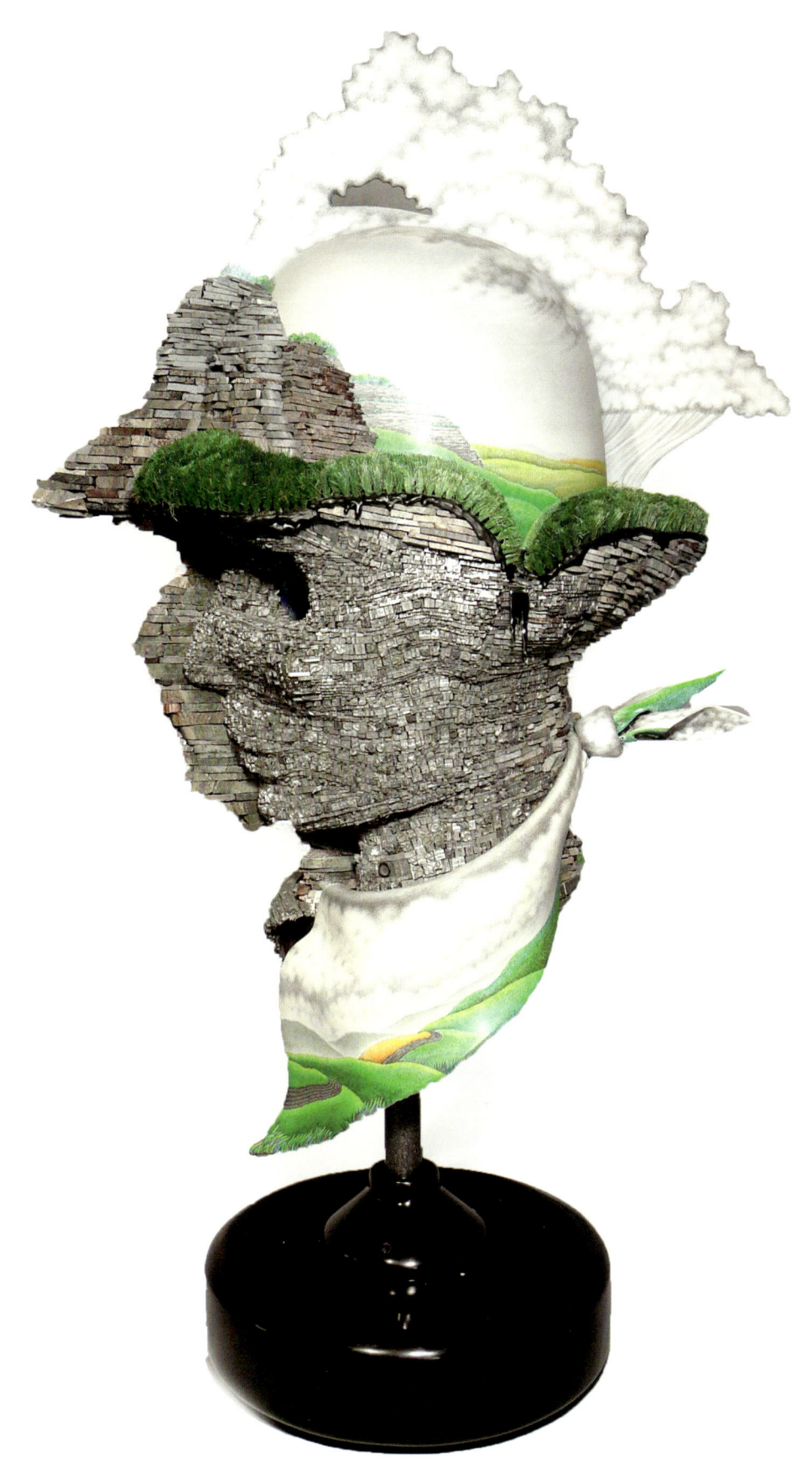

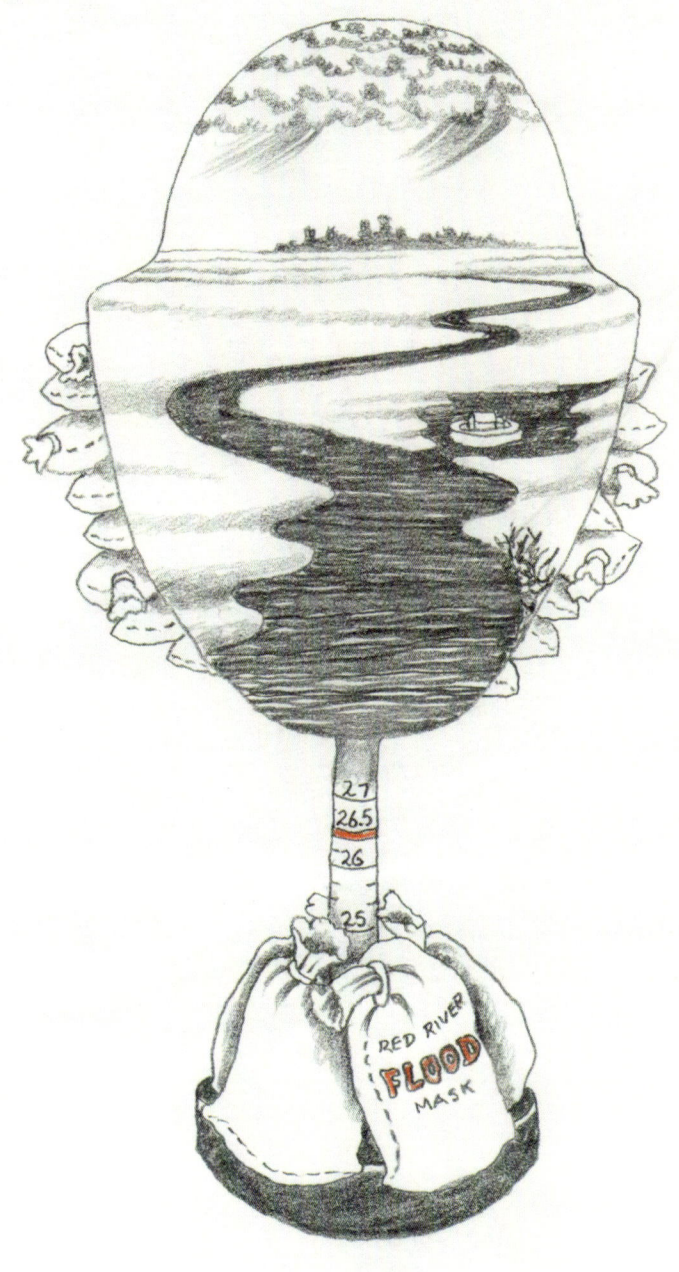

City skyline dark on top & hazy on horizon. Water very dark. Ring dike whitened. Color on roof of buildings. Light grey over entire landscape. Trees along riverbank in foreground. Reddish brown undercolor in foreground water. Turbulent sky along bottom of cloudbank.

Diane Tipona - 1997

Technical Approaches:
Sketchbooks and Processes

DON PROCH HAS ADOPTED a careful process for commencing a work. Some of his preparatory drawings are quick notes or sketches; others are meticulously worked-out thoughts. Proch explained the importance of his preparatory drawings and his practice of working out a piece before realizing it: "When you make a commitment to do an intensive piece, you can't allow for many mistakes. You can't find yourself three-quarters of the way through and then have to tear it down and basically start from scratch."[85]

His sketchbooks are rich, chronicling the development of specific works and detailing ongoing ideas. His many sketchbooks include notations for a number of works, all titled or described so that they are easily tied to the associated works. On one page, for instance, Proch focused on details of the neck scarf for *Bandana Mask* with this comment: "Bird in Eye—Black Field on neck scarf. Knot on right side of head." He changed his mind about the placement of the knot in the final sculpture. He moved it to the back of the work, pointing outward. Although Proch might change certain details when making the work, he rarely changes the actual structure of the work.

Proch has consistently maintained his long-established work routines, which reflect his highly disciplined approach to art making. The organization of his studio matches the meticulousness of his art. Materials, carefully organized in various containers, are laid out on a table beside a work in progress mounted on its turntable. Pieces of bone from Asessippi, in their natural state, from two to four centimetres long, fill one tin plate; others are sorted by colour. Proch found that bone naturally turned white over time, changing his chosen subtle palette of tans and greys, and thus substantially altering the sensibility of the work. Wanting to retain his deliberate colourations, he began dying tiny bone shards with natural materials. Next to the containers of bones are pie plates and bowls filled with bits of metal, wire, and the type from offset printing. Binder twine, silverpoint, graphite, chicken bones, chrome, catgut, and plexiglass are also at hand. On the wall above his work table is a maquette for a next *Drive-Thru*. The overall size, shapes, spaces, and construction details have been

109. Sketch for *Red River Flood Mask*, 1997.

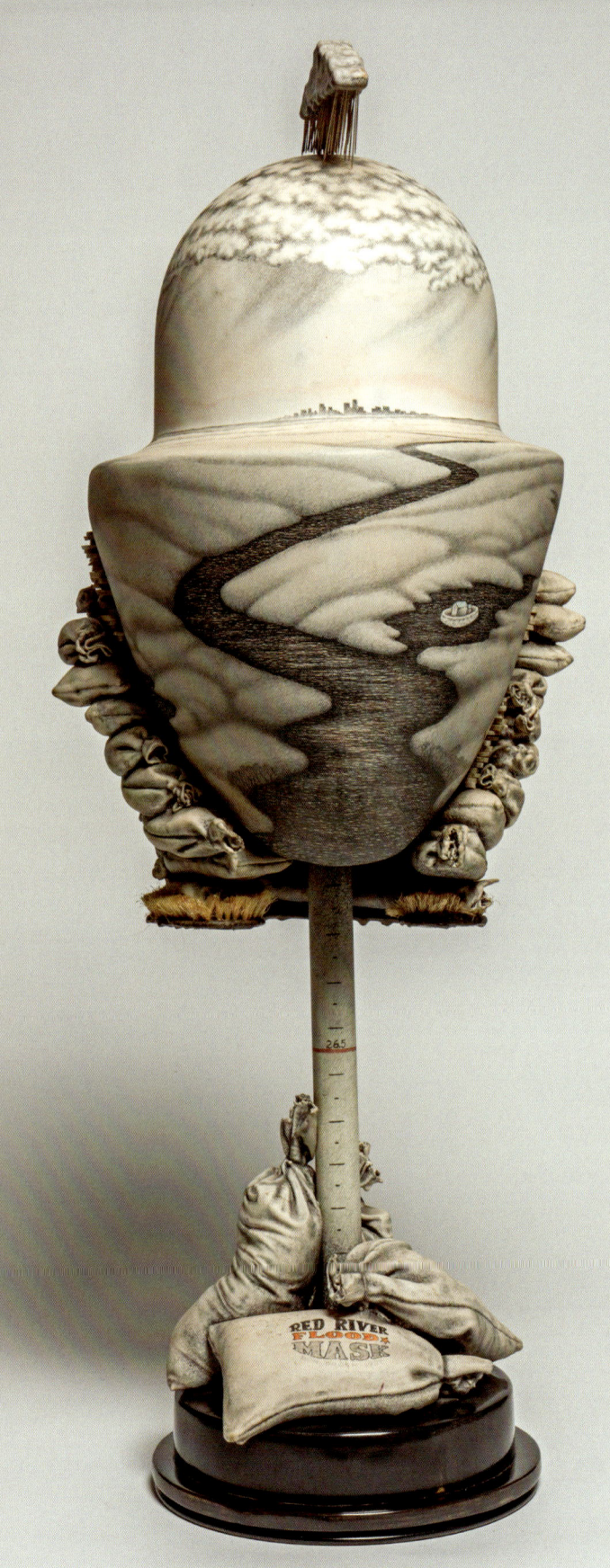

determined, and the perspective drawing for its landscape through the "barn doors" is sketched within.

The three-dimensional forms that Proch makes for drawing surfaces, in shapes reflecting his overall message, are built of fibreglass or wood. After sanding the form to a perfectly smooth finish, he draws in black and white, and in colour, with precision and dexterity, and appends elements related to his subject to the surface. As much as possible, Proch creates his sculptural forms outdoors during the summer because of the fibreglass particles and dust from sanding. He moves into the studio in the fall and winter to do the drawing and finishing.

Proch's masks, elevators, and later mappings and maskings show the evolution of his mature and unique visual language. Its precision was nascent in his student work. His characteristic, deliberate, and detailed tiny lines depict his microvision, which always merges into his macrovision. The layering of his surfaces and the various found materials that Proch uses—bones, polished and matte metals, grasses, twine, wire, and diverse objects from the farm—philosophically and symbolically deepen his message. His artistic evolution is clearly seen in his sketchbooks.

The visual thought process that Proch went through for *Red River Flood Mask* (1997), for instance, is particularly interesting. Recalling memories of recent catastrophes in Winnipeg, this work captures the largest flood of the century. Proch stacked many tiny sandbags around half the work, reminiscent of the millions of sandbags used to protect homes and buildings during the flood. The Red River flows through the other half of the work. Buildings in Winnipeg are depicted in the upper portion of the sculpture, and on the top Proch drew his characteristic stylized clouds and falling rain with piercing steel needles. The mask is mounted on a metal surveyor's pole complete with measurements to mark water levels. More sandbags are at the bottom of the pole. His notes and drawings for this work are precise, demonstrating the detail with

which Proch works out every aspect of a sculpture before he commences making it and the care in following his original concepts: "City skyline dark on top & hazy on horizon. Water very dark. Ring dike whitened. Color on roof of buildings. Light grey over entire landscape. Trees along riverbank in foreground. Reddish brown watercolor in foreground water. Turbulent sky along bottom of cloudbank." He continued with further sketches and notations on another page:

> Elevator closer on horizon line than distant city skyline. Horizon line above levels of bone and sandbag "dike."
>
> Ring dike around farm in "eye" area of mask.
>
> Cotton bags filled with cement, fibreglassed white and drawn on.
>
> Red stripe at 26.5 on surveying rod.
>
> Gradations noted on rod. Black fibreglass base on turntable.
>
> Sandbags supporting surveying rod.
>
> Title of mask on sandbag.
>
> Small separation between bags with chrome "water" running down in "eye" area of sandbag face. Sandbag shaded dark in area of other "eye."

Using an earlier iteration of the title for this work in his sketchbook, *Flood Plain Mask*, Proch began to work out its concept: "Sandbag base—ruler stem—cement centers. Edge of lake along rim of helmet. Ring dike from eye. Title and signature on sandbags (In print) Line all around Horizon. Bone below."

110. (OPPOSITE) *Red River Flood Mask*, 1997.

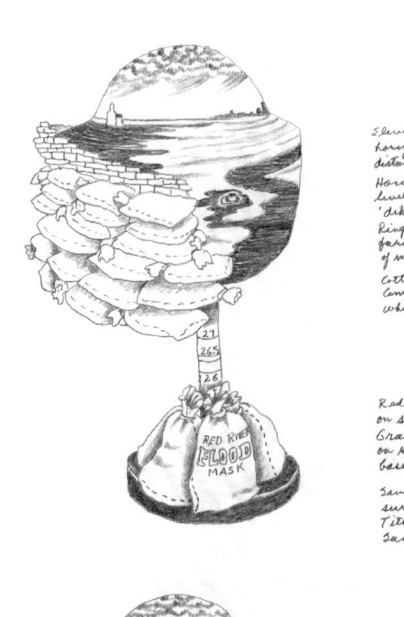

Elevator closer on
horizon line than
distant city skyline.
Horizon line above
level of base & Sandbag
'dike'.
Ring dikes around
farm in 'eye' area
of mask.
Cotton bags filled with
Cement, fiberglassed
white and drawn on.

Red Stripe at 26.5
on surveying rod.
Gradations noted
on rod. Black fiberglass
base on turntable.

Sandbags supporting
surveying rod.
Title of mask on
Sandbag.

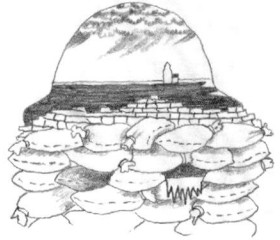

Small separation
between bags with
chrome 'water'
running down in
'eye' area of sandbag
faces. Sandbag Shaded
dark in area of other
'eye'.

Red River Flood Mask
Mask Проно - 1997

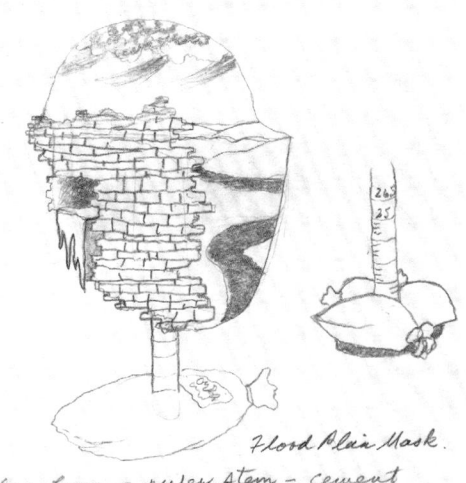

Flood Plain Mask.

Sandbag base - ruler stem - cement
Centers. Edge of lake along brim of
helmet.   Ring dike
farm-eye   Title &
Signature   on sandbags.
(Imprint)   line all around?
Horizon
(Boote below)

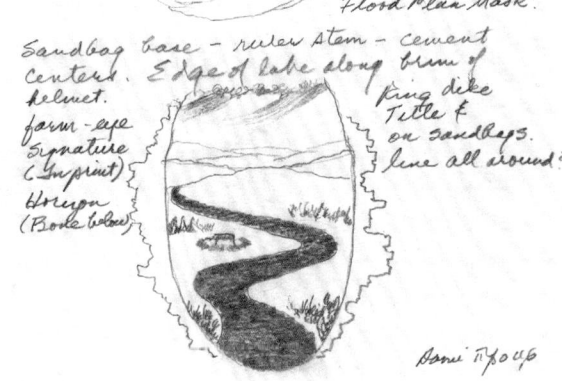

Dave Проно

111 and 112. Sketches for *Red River Flood Mask*, 1997.

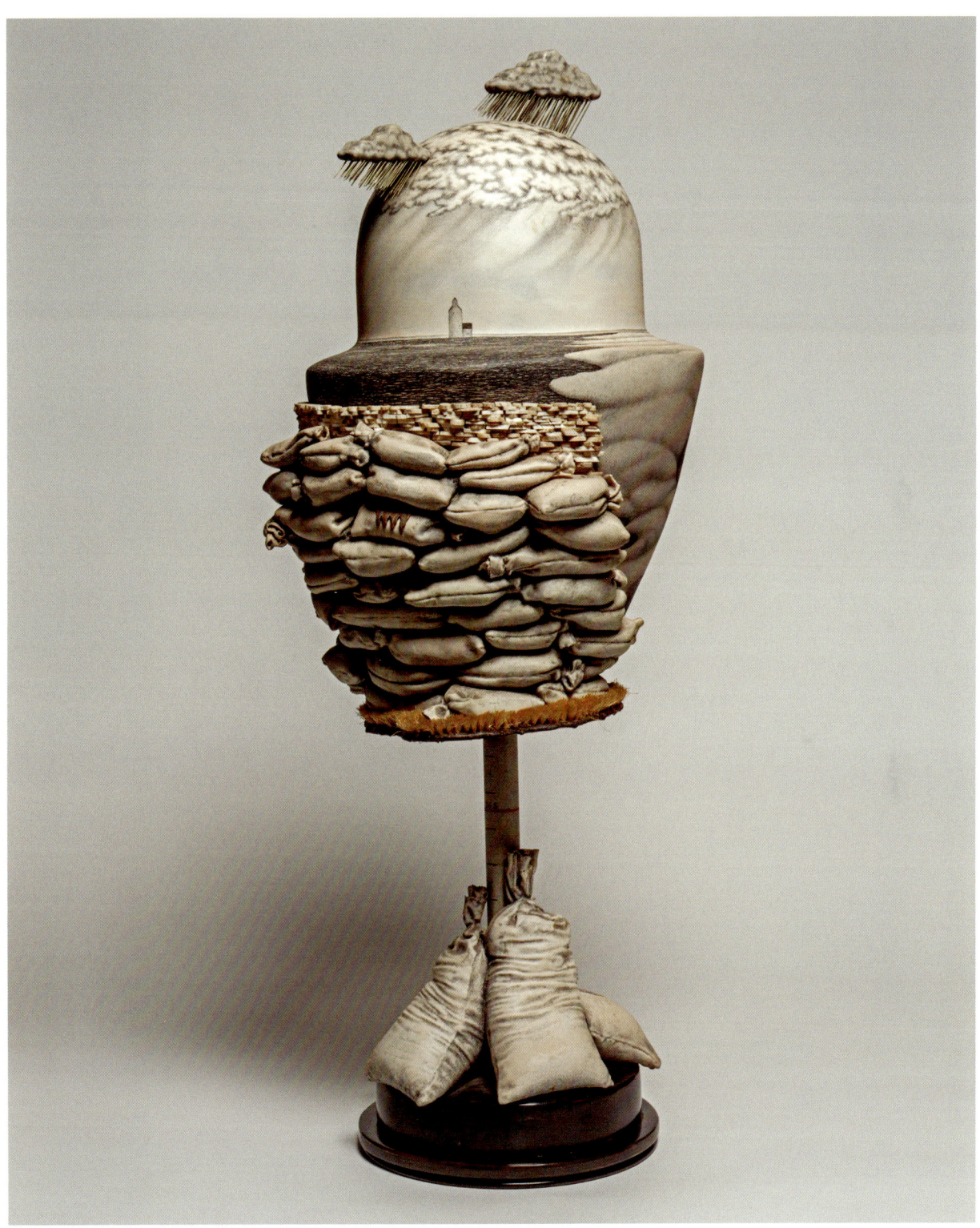

113. *Red River Flood Mask* (side view), 1997.

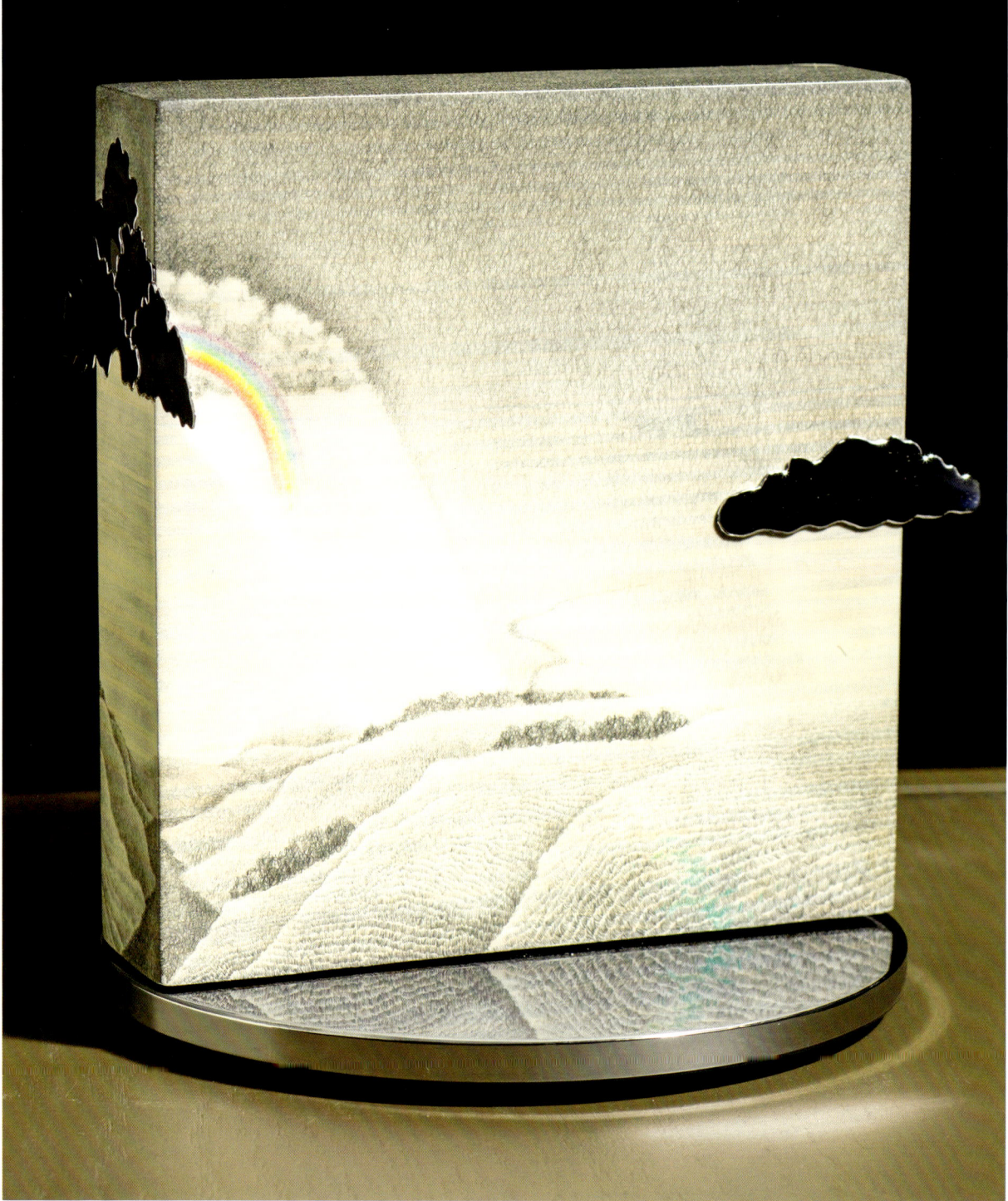

114. *Light Strata No. 5,* 1983.

Proch has incorporated reflective chrome elements in many of his works, including his works created on woodblocks, as well as his larger sculptures and masks. Beautiful and sophisticated, representing waterfalls and clouds, these chrome inserts project dual contrasting aspects of elegance and alarm. As the artist said, "I use a lot of high-tech stuff in my work because I want people to think about rural imagery fitting together with high-tech elements. In some of the block pieces I'm working on now I use a stereotypical prairie cloud shape, but it's coated in nickel oxide. We look out at [the] pretty cloud and we don't really know what it's carrying. So the recent pieces have an environmental concern."[86]

Having used reflective materials to great effect from the outset of his career, as seen in *Asessippi Tread* in 1970 and *Pincushion Man* in 1975, Proch also created reflective bases as turntables for many of his block pieces and some of his masks.

Light Strata No. 5 (1983), a pencil and coloured pencil work on wood, is one example, incorporating clouds fashioned with inlays of high-tech chrome on one side and on one edge of the piece. The formation of clouds on the end, pieced together like a puzzle, extends beyond that edge. A rainbow flows from one of the clouds. Proch's use of colour is again subtle and natural, and it echoes the rainbow above the horizon. In its exquisitely drawn rural landscape, repeated curves of the hills add to the depth and lyricism of the work; furrows intersect with the hills, setting up a visual counterpoint. The reflective chrome base adds to the three-dimensionality of the work. Proch prepared the surfaces for his woodblock works with the same fastidiousness as he did for his fibreglass pieces. The surfaces are perfectly smooth before he starts drawing. Proch began these block works because he liked the wood grain and "wanted to mix the natural grain of the wood with the kind of marks I made. The wood does influence the drawing. When you are drawing on it, you react to the way a particular grain goes."[87]

About the *Light Strata* series (1982–83), Proch wrote in some of his unpublished notes that

the "Light Strata" series is composed of drawing on wood with inlaid added materials (chromed copper, inlaid copper, neon light, nickel-plated chrome, and bone). The base for the drawing is layered laminated wood covered with a white translucent fibreglass that is sanded flat to form the drawing surface. Other materials are inlaid into parts of the drawing surface. The white fibreglass transforms the wood layer into a variety of hues of blues, greys, and purples that become part of the drawing, a strata of colour formed by materials and light.

The drawings create a feeling of light and atmosphere—directly in the drawing and indirectly in the materials used.[88]

111

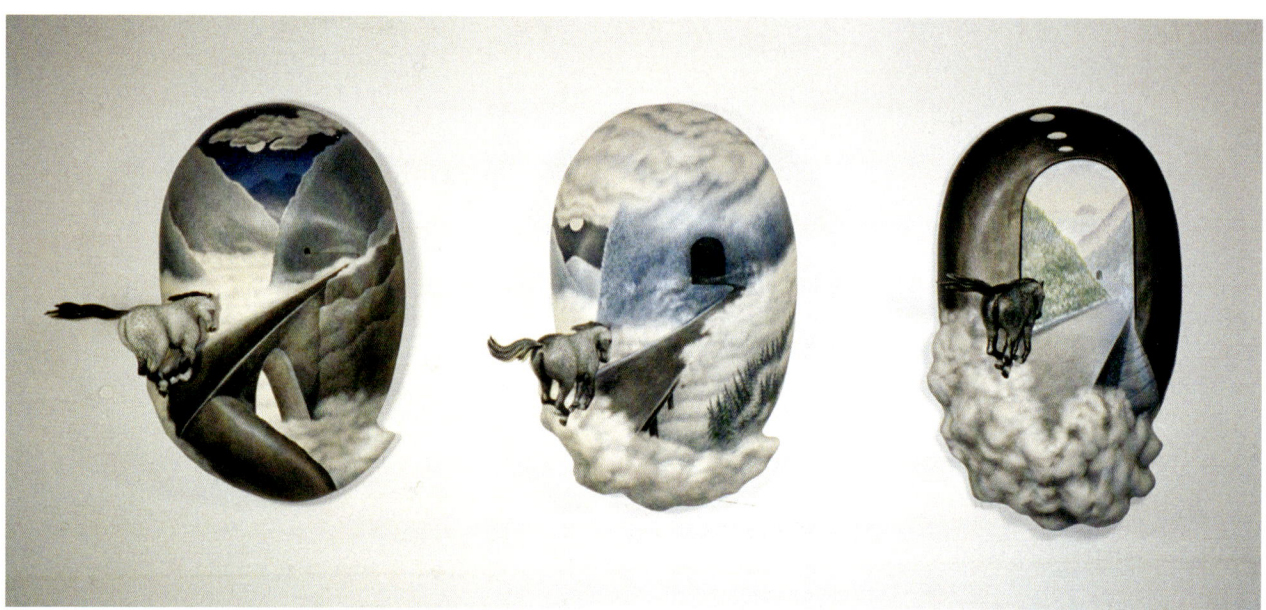

115. *The Journey (The Crossing, The Mist, The Sea)*, 1988.

116. (OPPOSITE) *The Journey* (detail), *The Crossing*, 1988.

117 and 118. (PAGES 114 AND 115) *The Journey* (detail), *The Mist, The Sea*, 1988.

Proch's transformations of specific images in different works become part of his storytelling. *The Journey* (1988) has three component parts: *The Crossing*, *The Mist*, and *The Sea*. In *The Mist*, the horse gallops over a bridge through the mist with trees below. In *The Sea*, the horse gallops along a highway, beside a forested mountain, like the Sea-to-Sky Highway in British Columbia. And in *The Crossing*, the horse gallops over a bridge above the clouds. Distinctive details of the bridge structure are revealed more in *The Crossing* than in *The Mist*, where the mist obscures most of the bridge itself. Is this the same horse that breaks free of the train in Colville's work to continue its journey across the country? Not surprisingly, Proch's sketchbooks and preliminary drawings include the horse for this triptych as well as the perspective and the overall compositional details of its landscape. The small bronzed horse hangs on a shelf in Proch's studio and it may feature again in future works.

Proch's technique is slow for both his two- and his three-dimensional works. Precision and texture, whether of bone, type, rolled necks of turtleneck sweaters, or metal, and carefully "built" components are evident throughout his oeuvre as Proch reclaims and transforms natural and functional objects. Sharp-pointed diagonals are repeated throughout his personal iconography. In *Prairie Sentinel* (1994), for instance, three clouds, in his stereotypical formation, float above and outside the central part of the work. Piercing the sky, sharp metal points extrude from elegant, soft cloud formations, echoing those drawn in the central portion of the work itself. These sharp protrusions, with their parallel lines of energy or force, recall the lines of force and motion of the early-twentieth-century Italian Futurists. The piercing energy of Proch's three-dimensional lines corresponds to that emanating from the rainbow in *Fire Fly*, his 1978 silkscreen print.

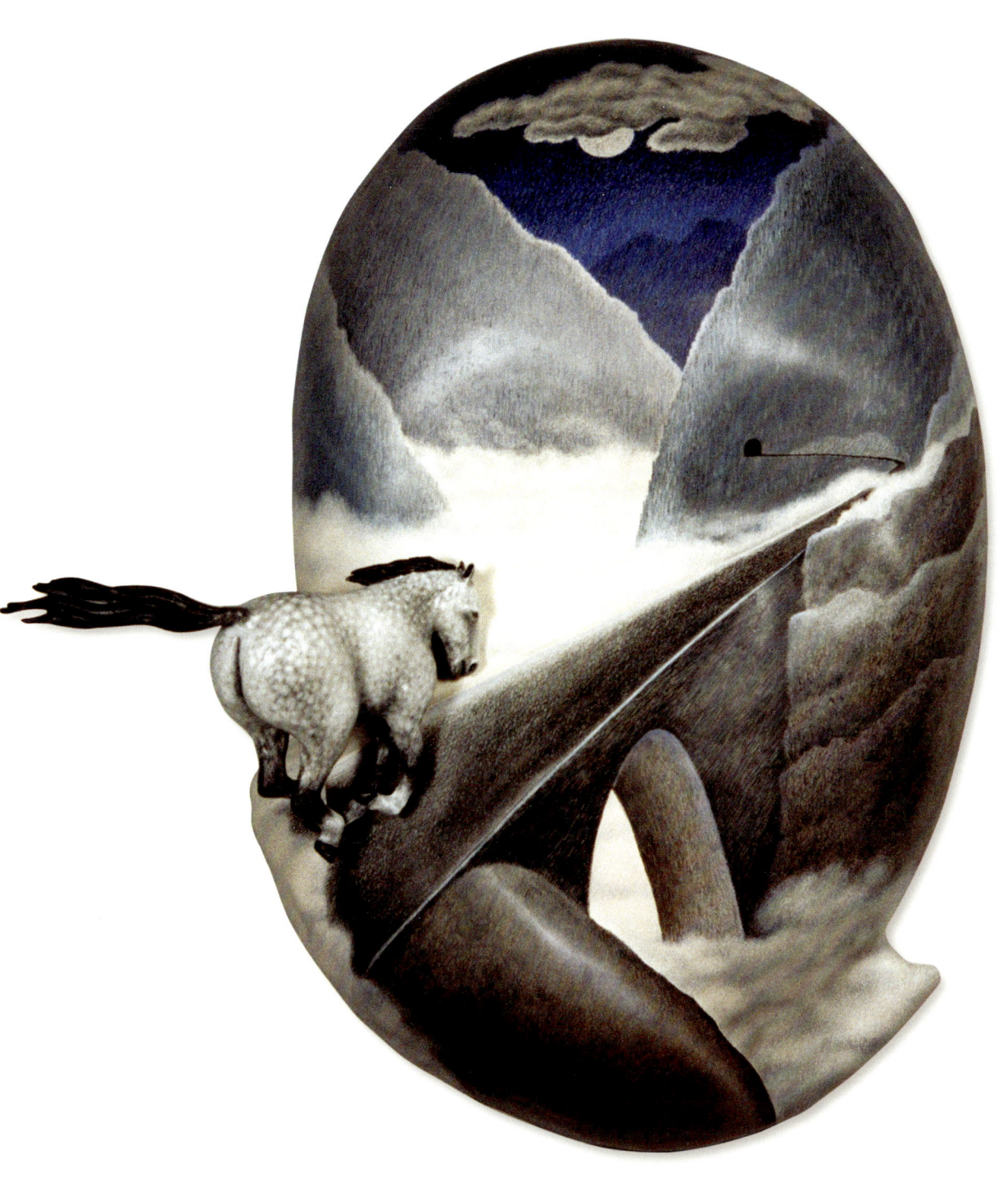

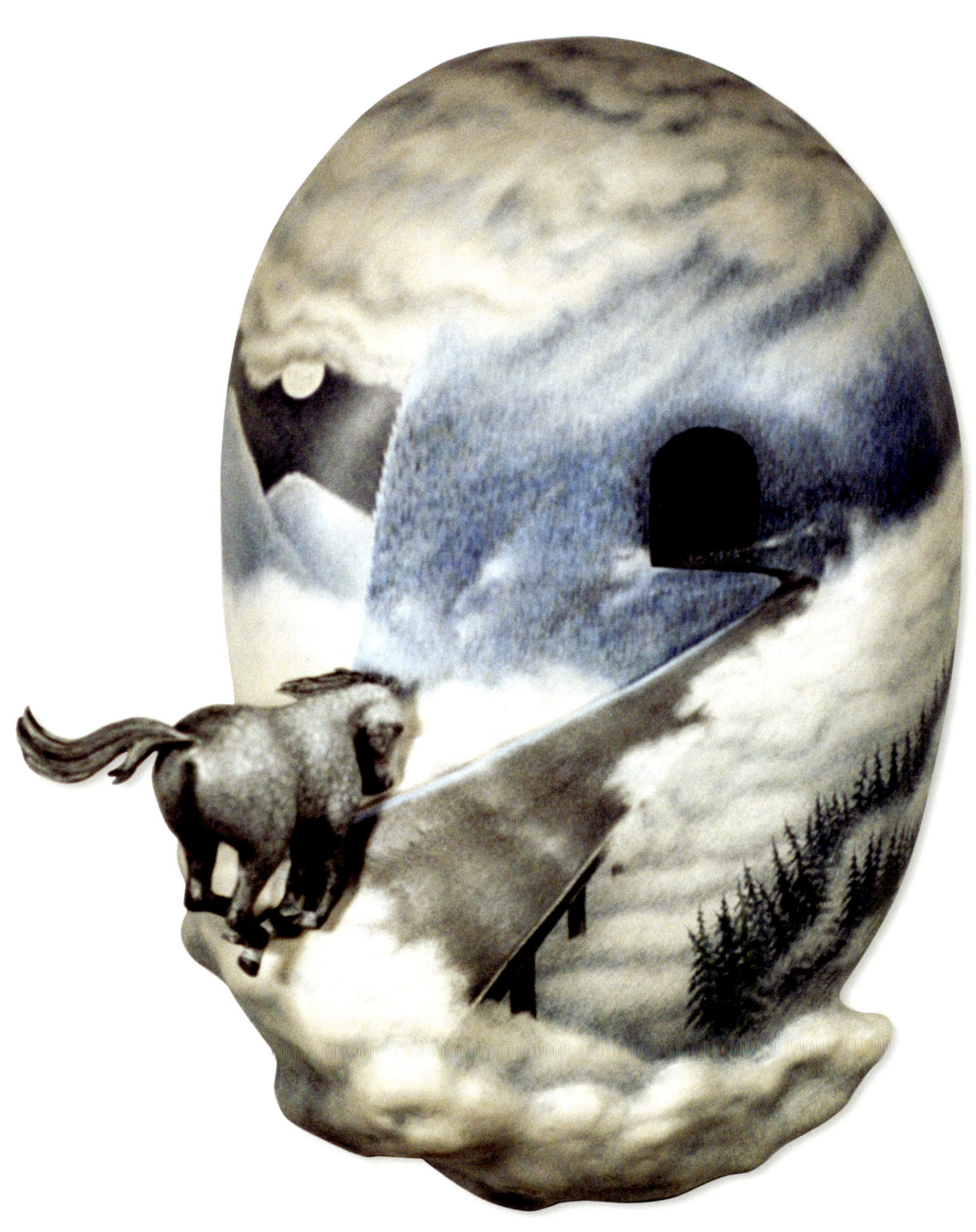

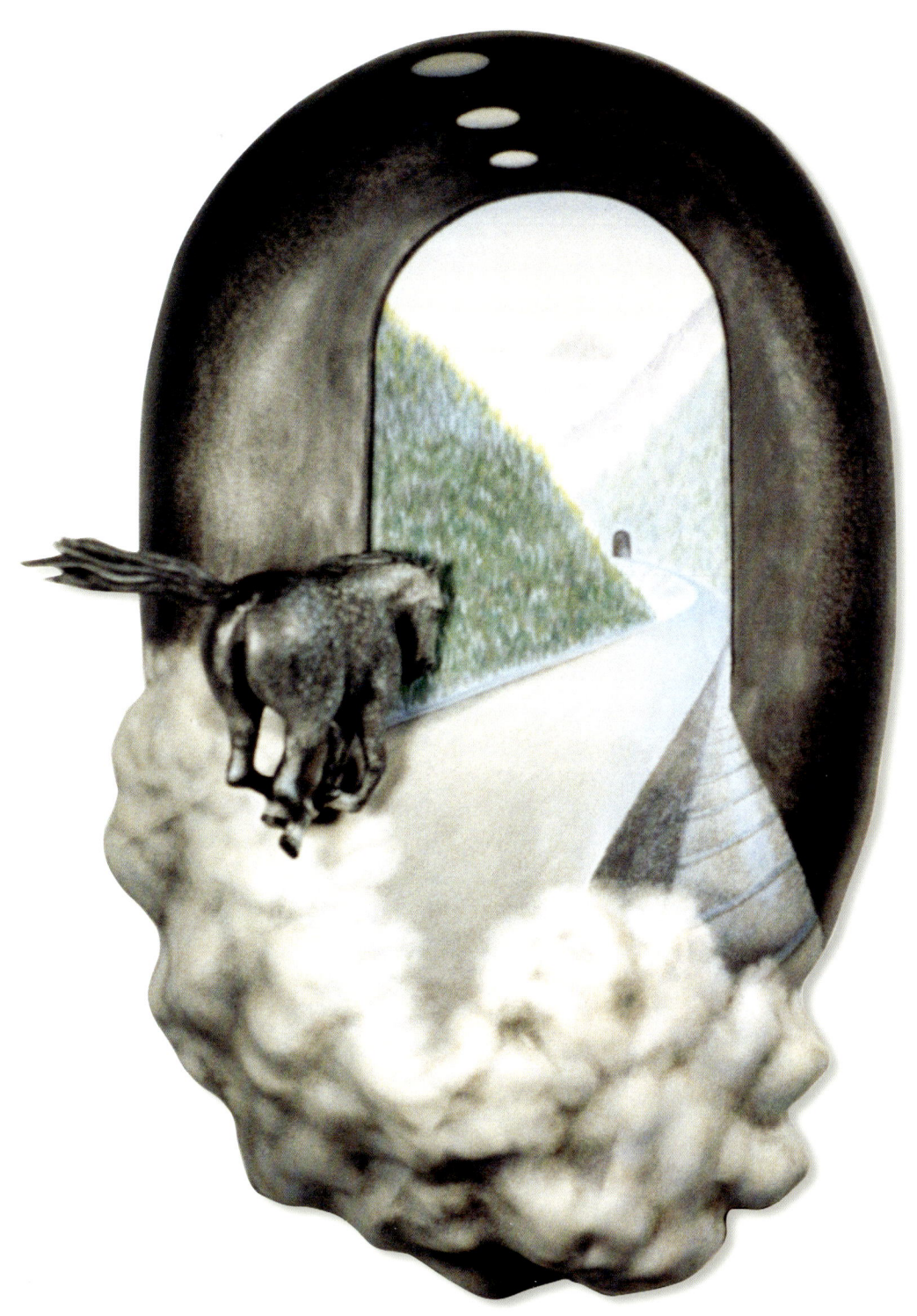

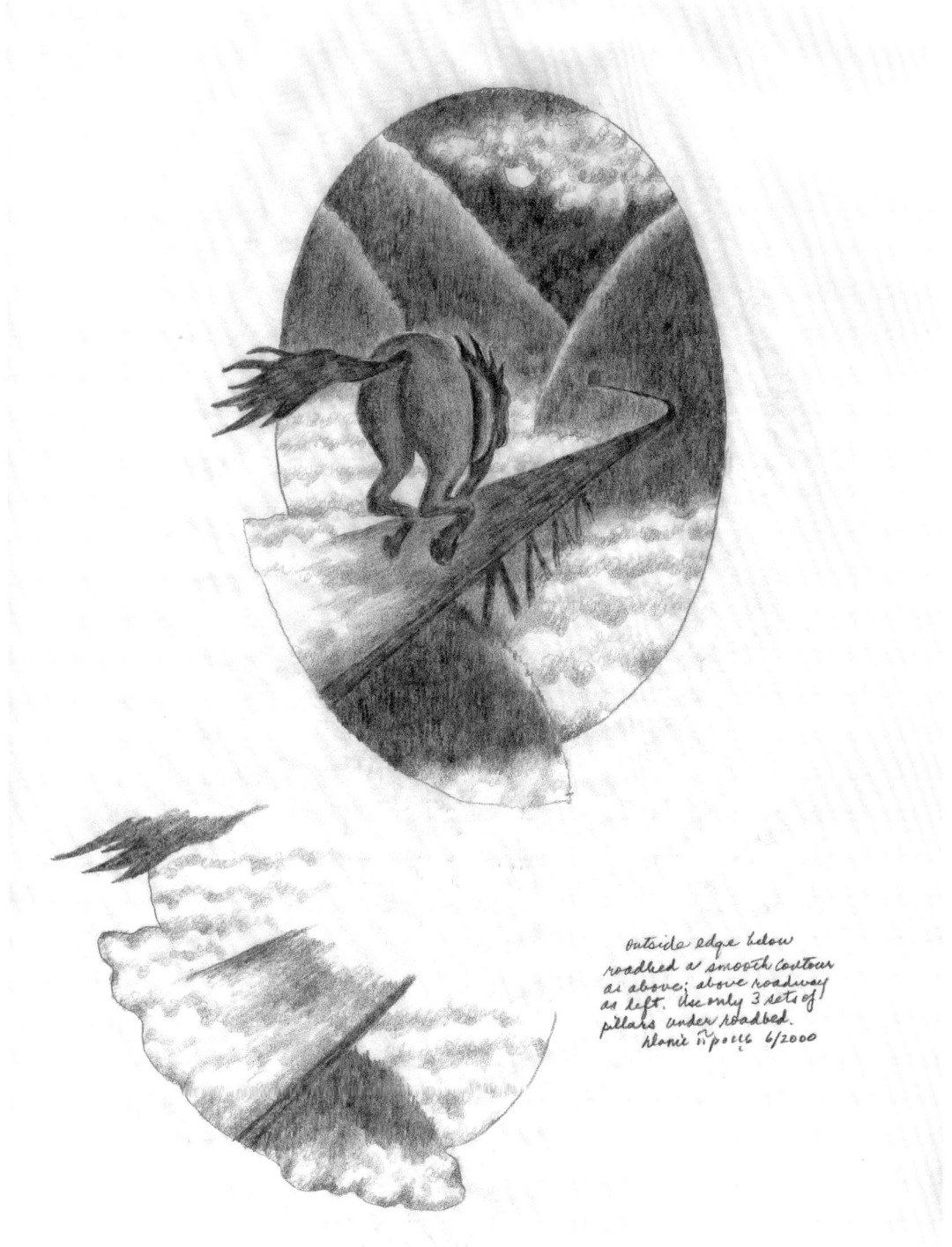

outside edge below
roadbed a smooth contour
as above; above roadway
as left. Use only 3 sets of
pillars under roadbed.
Alanie *πρειέ 6/2000

119. *The Journey*, drawing, 2000.

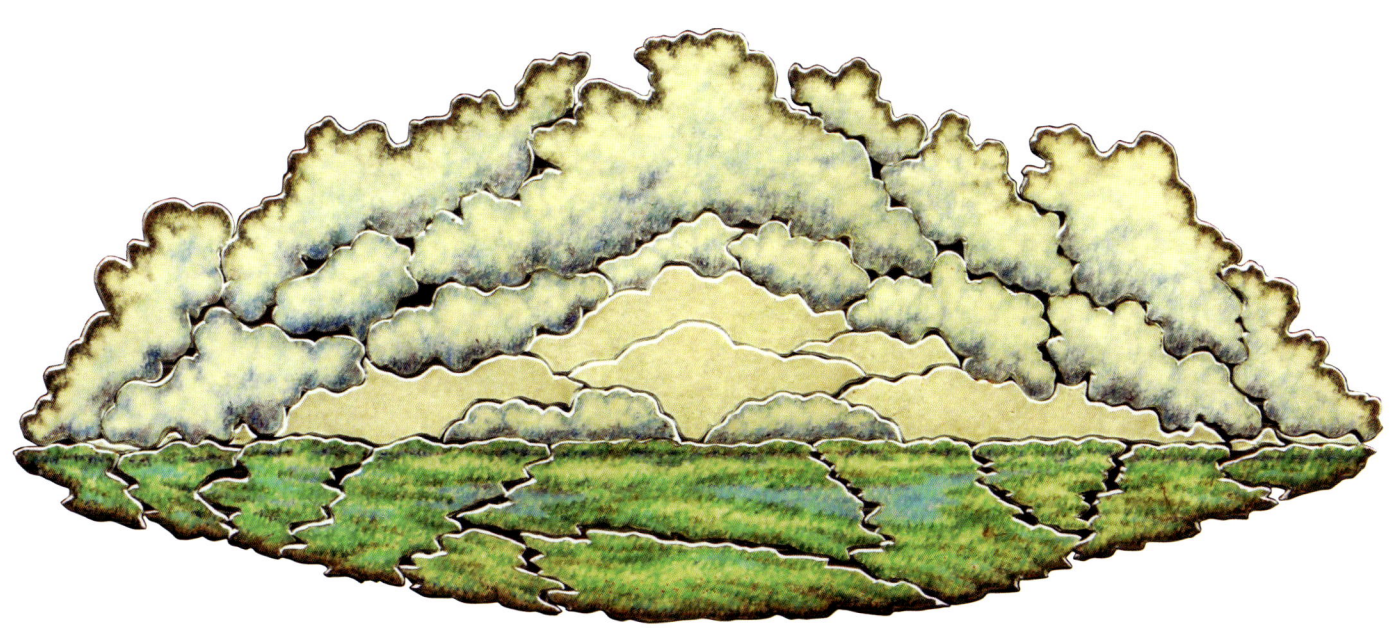

120. *Summersky*, 1982.

Proch opined that all the elements he added to his works "seem to have pointed ends on them. When I transform them I try to take away that end of it."[89] Robert Enright aptly elucidated that "there's always this pointed dialogue between the space above the horizon and the earth itself. The horizon is invariably the point of demarcation for that conflict."[90]

Proch's clouds are idiosyncratic, whether drawn, inlaid, sculpted, or appended. They are sensual at times, ominous at others. *Summersky* (1982), a twelve-foot, two-dimensional construction in the shape of a woman's lips, previews the shape that became Proch's iconic clouds. The landscape portrayed within the shape of *Summersky* is a simplified prairie cumulus cloud. Eroticizing the prairie, the horizon is the divide between the upper and lower lips. As for all of his works, Proch planned the composition in a preliminary drawing.

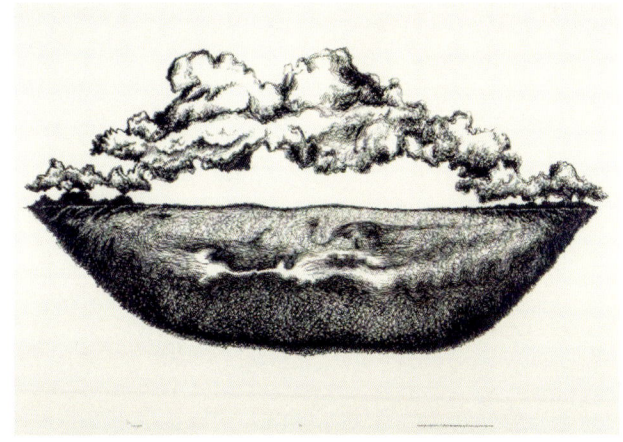

121. *Summerfield*, 1974.

Drawing: Pencil, Silverpoint, and Inlay

Proch's favourite medium is drawing, and drawings cover all his works—large installations, sculptures, masks, grain elevators, woodblocks, and fibreglassed board. Although most of his oeuvre is three-dimensional, Proch does not refer to himself as a sculptor: "I am not really a sculptor. I just draw on three-dimensional forms. I explore drawing." Of his process for his three-dimensional works, he says that "the construction is harsh, the drawing softening," and he reiterates the importance of drawing: "I stopped painting because I was not satisfied with them, so I felt I had to explore drawing more. It is the foundation of painting. I never returned to painting."[91] His drawings have always augmented the dichotomies of his messages, providing contrasts in each work between gentleness and toughness.

Red Wing (1998), a pencil and coloured pencil drawing on fibreglassed board, is a case in point, enhanced with nickel-plated copper, chrome, and black chrome on copper. Proch has combined a number of his "trademark" symbols in this work, such as the flowing golden Manitoba fields of grain, with a stream leading the viewer's eye toward the horizon. The vanishing point is cut off by a field. Ferns and grasses are in the foreground on both sides, and a red-winged blackbird is in the lower right. The seemingly serene scene is dominated by ominous clouds filling three-quarters of the composition. Off centre, within the moving parallels of his characteristic cloud formations, is a foreboding, stylized black cloud in chrome that emits dark lines of rain, the haunting negative presence of acid rain. Lightning erupts below. Sharp and dark threatening formations in the upper left enhance the sense of impending doom, threatening to disrupt the nostalgic tranquility of the scene below it. Such are the characteristic dichotomies in Proch's art.

The artist is quick to point out that his use of silverpoint, inspired by seeing a work by Picasso in New York, was learned in part from art history, though, as with other traditional media, Proch employs it in a truly contemporary way. He uses two methods of silverpoint. He draws with the end of a thin silver rod. He also draws with the edge of pure silver Canadian coins, either quarters or dimes made before 1967,[92] discovering this technique almost accidentally "when I dragged the side of a dime along the fibreglass surfaces. Its four ridges make four lines, and when you twist or turn the dime the lines become one. It has a good linear quality."[93] Each coin gave a different character to the drawing, the lines of a quarter being wider than those of a dime. Proch found that over time the colour of a silverpoint line changed as it oxidized, becoming softer, more like sepia, and increasing the contrast with his pencil lines and marks. He liked these changing effects and noted that the colour shift was even apparent where he had covered the lines with glaze.[94]

Proch's sensitively rendered colour also softens over time. Depth, light, and detail are conveyed with his subtle application of colour in his drawings. Proch almost caresses the surface with his pencil, sometimes applying colour on top of black and white. His precision in layering his colour produces his overall effect of delicacy, and the resulting fragile surface further reinforces his message.

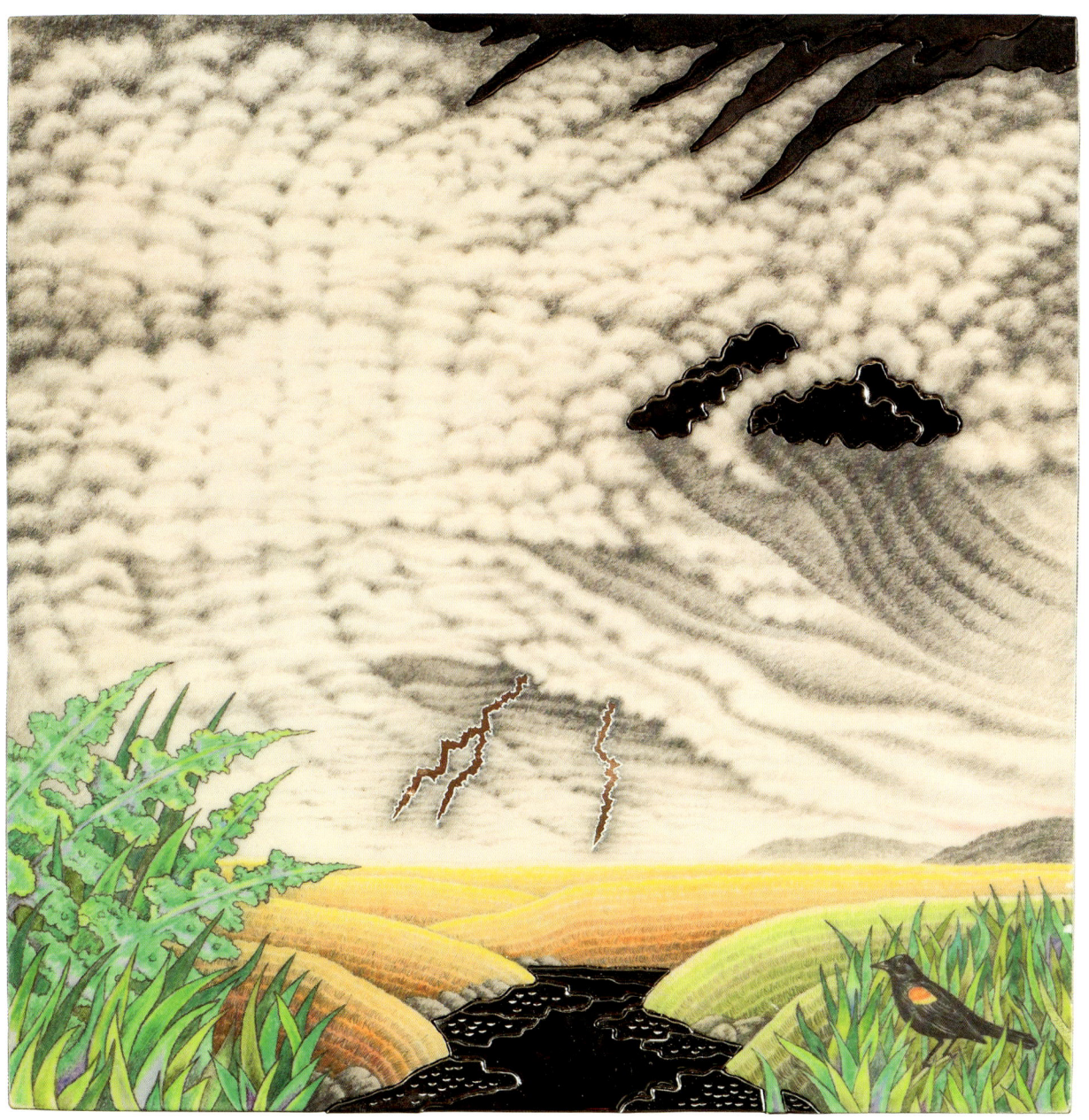

122. *Red Wing*, 1998.

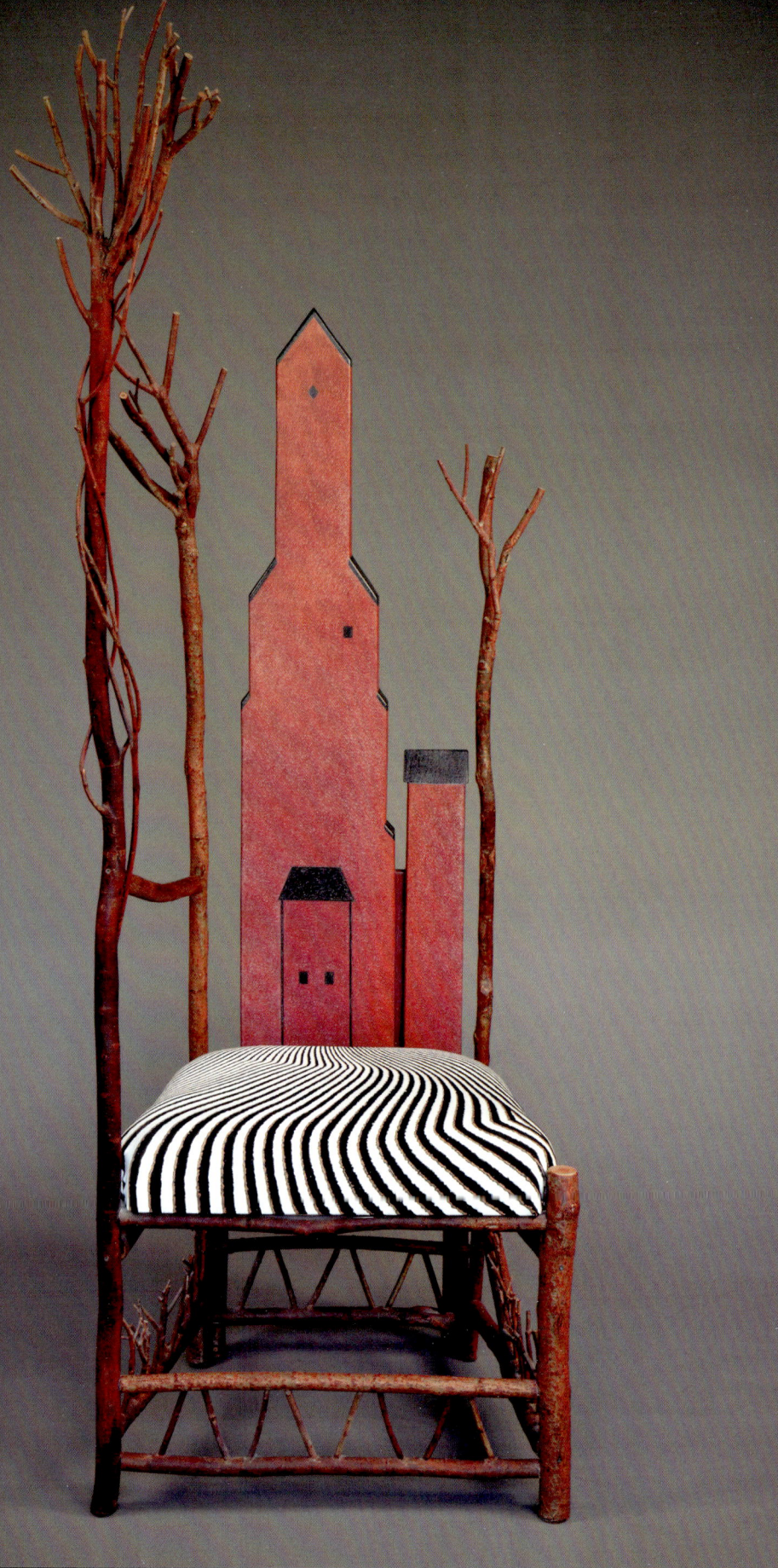

Epilogue: A Place Secure

THE 2008 SEATTLE FORUM on Public Art defined artists as "interpreters, translating themes from the world around us; a lens through which we can view, connect with and understand our own deeper feelings, fears and desires." The report for that forum concluded with the statement that "art makes it safe for us to come into contact with the wild, with our own playfulness. . . . Vibrancy in our community is a modulation between the wild and the ordered."[95]

Don Proch's work, in every medium, from his first installations in the 1970s to his stand-alone works of the twenty-first century, effectively mediates that tension between the natural world and the built environment. Proch gives his viewers a clear lens. His ordered and thoughtful works translate and connect the issues that consume him with those who engage with his art. The "wild" in his work portends environmental crisis. For decades, his evolving ideas have stretched traditional aesthetic norms as Proch has continued to incorporate new materials alongside old ones, such as combining silverpoint and pencil with high-tech chrome and oxides. His layering of his unique technical and iconographical dimensions evoke disquieting and seductive psychological impacts, at once beautiful and dissonant. His prairie values are clear as he mixes well-known traditions with the impending uncertain future.

Proch's art substantiates the inherent qualities of the world's most serious artists. His message is compelling. His unique creations of masks, grain elevators, paintings, prints, and drawings are intimate in presentation and simultaneously macro in scope, depth, and presence. This constant experimenter has consistently mixed new materials with old ones, farming materials with natural ones. Proch achieves deliberate, sensitive surfaces with contrasting textures and delicate and fastidious colouration. Each is rendered with technical perfection and precision—from the sanding of fibreglass or wood surfaces prior to drawing, to the polishing of chrome elements or the insertions of pieces of type or bone at varying depths. Every step is executed with particular care; his drawing is done with exactitude. Colours and the external and inlaid elements are specifically chosen to add substance and meaning.

123. *Elevator Chair*, 1990.

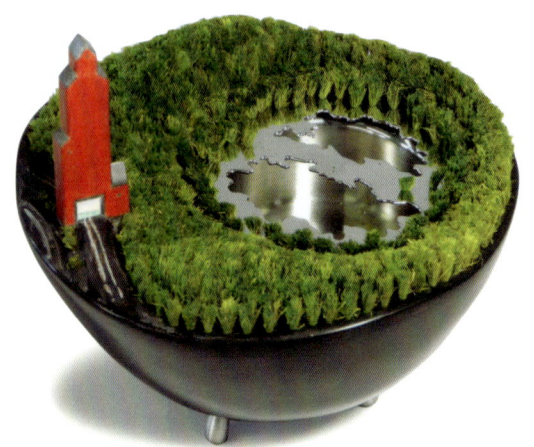

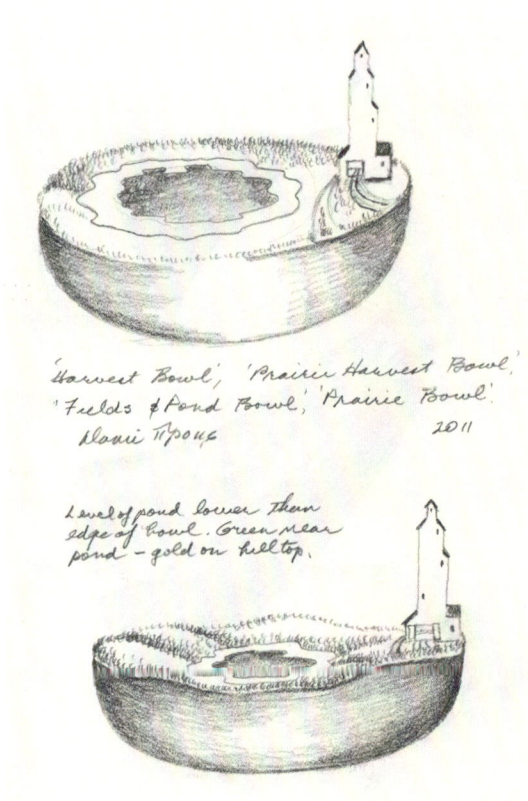

124. *Prairie Harvest Bowl*, 2011.

125. Sketch for *Prairie Harvest Bowl*, 2011.

Proch's research is precise; the detailed accuracy in his preliminary sketches and drawings is critical. Iconographical elements such as shifting horizons, skies, and landscapes interface with humanity, nature, and recurring prairie icons. His themes, materials, aesthetic approaches, and psychological depths have evolved over the years. His multi-layered sources—both conscious and unconscious— project contemporary societal concerns with honesty and integrity.

Proch's keen sense of humour is also obvious. His sculpture *Elevator Chair* (1990) has a grain elevator as its back; branches make up vertical extensions higher than the chair back on three of its four legs. Black-and-white patterns in the fabric on the seat are like furrows in a field in winter. The humour of *Prairie Harvest Bowl* (2011), a three-legged bowl 25 centimetres in diameter, also has a serious element. The bowl contains a lake, grasses, and a grain elevator, with a road running to it but not through it. The drive-through is blocked by a waterscape. The lake, in polished nickel-plated chrome, is contrasted in several parts, separated and surrounded by matte chrome. Once again Proch has balanced the wonder of nature with the devastation of climate change and pollution and, perhaps, the human hand in the damming of rivers, especially those in the West.

Unique in Canadian art as a whole, Proch's vision is particular, and his message is constant. Juxtaposing past and future societal concerns, farm and city, industry and "the hand," Proch has not been afraid to address the devastating effects of environmental pollution and climate change—flooding, acid rain, and severe storms. He clearly understands his audiences as he shares his observations, philosophy, and regional history. His means of expression and his visual approaches are his own, filled with his self-developed methods and images. Proch has had work in exhibitions in many parts of the world. Unfortunately, however, mounting a major retrospective of his art is virtually impossible given the fragility of his art and the many disparate public, private, and corporate collections in which he is represented.

Proch stands alone as a visionary and conscience for the prairies.

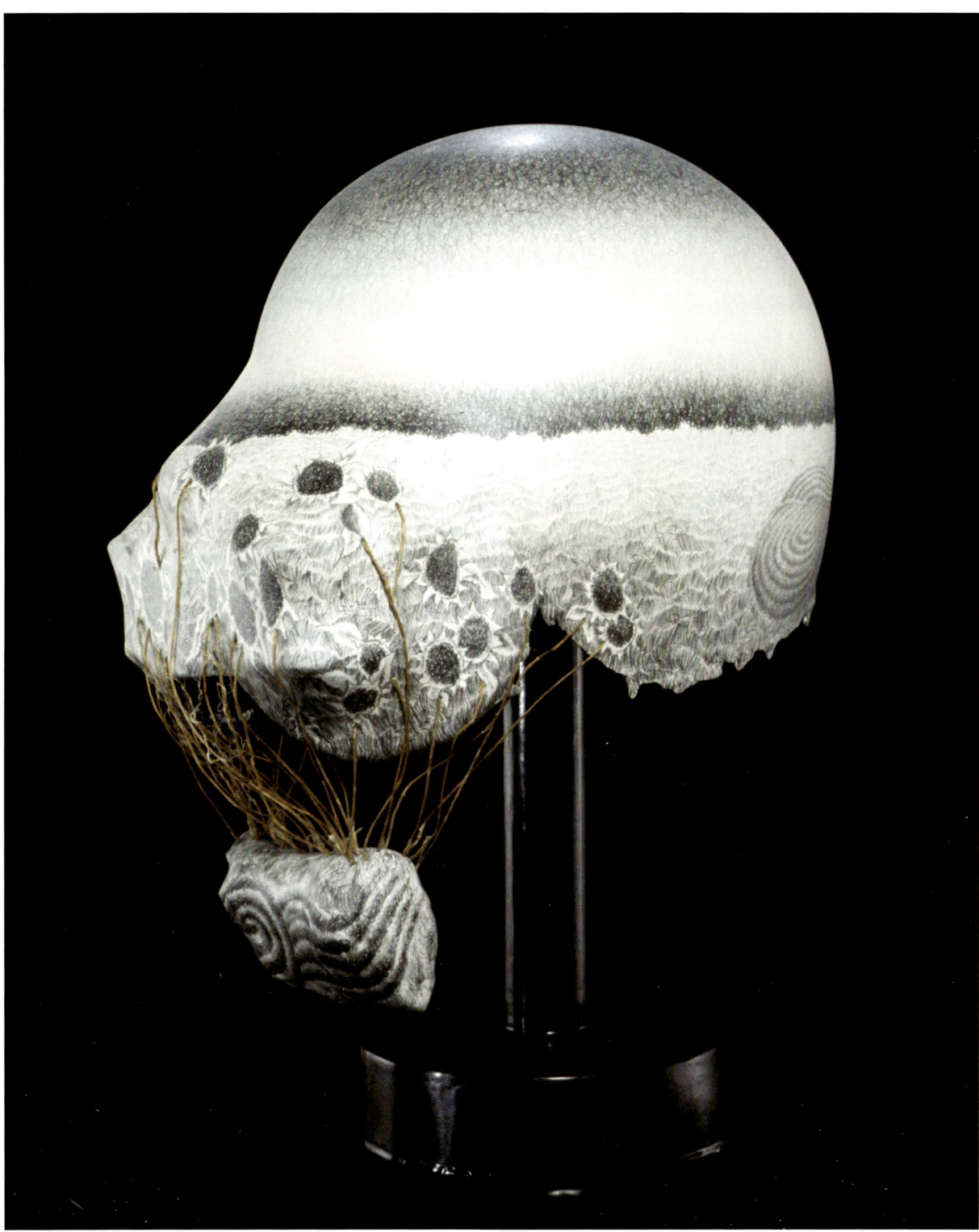

123

126. *Sunflower Shade Mask*, 1975.

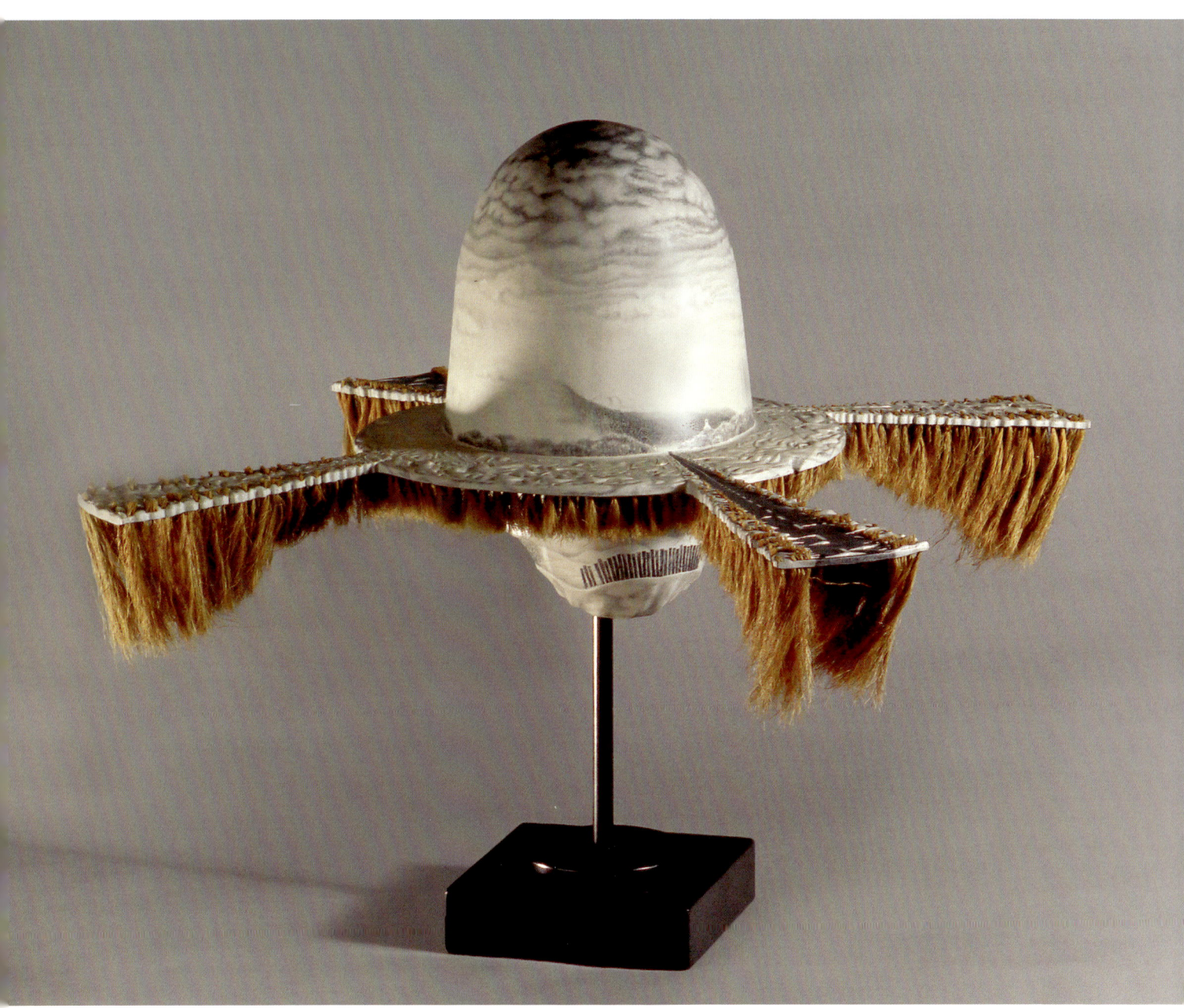

127. *No. 1 West Mask,* 1980.

ACKNOWLEDGEMENTS

A PROJECT SUCH AS authoring *Don Proch: Masking and Mapping* is a significant honour. Having followed this Manitoba artist's work over many decades, it has been an enriching experience to write about it and to spend hours with Don in his studio, researching images and sketchbooks, and fielding ideas about his work. I thank him for the opportunity to collaborate with him on this book. May it bring the depth, power, and sensitivity of his art to many.

My thanks also go to David Carr of the University of Manitoba Press, editor Glenn Bergen, and designer Frank Reimer, whose insights into Proch's work translated into this handsome volume.

Thanks go to all the owners of Don Proch's work for sharing them as they have through the reproductions included in the book. Collectors of his work are found from coast to coast, and internationally, and the works are in public, corporate, and private collections. Special appreciation goes to Andrew Kear and Nicole Fletcher of the Winnipeg Art Gallery and to the Buhler Gallery at St. Boniface Hospital.

Particular thanks go to the photographers who have captured Don Proch's work on film and in digital format, especially Ernest P. Mayer, who for many years has taken images of the work as it was completed. He has painstakingly recovered and digitized negatives and slides contemporary to the actual works. Alan McTavish, Ted Howorth, Leif Norman, and Don Hall have also taken images contained on these pages.

I also want to express my sincere gratitude to Sarah Yates for her advice on the text through its drafting stages. Thanks, too, go to all those who have written about Don Proch's work over the decades. Each has added immeasurably to our understanding of this innovative visionary and conscience for the prairies.

Patricia Bovey, FRSA, FCMA
December 2018

CHRONOLOGY

1964 Bachelor of Fine Arts, University of Manitoba

1966 Bachelor of Education, University of Manitoba

Awards and Exhibitions

1970s

Awards

1970 Purchase Award, Twelfth Winnipeg Show

Canada Council for the Arts Project Grant

1972–73 Canada Council for the Arts Grant

1973–74 Canada Council for the Arts Grant

1974–75 Canada Council for the Arts Grant

1975–76 Manitoba Arts Council Senior Arts Grant

1976–77 Manitoba Arts Council Senior Arts Grant

1978 Manitoba Arts Council Grant

1979 Canada Council Project Grant

Exhibitions

1970 *Twelfth Winnipeg Show*, Winnipeg Art Gallery

1972 *The Legend of Asessippi* (solo exhibition),
Winnipeg Art Gallery

1973 *Canada Trajectories*, Musée d'art moderne, Paris

Manitoba Mainstream, National Gallery of Canada, Ottawa

1974 *Western Canadian Painting*, Saidye Bronfman
Centre for the Arts, Montreal

1975 *Don Proch's Asessippi Clouds* (solo exhibition),
Winnipeg Art Gallery

Changing Visions: The Canadian Landscape,
Edmonton Art Gallery; Art Gallery of Ontario, Toronto

1976 *Western Untitled*, Glenbow Alberta Institute, Calgary

1977 *Don Proch* (solo exhibition), Musée d'art contemporain,
Montreal; Art Gallery of Windsor; Southern Alberta Art Institute,
Lethbridge

Sculpture on the Prairies, Winnipeg Art Gallery

The Screen Shop, Canadian Cultural Centre, Paris

1978 *Obsessions, Rituals, Controls*, Norman MacKenzie Art Gallery,
Regina

Artists, Prints, and Multiples, Winnipeg Art Gallery

1979 *The Canadian Landscape*, Art Gallery of Greater Victoria

Contemporary Canadian Prints, National Gallery of Canada,
Ottawa

1980s

Awards

1980 Manitoba Arts Council Senior Arts Grant

1985–86 Manitoba Arts Council Senior Arts Grant

1987–88 Canada Council for the Arts A Grant

Exhibitions

1980 *Works from the Canada Council Art Bank Collection*, Nabisco
Cultural Centre, New Jersey

Pluralities/1980/Pluralities, National Gallery of Canada, Ottawa

1981 *Winnipeg Perspective*, Winnipeg Art Gallery

1984 *Manitoba Artists Overseas*, Canada House, London, UK;
Canadian Cultural Centre, Brussels

1985 *Manitoba Artists Overseas*, Canadian Cultural Centre, Paris

Chicago International Art Exposition, Chicago

1986 *Los Angeles International Art Exposition*, Los Angeles

1987 *True North*, University of the Pacific Gallery,
Stockton, California

1988 *True North*, San Francisco State University Gallery

1989 *Political Landscapes #1*, Royal Academy of Arts, Toronto; Tom
Thomson Memorial Gallery, Owen Sound, ON; Billboard Art,
South Wall, Owen Sound, ON

Chicago International Art Exposition, Chicago

1990s

Exhibitions

1996 *Prairie Theism*, Winnipeg Art Gallery

1996–97 *The Electrified Collection*, Winnipeg Art Gallery

1997 *Drawing the Line*, Winnipeg Art Gallery

The Royal Canadian Academy of Arts Prairie Region Exhibition,
Winnipeg Art Gallery

1997–98 *Grainscapes*, Oseredok Ukrainian Cultural and Educational
Centre, Winnipeg

1998 *Breaking the Line: When Is a Drawing Not a Drawing?*, Winnipeg
Art Gallery

The Royal Canadian Academy of Arts Prairie Region Exhibition,
Norman MacKenzie Art Gallery, Regina

The City as A Memory, Chicago Atheneum

2000s Forward

Exhibitions

1990–2002 *Spring and Fall Exhibitions*, Douglas Udell Gallery,
Vancouver and Edmonton

2001 *Curieux univers*, University of Montreal Gallery

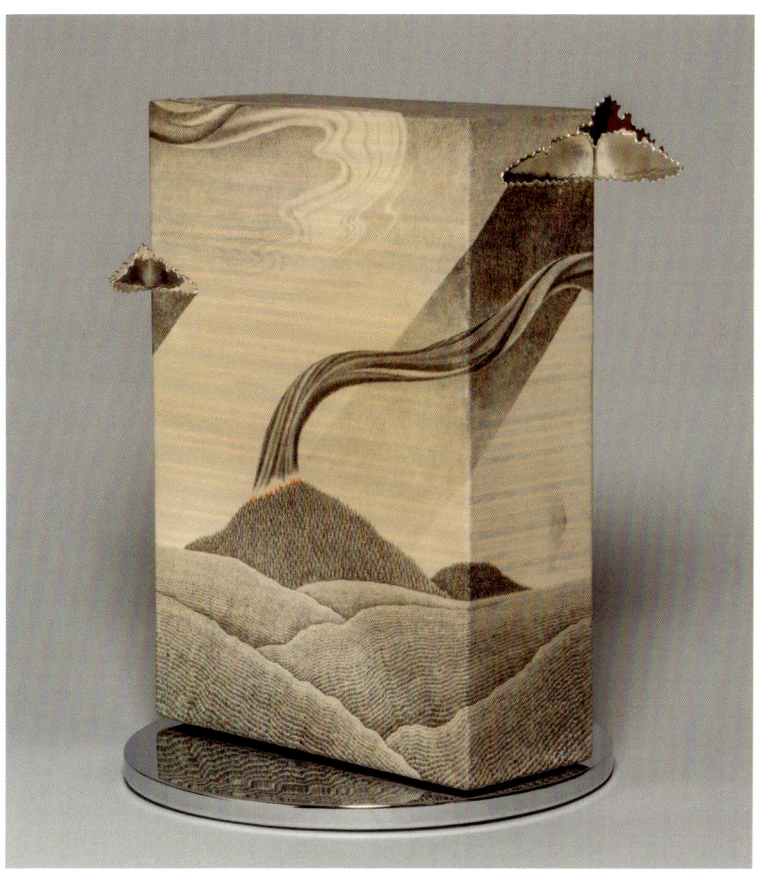

128. *Distant Fire*, 1985.

2002, 2003 *Toronto International Art Expo*, Toronto

2009 *Flight Dreams*, Art Gallery of Nova Scotia, Halifax

2002–present *Annual exhibitions*, Mayberry Fine Art, Winnipeg and Toronto

2015 *Manitoba Insights: The Ken Hughes Gift*, Buhler Gallery, St. Boniface Hospital, Winnipeg

2017 *Visual Celebrations II*, Buhler Gallery, St. Boniface Hospital, Winnipeg

2018 *Screening the 70s*, Buhler Gallery, St. Boniface Hospital, Winnipeg

Selected Public and Corporate Collections

Art Gallery of Ontario, Toronto

Art News Collections, New York

Bronfman Collection, Montreal

Buhler Gallery, St. Boniface Hospital, Winnipeg

Canada Council Art Bank, Ottawa

CIL Collection, Toronto

Crown Life Insurance Company, Toronto

Exxon Collection, Calgary

Glenbow Alberta Institute, Calgary

Manitoba Telephone, Winnipeg

Mississauga Public Library, Mississauga

National Gallery of Canada, Ottawa

Norman MacKenzie Art Gallery, Regina

Power Corporation

Province of Manitoba Art Collection

Richardson Foundation Collection, Winnipeg and Toronto

Royal Bank of Canada, Winnipeg

Scarborough College, University of Toronto

Shell Canada Collections, Calgary

Shelter Corporation, Winnipeg

University of Manitoba, School of Art Collection, Winnipeg

University of Saskatchewan, Saskatoon

University of Winnipeg

Vancouver Art Gallery

Winnipeg Art Gallery

Winnipeg Convention Centre

LIST OF ILLUSTRATIONS

1. Don Proch beside *Pincushion Man*, 1975. Photo by Ernest Mayer.

2. Hockey Game: Manitoba vs. Saskatchewan, c. 1975, in Regina. Back row, left to right: Don Proch, Joe Fafard. Middle row: Russ Yuristy, David Thauberger, Bill Lobchuk. Front: Tony Tascona. Photo by Don Hall.

3. Don Proch's paternal grandparents, Mary and George Proch.

4. Don Proch's maternal grandparents, Mary and Luke Burtnyk, Ethelbert, Manitoba.

5. Don Dudar and Don Proch, 1950.

6. Don Proch's mother, Nastya (Nellie) Proch, c. 1940.

7. Don Proch's father, Don Proch Sr., in the late 1930s in Hamilton.

8. *School of Art*, 1961, pen and ink on paper, 35.6 x 50.8 cm. Collection of the artist.

9. Don Proch, 1962, studio on Hargrave Street, Winnipeg.

10. *Dick Williams' Print Studio*, 1962, pen and ink on paper, 30.48 x 45.72 cm. Collection of the artist.

11. *A & W*, 1964, oil on canvas, 122 x 122 cm. Collection of the artist.

12. The Grand Western Canadian Screen Shop on Princess Street. Photo by Ted Howorth.

13. *Granite I*, 1979, silkscreen, 65/100, 20.3 x 61 cm. Collection of St. John's College. Photo by Ernest Mayer.

14. Stewart MacPherson (left), Don Proch, and Don Proch Sr. (right), at Stewart's Shop, Roseisle, Manitoba, 1978.

15. Don Proch assembling *Motria's Hair*, 1971, at his studio on Princess Street. Photo by Ernest Mayer.

16. Don Proch in the Asessippi Valley, c. 1978. Photo by Ernest Mayer.

17. *Paterson Elevator*, 1954, oil on canvas, 35.56 x 30.48 cm. Collection of the artist.

18. *Asessippi Tread*, 1970, silverpoint, graphite, fibreglass, wood, steel, 42.5 x 84.5 x 197 cm. Collection of the Winnipeg Art Gallery. Photo by Ernest Mayer.

19. *Asessippi Tread* (detail), 1970. Collection of the Winnipeg Art Gallery. Photo by Ernest Mayer.

20. *Asessippi Tread* (detail), 1970. Collection of the Winnipeg Art Gallery. Photo by Ernest Mayer.

21. *Asessippi Tread* (side view), 1970. Collection of the Winnipeg Art Gallery. Photo by Ernest Mayer.

22. *Motria's Hair*, 1972, wood, gesso, silverpoint, graphite, chrome, steel, fibreglass, hay, 57 x 170 x 26 cm. Collection of the Winnipeg Art Gallery. Photo by Ernest Mayer.

23. Don Proch and Glen Tinley on the coast of Portugal. Photo by Ted Howorth.

24. *Asessippi Retread*, 1978, silkscreen print, 23.5 x 63.5 cm. Collection of the Winnipeg Art Gallery. Photo by Ernest Mayer.

25. Don Proch and Don Proch Sr. working on *Velocipede* in the workshop, 1976. Photo by Cal Bailey.

26. Don Proch and Don Proch Sr. working on *Velocipede* in the workshop, 1976. Photo by Cal Bailey.

27. *Velocipede*, 1976, silverpoint, coloured pencil and graphite on chromed steel, stainless steel, and mirrored plexiglass construction, 2,243.8 x 152.4. x 121.9 cm. Collection of the Canada Council Art Bank. Photo by Ernest Mayer.

28. *Legend of Asessippi* Exhibition Installation, 1972. Photo by Ernest Mayer.

29. *Legend of Asessippi* Exhibition Installation, 1972. Photo by Ernest Mayer.

30. *Legend of Asessippi* Exhibition Installation, 1972. Photo by Ernest Mayer.

31. *Chicken Block*, 1972, site-specific installation at the Winnipeg Art Gallery, 701 x 1,524 x 45.7 cm. Photo by Ernest Mayer.

32. Constructing *Chicken Block*.

33. Don, and Steve Chachula of Inglis, Manitoba, working towards Don's 1972 WAG exhibition, *The Legend of Asessippi*. Photo by Ernest Mayer.

34. *Pincushion Man (Wearing Brushcut, Listening for Buffalo Mask)*, 1975, fibreglass, gesso, graphite, plexiglass, chrome, neon tubes, plastic, 80 x 488 x 244 cm. Collection of Winnipeg Art Gallery. Photo by Ernest Mayer.

35. Studies for *Pincushion Man*, 1975, pencil on paper. Collection of the Winnipeg Art Gallery. Photo by Ernest Mayer.

36. Studies for *Pincushion Man*, 1975, pencil on paper. Collection of the Winnipeg Art Gallery. Photo by Ernest Mayer.

37. Studies for *Pincushion Man*, 1974, pencil on paper. Collection of the Winnipeg Art Gallery. Photo by Ernest Mayer.

38. *Asessippi Laser Racer*, 1975, silverpoint and graphite drawing on a fibreglass construction, Honda 350 motorcycle, ruby red laser, catgut, animal bone, h. 182.88 cm, w. 121.92 cm; l. 1,524 cm. Collection: stolen. Photo by Ernest Mayer.

39. *Field, In Situ*, 1980, binder twine (sisal), cast fibreglass, wood, lights, 25 x 914 x 1,524 cm. Site-specific and destroyed. Photo by Ernest Mayer.

40. *Field, In Situ*, 1980. Photo by Ernest Mayer.

41. *Field, In Situ*, 1980. Photo by Ernest Mayer.

42. *Field, In Situ*, 1980. Photo by Ernest Mayer.

43. *Field, In Situ*, 1980. Photo by Ernest Mayer.

44. *Field*, National Gallery of Canada Installation, *Pluralities* Exhibition, 1980, binder twine, sisal, cast fibreglass, wood and photographs, 25 x 914 x 1,524 cm.

45. Sketches for *Asessippi Valley with Yellow-Throated Vireo*, 2003, pencil on paper. Collection of the artist.

46. *Prairie Waters*, 2018, 182.9 x 152.4 cm, pencil and coloured pencil on a fibreglassed board with chromed copper waterdrops, chromed copper water details, chromed horseshoe nail, and stainless steel "horseshoe." Photo by Don Proch.

47. *Horizon Detail*, 1974, silkscreen print, with roller bearing powdered graphite mixed with bronzing varnish, 71.2 x 101.6 cm. Collection of the Buhler Gallery, St. Boniface Hospital, Winnipeg. Photo by Ernest Mayer.

48. *Fire Fly*, 1978, silkscreen print, A/P, 71 x 56 cm. Collection of the Buhler Gallery, St. Boniface Hospital from the K.J. Hughes Collection, gift of his family and the Winnipeg Art Gallery. Photo by Ernest Mayer.

49. *Walking Plow*, 1972, silkscreen on gessoed canvas, 106.7 x 121.5 cm. Collection of the Winnipeg Art Gallery. Photo by Ernest Mayer.

50. *Luke's Cultivator*, 1974, silkscreen print, 3/10, 111.7 x 122.5 cm. Collection of the Winnipeg Art Gallery. Photo by Ernest Mayer.

51. *Woodsmoke*, 1977, silkscreen print, 55.9 x 71.1 cm. Private collection. Photo by Ernest Mayer.

52. *Hummingbird Watching Mask* (detail), 1974. Hummingbird carved by Bertie Duncan. Photo by Ernest Mayer.

53. *Hummingbird Watching Mask*, 1974, silverpoint and graphite drawing on fibreglass, carved wood, orange lighted interior and barbed wire construction, h. 33.02 cm. Private collection. Photo by Ernest Mayer.

54. *Humming Bird Watching Mask* (side view), 1974.

55. *Rainbow Mask*, 1976, graphite and silverpoint on fibreglass, h. 50.8 cm. Collection of the Glenbow Alberta Institute, Calgary. Photo by Ernest Mayer.

56. *Manitoba Mining Mask* (front view), 1976, silverpoint and graphite on fibreglass, stainless steel and bone 62 x 32.3 x 36 cm. Collection of the University of Saskatchewan, Saskatoon. Photo by Ernest Mayer.

57. *Manitoba Mining Mask* (back view), 1976.

58. *Night Landing Mask*, 1982, silverpoint, graphite, fibreglass, leather, steel, polyester resin, fibre optics, bone, electrical components, 66.5 x 63.2 x 43 cm. Collection of the Winnipeg Art Gallery. Photo by Ernest Mayer.

59. *Delta Night Mask – Homage à Kelly Clark*, 1984, silverpoint and graphite drawing on a fibreglass construction, steel and fibre optics, 84.5 x 36 x 42 cm. MacKenzie Art Gallery, University of Regina Collection, purchased with the assistance of the Canada Council Art Bank.

60. *Delta Night Mask – Homage à Kelly Clark* (side view), 1984.

61. Sketch for *Waterfront Reading Mask*, 2010. Collection of the artist.

62. Don Proch working on *Waterfront Reading Mask*, 2010. Photo by Alan McTavish.

63. *Waterfront Reading Mask* (detail), 2010. Photo by Alan McTavish.

64. Sketches for *Waterfront Reading Mask*, 2009. Collection of the artist.

65. *Waterfront Reading Mask*, 2010, silverpoint, pencil and coloured pencil on a fibreglass, dyed bone, wood and electrical construction, 76.2 x 25.4 x 43.18 cm. Private collection. Photo courtesy of Mayberry Fine Art.

66. *Chicken Bone Mask*, 1978, silverpoint and pencil and chicken bones on fibreglass, 43.18 x 27.94 x 27.94 cm. Private collection. Photo by Don Hall.

67. *Chicken Bone Mask* (side view), 1978. Photo by Don Hall.

68. *Wild Bill Lobchuk Back Forties Mask*, 1976, silverpoint and pencil and grass on fibreglass, 66.04 x 35.56 x 43.18 cm. Private collection. Photo by Ernest Mayer.

69. *Blue Canoe Mask*, 1985, silverpoint and pencil and coloured pencil on fibreglass, 91.44 x 30.48 x 76.2 cm. Private collection. Photo by Ernest Mayer.

70. *Balance – Homage à Cicansky*, 2010, pencil and coloured pencil on a cast bronze, wood, steel and bone construction, 50.8 x 50.8 x 7.62 cm. Private collection. Photo by Don Proch.

71. *Joe – A Portrait*, 2016, silverpoint, graphite and coloured pencil on fibreglass board, 40.64 x 35.56 cm. Private collection. Photo by Don Proch.

72. Sketch for *The Gord Landscape with Passing Comet*, 2017. Collection of the artist.

73. *The Gord Landscape with Passing Comet*, 2017, silverpoint, graphite, coloured pencil, inlaid bone, chicken bone, chrome pins, carved wood, chrome plated on copper, on fibreglass form, 71.12 x 30.48 x 35.56 cm. Private collection. Photo courtesy of Mayberry Fine Art.

74. Sketches for *The Gord Landscape with Passing Comet*, 2017. Collection of the artist.

75. Sketches for *The Gord Landscape with Passing Comet*, 2017. Collection of the artist.

76. *Great Plains Mask* (left side), 1986, silverpoint, pencil and coloured pencil on a fibreglass, chicken bone, chrome brass pins, and inlaid animal bone construction, 101.6 x 35.6 x 55.9 cm. Private collection. Photo by Don Hall.

77. *Great Plains Mask* (right side), 1986. Photo by Don Hall.

78. *The Farm As A Memory Mask* (left angle), 2000, silverpoint, graphite and coloured pencil, drawn on cast porcelain, 30.48 x 25.4 x 5.08 cm. Private collection. Photo by Don Proch.

79. *The Farm As A Memory Mask* (right angle), 2000. Photo by Don Proch.

80. Sketch of *The Farm As A Memory Mask*, 2000. Collection of the artist.

81. *Bandana Mask*, 2013, silverpoint, pencil and coloured pencil on a fibreglass and dyed bone construction, h. 91.4 cm. Private collection. Photo courtesy of Mayberry Fine Art.

82. Sketches for *Bandana Mask*, 2013. Collection of the artist.

83. Sketches for *Bandana Mask*, 2011. Collection of the artist.

84. Drawing, 1999, pencil and coloured pencil, 30.48 x 22.86 cm. Collection of the artist.

85. *Night Rail*, 1976, silkscreen print, 38/50, frame: 49.3 x 45.5 cm, image 36 x 32 cm. Collection of the Buhler Gallery, St. Boniface Hospital, from the K.J. Hughes Collection, gift of his family. Photo by Leif Norman.

86. Sketch for *Incline*, 1976, pencil on paper. Collection of the artist.

87. *Rocky Mountain Mask*, 1976, silverpoint and graphite drawing on a fibreglassed and inlaid silver wire construction, h. 35.56 cm. Collection of the Nickle Galleries, University of Calgary. Purchased with funds from Dr. W. Campbell and the Government of Canada. Photo by Ernest Mayer.

88. *Prairie Monolith*, 1996, silverpoint, pencil and coloured pencil on a fibreglass, chromed copper and sisal construction, h. 91.44 cm. Collection of Oseredok Ukrainian Cultural and Educational Centre, Winnipeg. Photo by Ernest Mayer.

89. *Root Systems*, 1995, animal bone, fibreglass, sisal, steel, pencil and coloured pencil, h. 93.98 cm. Private collection.

90. Sketch for *Prairie Monolith*, 1996, pencil and coloured pencil on paper, 30.48 x 22.86 cm. Collection of the artist.

91. *Home Grain*, study, 1998, pencil and coloured pencil on paper, 30.48 x 22.86 cm. Collection of the artist.

92. *Prairie Drive-Thru*, 1988, graphite, coloured pencil, chromed copper, laminated plywood, fibreglass, 57.2 x 30.5 x 14 cm. Collection of the Winnipeg Art Gallery, gift of Allan MacDonald.

93. *Prairie Trail*, 2002, silverpoint, pencil, coloured pencil on fibreglassed wood, chromed copper, h. 78.74 cm. Private collection. Photo courtesy of Mayberry Fine Art.

94. *Flourishing*, 2008, silkscreen print, 55.88 x 38.1 cm. Commissioned by the University of Manitoba. Private collection. Photo by Leif Norman.

95. *Through the Artist's Eye Moon and Pine Bough* (side view), 1990, graphite, coloured pencil, laminated plywood, fibreglass, animal bone, chicken wing bones, chromed pins, copper, light bulb, 150 x 20.3 x 24.7 cm. Collection of the Winnipeg Art Gallery. Photo by Ernest Mayer.

96. *Through the Artist's Eye Moon and Pine Bough* (front view), 1990. Photo by Ernest Mayer.

97. *Colville's Horse Races through the Prairie Drive-Thru Gallery, Brushing Past John Nugent's "No. 1 Hard," Heading West to Haida Gwaii*, 2016, silverpoint, pencil and coloured pencil on a fibreglass, wood, welded steel, dyed sisal and cast bronze horse, 101.6 x 91.4 x 25.4 cm. Private collection. Photo by Ernest Mayer.

98. Sketches for *Colville's Horse Races through the Prairie Drive-Thru Gallery, Brushing Past John Nugent's "No. 1 Hard," Heading West to Haida Gwaii*, 2013, pencil, 30.48 x 22.86 cm. Collection of the artist.

99. Sketches for *Colville's Horse Races through the Prairie Drive-Thru Gallery, Brushing Past John Nugent's "No. 1 Hard," Heading West to Haida Gwaii*, 2013, pencil, 30.48 x 22.86 cm. Collection of the artist.

100. *Colville's Horse Races through the Prairie Drive-Thru Gallery, Brushing Past John Nugent's "No. 1 Hard," Heading West to Haida Gwaii* (detail), 2016. Photo by Ernest Mayer.

101. *Colville's Horse Races through the Prairie Drive-Thru Gallery, Brushing Past John Nugent's "No. 1 Hard," Heading West to Haida Gwaii* (detail), 2016. Photo by Ernest Mayer.

102. Sketch for *Typeface Mask*, 2015, pencil and coloured pencil, 30.48 x 22.86 cm. Collection of the artist.

103. Sketch for *Typeface Mask*, 2012, pencil, 30.48 x 22.86 cm. Collection of the artist.

104. Sketch for *Typeface Mask*, 2014, pencil, 30.48 x 22.86 cm. Collection of the artist.

105. Sketch for *Typeface Mask*, 2014, pencil, 30.48 x 22.86 cm. Collection of the artist.

106. Sketch for *Typeface Mask*, 2015, pencil, 30.48 x 22.86 cm. Collection of the artist.

107. *Typeface Mask* (detail), 2017. Photo courtesy of Mayberry Fine Art.

108. *Typeface Mask*, 2017, bone, metal type, wood, electric typewriter ball, sisal, fibreglass, silverpoint, pencil and coloured pencil, h. 91.44 cm. Private collection. Photo courtesy of Mayberry Fine Art.

109. *Red River Flood Mask*, sketch, 1997, pencil, 30.48 x 22.86 cm. Collection of the artist.

110. *Red River Flood Mask*, 1997, silverpoint, pencil and coloured pencil on a fibreglass, wood, sisal, and chrome pin construction, 82.6 x 33 x 33 cm. Collection of the Winnipeg Art Gallery, gift of Allan MacDonald. Photo by Ernest Mayer.

111. *Red River Flood Mask*, sketch, 1997, pencil, 30.48 x 22.86 cm. Collection of the artist.

112. *Red River Flood Mask*, sketch, 1997, pencil, 30.48 x 22.86 cm. Collection of the artist.

113. *Red River Flood Mask* (side view), 1997. Photo by Ernest Mayer.

114. *Light Strata No. 5*, 1983, pencil and coloured pencil on wood, chrome. Collection of the Buhler Gallery, St. Boniface Hospital, from the K.J. Hughes Collection, gift of his family. Photo by Leif Norman.

115. *The Journey (The Crossing, The Mist, The Sea)*, 1988, pencil, silverpoint, coloured pencil, cast bronze, cast porcelain, steel on wood construction, *The Crossing*: 55.88 cm, *The Mist*: 55.88 cm, *The Sea*: 58.42 cm. Private collection. Photo by Don Proch.

116. *The Journey* (detail), *The Crossing*. Photo by Don Proch.

117. *The Journey* (detail), *The Mist*. Photo by Don Proch.

118. *The Journey* (detail), *The Sea*. Photo by Don Proch.

119. *The Journey*, drawing, 2000, pencil on paper. Collection of the artist.

120. *Summersky*, 1982, silverpoint and pencil on fibreglassed board, 182.88 x 365.76 x 7.62 cm. Collection of CIL, Toronto. Photo by Ernest Mayer.

121. *Summerfield*, 1974, silkscreen, 86.5 x 119.4 cm, image: 57.3 x 112.2 cm. Collection of the Winnipeg Art Gallery, gift of Dr. and Mrs. R.E. Beamish.

122. *Red Wing*, 1998, pencil and coloured pencil on fibreglassed board with nickel-plated copper, chrome, and black chrome on copper, 35.36 x 25.4 cm. Collection of the Buhler Gallery, St. Boniface Hospital, from the K.J. Hughes Collection, gift of his family. Photo by Leif Norman.

123. *Elevator Chair*, 1990, coloured pencil, painted canvas, and diamond willow, 182.88 x 60.96 x 60.96 cm. Private collection. Photo by Don Proch.

124. *Prairie Harvest Bowl*, 2011, coloured pencil on a chrome copper wooed and dyed sisal construction, d. 25.4 cm. Private collection. Photo by Don Proch.

125. Sketch for *Prairie Harvest Bowl*, 2011, pencil. Collection of the artist.

126. *Sunflower Shade Mask*, 1975, pencil, silverpoint, catgut on fibreglass. Private collection. Photo by Ernest Mayer.

127. *No. 1 West Mask*, 1980, fibreglass, graphite, silverpoint, sisal, metal, 73.5 x 54.9 cm. Collection of the Winnipeg Art Gallery. Photo by Ernest Mayer.

128. *Distant Fire*, 1985, fibreglass, wood, pencil, coloured pencil, silverpoint, chromed nickel, 36 x 35 x 21 cm. Collection of the University of Manitoba, gift of Anna and Lyle Silverman. Photo by Ernest Mayer.

NOTES

1. Don Proch was born in 1942, though a number of references to him and his work in both publications and some collection databases have that year erroneously as 1944.

2. The T. Eaton Company, a Canadian department store, had a vibrant mail-order department. Its Winnipeg store serviced western and northern Canada.

3. Don Proch in conversation with Patricia Bovey, April 2016.

4. Ibid.

5. Proch in conversation with Patricia Bovey, July 2017.

6. Proch in conversation with Bovey, November 2017.

7. Bill Lobchuk in conversation with Patricia Bovey, February 2014.

8. Angela Davis, *The Grand Western Canadian Screen Shop: Printing, People, and History* (Regina: MacKenzie Art Gallery, 1992), 43.

9. Lobchuk in conversation with Bovey, February 2014.

10. Davis, *The Grand Western Canadian Screen Shop*, 43.

11. Lobchuk in conversation with Bovey, February 2014.

12. Ibid.

13. Proch in conversation with Bovey, April 2017.

14. Lobchuk in conversation with Bovey, January 2018.

15. Adele Freedman, "The Magic Masks of Asessippi: Don Proch Is the Shaman of Prairie Art," *Saturday Night*, (January–February 1977): 41.

16. Larysa Briukhovets'ka, "In the Artist's Studio: The Earth as Object of Beauty," *Kyiv Journal* 4 (1991) [translated typescript].

17. Proch in conversation with Bovey, November 2017.

18. Proch in conversation with Bovey, April 2017.

19. Freedman, "The Magic Masks of Asessippi," 41.

20. Philip Fry, *The Legend of Asessippi* (Winnipeg: Winnipeg Art Gallery, 1972).

21. Freedman, "The Magic Masks of Asessippi," 38.

22. Ibid.

23. Don Proch, interviewed by Robert Enright, "They Don't Make Horseshoe Nails Like They Used To," *Border Crossings* 9, no. 2 (1990): 11.

24. Don Proch in correspondence with Patricia Bovey, August 2017.

25. Proch in Enright, "They Don't Make Horseshoe Nails Like They Used To," 10.

26. Ibid., 9.

27. Ibid., 11.

28. Briukhovets'ka, "In the Artist's Studio."

29. John Graham, "Asessippi Lauded," *Winnipeg Free Press*, 14 November 1975.

30. Proch in conversation with Bovey, April 2017.

31. Proch in Enright, "They Don't Make Horseshoe Nails Like They Used To," 15.

32. Ibid.

33. Patricia Vervoort, "Masking and Mapping the Prairie Landscape: Fragments in 2-D and 3," *British Journal of Canadian Studies* 6, no. 1 (1991): 138.

34. Quoted in ibid., 138.

35. Ibid.

36. William Kirby, "Urban and Rural Relationship Explored," *Winnipeg Free Press*, 11 January 1975, 17.

37. Proch in conversation with Bovey, November 2017.

38. Ernest Mayer in conversation with Patricia Bovey, April 2018.

39. Proch in conversation with Bovey, January 2018.

40. Proch in correspondence with Bovey, August 2017.

41. Lobchuk in conversation with Bovey, November 2017.

42. Ken Hughes, "Don Proch," in *Manitoba Art Monographs: Kelly Clark, E.J. (Ted) Howorth, Bill Lobchuk, Don Proch, Tony Tascona, Esther Warkov* (Winnipeg : Manitoba Dept. of Cultural Affairs and Historical Resources, 1982), 174, 176.

43. Ibid., 181–82.

44. Ibid., 195.

45. Ibid., 197.

46. Peter Mellen, *Landmarks of Canadian Art* (Toronto: McClelland and Stewart, 1978), 251, 254.

47. William Kirby, "Introduction," in *Don Proch: Travelling Exhibition* (Winnipeg: Winnipeg Art Gallery, 1977).

48. Vervoort, "Masking and Mapping the Prairie Landscape," 132.

49. Graham, "Asessippi Lauded."

50. Briukhovets'ka, "In the Artist's Studio."

51. Don Proch, "Artist's Statement," in *Flight Dreams* (Halifax: Art Gallery of Nova Scotia, 2009), 49.

52. Proch in conversation with Bovey, November 2017.

53. Michelle Lavalle, "When I think of the land. . . ." MacKenzie Art Gallery website, http://www.mackenzieartgallery.ca/engage/exhibitions/when-i-think-of-the-land.

54. Proch in conversation with Bovey, April 2017.

55. Graham, "Asessippi Lauded."

56. Karen Allen, "Criss-Crossing the Boundaries," in *The Winnipeg Perspective 1981—Ritual* (Winnipeg: Winnipeg Art Gallery, 1981).

57. Joan Sadler, "Don Proch's Prairie," *Winnipeg Tribune Magazine*, 26 January 1980, 20.

58. Quoted in ibid., 20.

59. Allen, "Criss-Crossing the Boundaries."

60. Clyde McConnell, *True North/Far West* (Stockton, CA: University of the Pacific Gallery, 1987), 5.

61. Graham, "Asessippi Lauded."

62. Vervoort, "Masking and Mapping the Prairie Landscape," 131.

63. Graham, "Asessippi Lauded."

64. Proch in conversation with Bovey, November 2017.

65. Ibid.

66. Ibid.

67. Proch in Enright, "They Don't Make Horseshoe Nails Like They Used To," 13.

68. Proch in correspondence with Bovey, August 2017.

69. Ibid.

70. Steve Prystupa.

71. Don Proch, sketchbook notes.

72. Garth von Buchholz, "Galleries and Museums re Grain Scapes," *Winnipeg Free Press*, November 1997.

73. Proch, sketchbook, dated 1996.

74. Proch, sketchbook, dated 1998.

75. von Buchholz, "Galleries and Museums re Grain Scapes."

76. Proch, sketchbook, dated 1997.

77. The artist's spelling of "drive-thru" in the title of the work is intended to be colloquial, in keeping with the spirit of the Screen Shop and his own approach to his work and society.

78. Proch in correspondence with Bovey, January 2018.

79. Proch in correspondence with Bovey, August 2017.

80. Proch in conversation with Bovey, November 2017.

81. Proch in correspondence with Bovey, August 2017.

82. Proch, sketchbook notes.

83. Proch, sketchbook notes regarding *Typeface Mask*.

84. Proch in conversation with Bovey, 2017.

85. Proch in Enright, "They Don't Make Horseshoe Nails Like They Used To," 12.

86. Ibid., 11.

87. Ibid., 12–13.

88. Proch, unpublished notes.

89. Proch in Enright, "They Don't Make Horseshoe Nails Like They Used To," 15.

90. Ibid.

91. Proch in conversation with Bovey, 2017.

92. The pre-1967 date for the silver coins is important since after 1967 the Canadian Mint added other metals to the silver, rendering the later coins of no use for this artistic technique. His father bought rolls of pre-1967 quarters for Proch for future use.

93. Proch in conversation with Bovey, 2017.

94. Ibid.

95. *Seattle Forum on Public Art*, 2008.

SELECTED BIBLIOGRAPHY

Allen, Karen. "Criss-Crossing the Boundaries." In *The Winnipeg Perspective 1981—Ritual*. Winnipeg: Winnipeg Art Gallery, 1981.

Besant, Derek Michael. "'Western Untitled' at the Glenbow Centre." *Artmagazine* 8 (1976): 14–17.

Bovey, Patricia. *Manitoba Insights: The Ken Hughes Gift*. Winnipeg: Buhler Gallery, St. Boniface Hospital, 2015.

———. *Visual Celebrations*. Winnipeg: Buhler Gallery, St. Boniface Hospital, 2017.

Bovey, Patricia, and Leona Herzog. *Visual Celebrations II*. Winnipeg: Buhler Gallery, St. Boniface Hospital, 2017.

Bringhurst, Robert, Geoffrey James, Russell Keziere, and Doris Shadbolt, eds. *Visions: Contemporary Art in Canada*. Vancouver: Douglas and McInytre, 1983.

Briukhovets'ka, Larysa. "In the Artist's Studio: The Earth as Object of Beauty." *Kyiv Journal* 4 (1991) [translated typescript].

Cerrito, Joann. *Contemporary Artists*. 4th ed. New York: St. James Press, 1996.

Cooley, Dennis. *Draft: An Anthology of Western Canadian Poetry*. Winnipeg: Turnstone Press, 1981. [Proch's *Chicken Bone Mask* on the cover.]

———, ed. *Essays on Canadian Writing* (Prairie Poetry Issue) 18–19 (1980). [Proch's *Night Wind Mask* on the cover.]

Enright, Robert. "Proch a Leader in Prairie Art." *Winnipeg Free Press*, 21 June 1980, 35.

———. "Contemporary Art for Gallery Birthday," *Winnipeg Free Press*, 12 July 1980, 31.

———. "They Don't Make Horseshoe Nails Like They Used To." *Border Crossings* 9, no. 2 (1990): 6–15.

Farrante, Angela, and Roy MacGregor. "The Heirs Apparent: Presenting the Canadians We'll Soon Be Talking About." *Maclean's* (January–February 1978): 29–40.

Fenton, Terry, and Karen Wilkin. *Modern Painting in Canada: Major Movements in Twentieth Century Canadian Art*. Edmonton: Hurtig Publishers and Edmonton Art Gallery, 1978.

Freedman, Adele. "The Magic Masks of Asessippi: Don Proch Is the Shaman of Prairie Art." *Saturday Night* 92, no.1 (January–February 1977): 38–41, 44–45.

Friesen, Patrick, dir. *Don Proch: The Spirit of Asessippi*. Winnipeg: Manitoba, Department of Education, 1984.

Fry, Philip. *The Legend of Asessippi*. Winnipeg: Winnipeg Art Gallery, 1972.

———. "Prairie Space Drawing." *Artscanada* 29, no. 3 (1972): 40–56.

Grace, Sherrill. *Canada and the Idea of North*. Montreal: McGill-Queen's University Press, 2007.

Graham, John. "Proch is Innovative." *Winnipeg Free Press*, 14 March 1975.

———. "Asessippi Lauded." *Winnipeg Free Press*, 14 November 1975.

Gunter, Jodi. "All of Art's Extremes Seen in Winnipeg Show." *Winnipeg Free Press*, 13 November 1970, 29.

Herzog, Leona. *Screening the 70s: Celebrating the 50th Anniversary of the Grand Western Canadian Screen Shop*. Winnipeg: Buhler Gallery, St. Boniface Hospital, 2018.

Hogbin, Stephen, ed. *Political Landscapes #1: Canadian Artists Exploring Perceptions of the Land*. Owen Sound, ON: Tom Thomson Memorial Art Gallery, 1989.

Hughes, Kenneth. "Asessippi Everywhere: The Art of Don Proch." *Canadian Dimension* 13, no. 3 (August–September 1978): 26–37.

———. "Don Proch." In *Manitoba Art Monographs: Kelly Clark, E.J. (Ted) Howorth, Bill Lobchuk, Don Proch, Tony Tascona, Esther Warkov*, 169–250. Winnipeg: Manitoba, Cultural Affairs and Historical Resources, 1982.

Kamienski, Jan. "Symbolism Links Three Gallery Shows." *Winnipeg Tribune*, 26 August 1972, 20.

Kerr, Don. "Don Proch—Manitoba Artists." *NeWest Review* (Special Winnipeg Issue), November 1982.

Kirby, William. "Urban and Rural Relationship Explored." *Winnipeg Free Press*, 11 January 1975, 17.

———. "Don Proch." Exhibition review. *Artscanada* 32 (March 1975): 59–60.

———. *Don Proch's Asessippi Clouds*. Winnipeg: Winnipeg Art Gallery, 1975.

———. "Introduction." In *Don Proch: Travelling Exhibition*. Winnipeg: Winnipeg Art Gallery, 1977.

Lavalle, Michelle. "When I think of the land. . . ." MacKenzie Art Gallery website, http://www.mackenzieartgallery.ca/engage/exhibitions/when-i-think-of-the-land.

Ling Wong, Judy. "Arts London Review." Canada House, 15 October 1984.

Livingstone, David. "Turning Prairie into Art." *Globe and Mail*, 29 January 1977, A2.

Lowndes, Joan. "Western Triptych, First Panel, Calgary." *Artscanada* 33 (December 1976–January 1977): 44–51.

McConnell, Clyde. *True North/Far West*. Stockton, CA: University of the Pacific Gallery, 1987.

Mellen, Peter. *Landmarks of Canadian Art*. Toronto: McClelland and Stewart, 1978.

Michel, Jacques. "La trajectoir Canadienne aujourd'hui." *La Monde*, 6 July 1973.

Pagé, Suzanne. *Canada Trajectories 73*. Paris: Musée d'art moderne, 1972.

Pelensky, Oksana. *Biennale of the Ukrainian Fine Arts: Painting, Graphic, Sculpture*. Lviv: Ukrainian-American Renaissance Foundation, 1991.

Phillips, Carol. *Obsessions, Rituals, Controls: An Exhibition of Sculptural Works*. Regina: Norman MacKenzie Art Gallery, 1978.

Robitaille, Louis-Bernard. "Le Canada anglais découvert à Paris." *La Presse*, 14 July 1973.

Sadler, Joan. "Don Proch's Prairie." *Winnipeg Tribune Magazine*, 26 January 1980, 19–20.

Shaul, Sandra. "Canadian Art in Paris." *Artmagazine* 5 (1973): 9–36.

Thompson, Don, dir. *Visions: Artists and the Creative Process*. Toronto: TV Ontario, 1983.

Vervoort, Patricia. "Masking and Mapping the Prairie Landscape: Fragments in 2-D and 3." *British Journal of Canadian Studies* 6, no. 1 (1991): 129–40.

von Buchholz, Garth. "Galleries and Museums re Grain Scapes." *Winnipeg Free Press*, November 1997.

Warnod, Jeanine. "Expériences canadiennes." *Le Figaro*, 20 June 1973.

Wilkin, Karen. "Rugged Individualists with No Urge to Roam." *ARTnews* 78, no. 2 (February 1979): 84–88.

Woloski, Rosalie. "A Paris Showing for Two Winnipeg Artists." *Winnipeg Tribune*, 19 May 1973, 24.

Yates, Sarah. "The Canadian Influence in Paris." *Artmagazine* 9 (October/November 1977): 22–26.

———. "Winnipeg: The Grand Western Canadian Screen Shop." *Artmagazine* 8 (1977).

Zack, Bandanna. "Canadian Artists in Exhibition." In *The Roundstone*. Toronto: Toronto Arts Council, 1973.

133

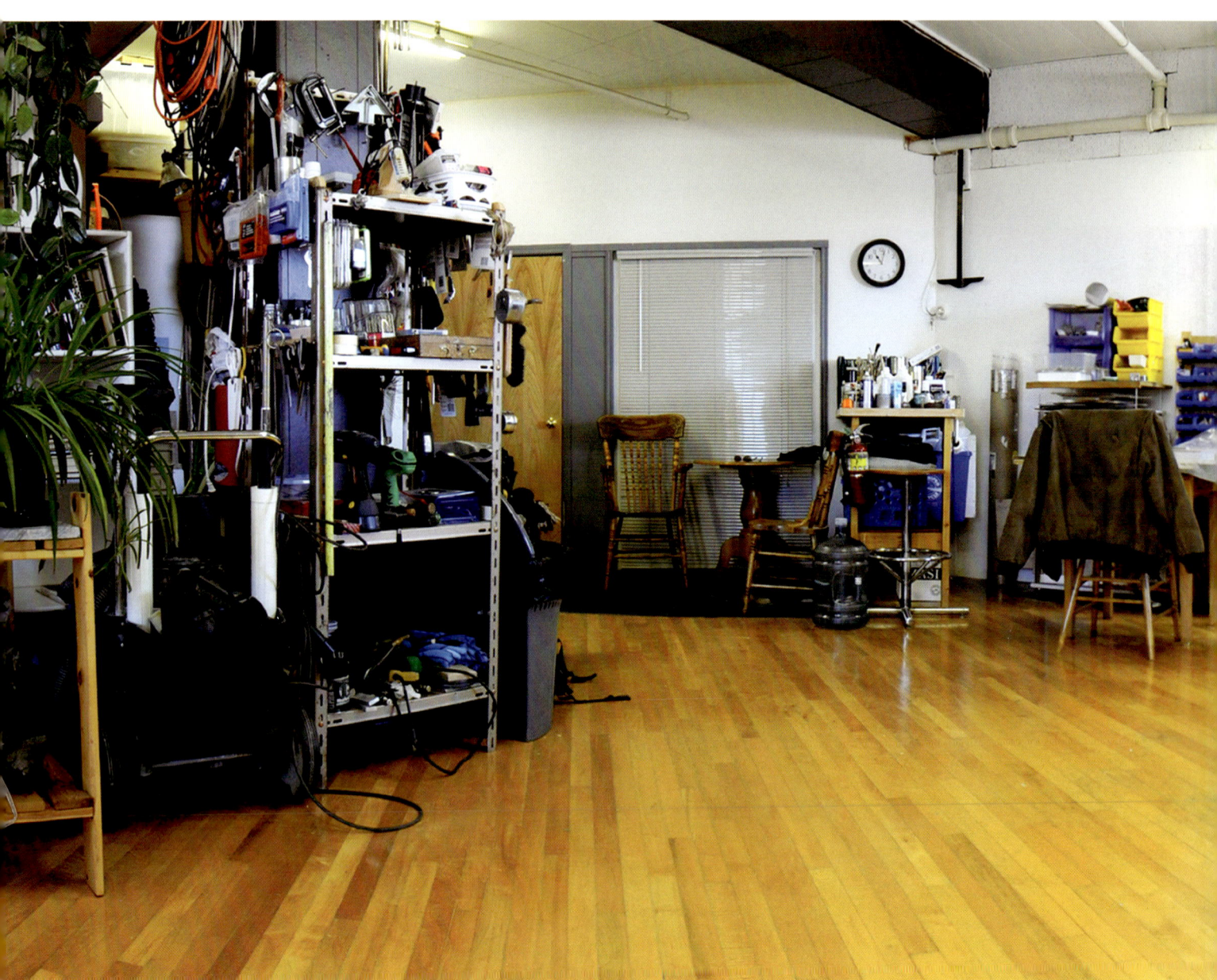

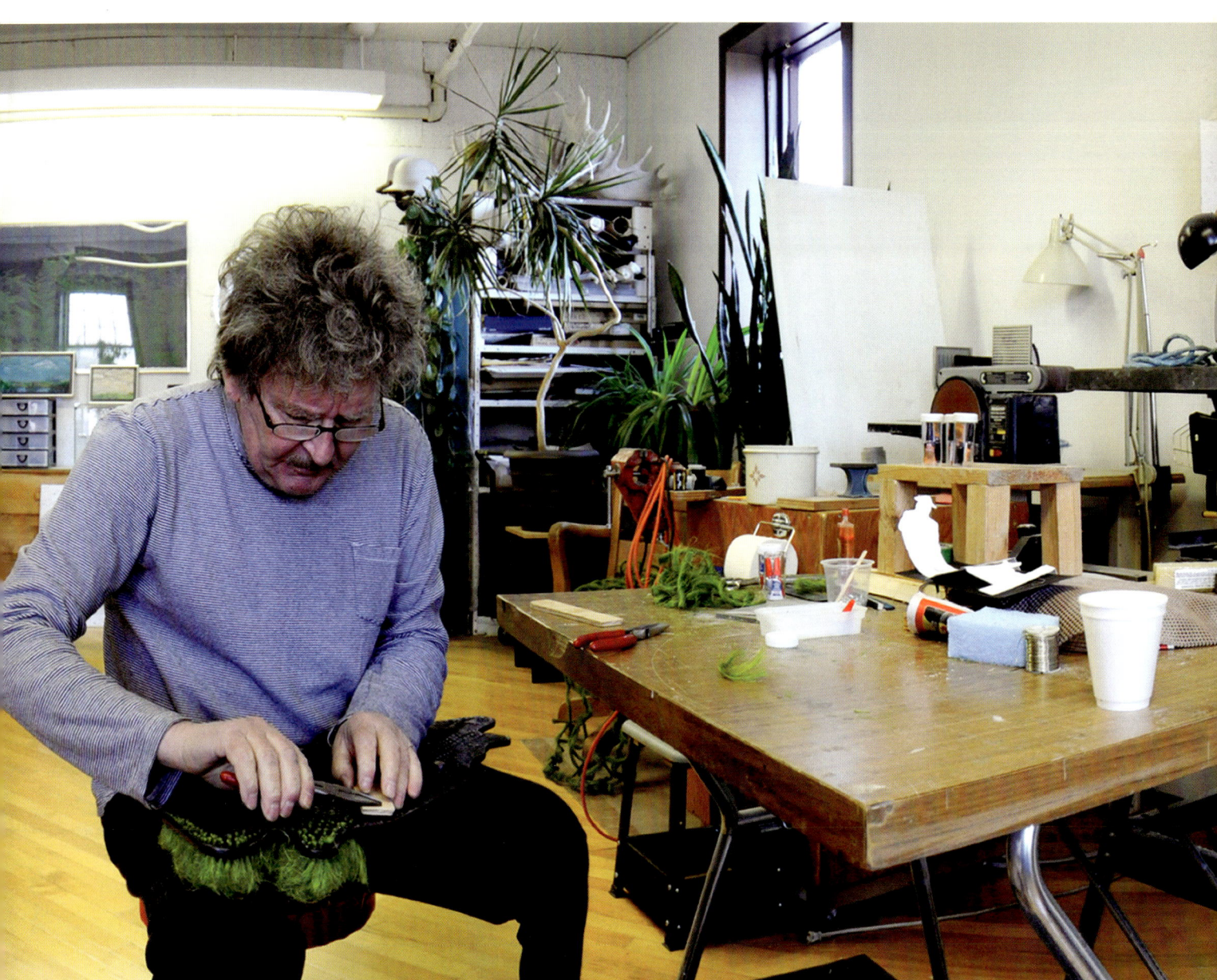

Slavi Просіб